FAIR TRIALS

The right to a fair trial has become an issue of increasing public concern, following a series of high profile cases such as the *Bulger* case, *Khan (Sultan)* and *R v DPP ex p Kebilene*. In determining the scope of the right, we now increasingly look to the ECHR, but the court has given little guidance, focusing on reconciling procedural rules rather than addressing the broader issues. This book addresses the issue of the meaning of the right by examining the contemporary jurisprudence in the light of a body of historical literature which discusses criminal procedure in a European context. It argues that there is in fact a European criminal procedural tradition which has been neglected in contemporary discussions, and that an understanding of this tradition might illuminate the discussion of fair trial in the contemporary jurisprudence.

This challenging new work elucidates the meaning of the fair trial, and in doing so challenges the conventional approach to the analysis of criminal procedure as based on the distinction between adversarial and inquisitorial procedural systems. The book is divided into two parts. The first part is dominated by an examination of the fair trial principles in the works of several notable European jurists of the nineteenth century, arguing that their writings were instrumental in the development of the principles underlying the modern conception of criminal proceedings. The second part looks at the fair trials jurisprudence of the ECHR, and it is suggested that although the Court has neglected the European tradition, the jurisprudence has nevertheless been influenced, albeit unconsciously, by the institutional principles developed in the nineteenth century.

Volume 4 in the Criminal Law Library series

Criminal Law Library

Fair Trials

The European Criminal Procedural Tradition and the European Court of Human Rights

SARAH J SUMMERS

·HART·
PUBLISHING

OXFORD AND PORTLAND, OREGON
2007

Published in North America (US and Canada) by
Hart Publishing
c/o International Specialized Book Services
920 NE 58th Avenue, Suite 300
Portland, OR 97213-3786
USA
Tel: +1 503 287 3093 or toll-free: (1) 800 944 6190
Fax: +1 503 280 8832
E-mail: orders@isbs.com
Website: www.isbs.com

Hart Publishing, 16C Worcester Place, OX1 2JW
Telephone: +44 (0)1865 517530 Fax: +44 (0)1865 510710
E-mail: mail@hartpub.co.uk
Website: http://www.hartpub.co.uk

British Library Cataloguing in Publication Data
Data Available

ISBN 978-1-84113-730-8 (hardback)

Typeset by Columns Design Ltd, Caversham
Printed and bound in Great Britain by
TJ International Ltd, Padstow, Cornwall

For my family
and for Sari and his family

Acknowledgments

Many thanks

To Jim Murdoch for allowing me to participate in his award-winning 'European Human Rights Project' at the University of Glasgow and for his useful insights on Chapters 4 and 5. To Christian Schwarzenegger for letting me commandeer many books from his wonderful collection of historical works on criminal law and procedure.

To Lindsay Farmer for suggesting that I consider writing a PhD, for his continued support and encouragement even after I decided to write it in Zurich rather than Glasgow and for his many helpful comments and criticisms. To Stefan Trechsel for providing me with the perfect 'day job' and for his valuable comments on the text, and to both Stefan and Franca for welcoming me to Switzerland.

To Sararard Arquint for his readiness to discuss many of the ideas set out in this book and to my family for everything.

This book is based on the author's doctoral thesis written at the University of Zurich under the co-supervision of Professor Lindsay Farmer (Glasgow) and Professor Stefan Trechsel (Zurich). All translations are by the author, unless otherwise stated.

Contents

Tables of Cases

Decisions and Reports of European Commission of Human Rights and European Court of Human Rights

Introduction

ARTICLE 6 OF THE European Convention on Human Rights has become the defining standard within Europe for determining the fairness of criminal proceedings. Its success has been attributed to the fact that it is not based on a particular model of criminal procedure. In this regard it is no coincidence that much of the literature on comparative criminal procedure law continues to adhere to an understanding of European criminal procedural systems as divided into two groups: the accusatorial and the inquisitorial. In Part One, this understanding of European criminal proceedings is challenged by an examination of the work of various important European jurists of the nineteenth century. It is argued that their writings on the nature and form of criminal proceedings were instrumental in the developing conception of the principles which underlie the modern conception of criminal proceedings. Further it is claimed that on the basis of their work it is possible to identify a common European conception of criminal proceedings.

In Part Two, the fair trials jurisprudence of the European Court of Human Rights is analysed in order to determine whether it can be said to be following the European criminal procedural tradition. It is suggested that although the European tradition has been neglected by the Court, the jurisprudence has nevertheless been influenced, albeit unconsciously, by the institutional principles developed in the nineteenth century. Only through letting go of the accusatorial–inquisitorial typology and devoting more consideration to the European procedural tradition will it be possible, however, for the Court to develop a more coherent and consistent vision of the rights set out in Article 6.

Finally the implications associated with construing fairness principally in terms of individual rights are assessed. Not only is this at odds with the European procedural tradition, it also excludes broader consideration of procedural fairness in the context of the criminal justice system. The rights-based approach has contributed to the failure to come to terms with the implications of the separation of criminal proceedings into the investigative phase and the determinative trial. In one crucial sense, this means that there has been little progress in the development of our understanding of criminal proceedings since the nineteenth century. The fairness of the trial continues to be the primary means of legitimising the criminal process, but the trial is nevertheless heavily dependent on the under-regulated investigation to ensure the effectiveness of the system of prosecutions. A more coherent understanding of fairness requires recognition of the reliance of the role of the defence (and therefore the rights of the accused) on the institutional structure of the proceedings.

Part One

1

The Enduring Legacy of 'Inquisitorial' and 'Accusatorial' Procedural Forms in the Debate on Comparative Criminal Procedure

A The Enduring Legacy of the Inquisitorial/Accusatorial Divide

I T MAY BE uncontroversial to suggest that European criminal procedure law has, in the last 20 years, enjoyed something of a renaissance. It may be less controversial still to attribute this, at least in part, to the considerable case law amassed by the European Court (the Court) and Commission of Human Rights in their interpretation and application of Articles 5 and 6 of the European Convention on Human Rights (ECHR). But acceptance of this consensus would be to ignore the inherent tension in the phrase 'European criminal procedure law'. While the Strasbourg case law has undoubtedly influenced the procedural laws of the member states, it has done little to reconcile these or to situate them within some kind of European criminal procedural tradition.

The renewed interest in the regulation of the application of the substantive law cannot be said to have contributed much to the examination of the essence and form of procedural law and procedural rights. Instead, the debate on systems of criminal procedure and on the nature of procedural rights has been dominated by simplistic comparative examinations. Rather than addressing normative concerns such as how procedural systems should look or the role that procedural rights should play, the comparative criminal procedure law scholarship has been preoccupied with the descriptive classification of systems. This has not only served to cast doubt on the merits of comparative criminal procedure law as a legitimate discipline,[1] but has also meant that the emerging case law and principles of the ECHR in the field of criminal procedure have not been properly evaluated.

Much of the literature on comparative criminal procedure rests on underlying assumptions which are seldom tested, but which nevertheless exert considerable influence on the conclusions reached. Undoubtedly the most familiar and dominant of these is the belief that there are 'two main approaches to criminal procedure in most of the world: the inquisitorial and the accusatorial'.[2] It is highly unusual for any work that aims to describe, define or compare criminal procedure to eschew reference to these terms.[3] According to Jörg, Field and Brants, the criminal justice systems of England and Wales and the Netherlands are 'typical examples of adversarial and inquisitorial systems, respectively'.[4] 'The English and American systems are adversarial; in contrast, Continental European systems, like the French and Italian, are inquisitorial', writes Carey,[5] while Malsch and Freckelton contrast 'adversarial, or party-centred systems—such as those in the United States, the United Kingdom and Australia—and the court-centred or inquisitorial systems—such as that which exists in the Netherlands'.[6] Fairchild and Dammer are content to lump together 'France, German, China and even, in some respects, Japan' as examples of 'inquisitorial systems',[7] while Van Kessel simply refers to 'today's Continental inquiry systems of criminal justice'.[8] The adversarial–inquisitorial typology is by no means restricted to the English

---

[1] P Roberts, 'On Method: The Ascent of Comparative Criminal Justice' (2002) 22 *Oxford Journal of Legal Studies* 539 at 539–41. For an analysis of the problems of the comparative methodology more generally see P Legrand, 'Public Law, Europeanisation and Convergence: Can Comparativists Contribute?' in P Beaumont, C Lyons and N Walker (eds), *Convergence and Divergence in European Public Law* (Oxford, Hart Publishing, 2002).

[2] CM Bradley, 'The Convergence of the Continental and the Common Law Model of Criminal Procedure' (1996) 7 *Criminal Law Forum* 471 at 471.

[3] See JD Jackson, 'The Effect of Human Rights on Criminal Evidentiary Processes: Towards Convergence, Divergence or Realignment' (2005) 68 *MLR* 737 at 740.

[4] N Jörg, S Field and C Brants, 'Are Inquisitorial and Adversarial Systems Converging?' in C Harding, P Fennel, N Jörg and B Swart (eds), *Criminal Justice in Europe: A Comparative Study* (Oxford, Clarendon Press, 1995).

[5] J Carey, 'Charles Laughton, Marlene Dietrich and the Prior Inconsistent Statement' (2005) 36 *Loyola University of Chicago Law Journal* 433 at 441.

[6] M Malsch and I Freckelton, 'Expert Bias and Partisanship: A Comparison between Australia and the Netherlands' (2005) 11 *Psychology, Public Policy and Law* 42 at 42.

[7] E Fairchild and HR Dammer, *Comparative Criminal Justice Systems* (Belmont, Cal, Wadsworth Publishing, 2001) at 146. Several American commentators regard Germany as paradigmatic of the inquisitorial tradition: see eg RK Christensen, 'Getting to Peace by Reconciling Notions of Justice: The Importance of Considering Discrepancies Between Civil and Common Legal Systems in the Formation of the International Criminal Court' (2001) 6 *UCLA Journal of International Law and Foreign Affairs* 391 at 403; J Kokott, *The Burden of Proof in Comparative and International Human Rights Law: Civil and Common Law Approaches with Special Reference to the American and German Legal Systems* (The Hague, Kluwer Law, 1998).

[8] G van Kessel, 'European Perspectives on the Accused as a Source of Testimonial Evidence' (1998) 100 *West Virginia Law Review* 799 at 799.

language literature and it is not uncommon for 'continental European' commentators to position their systems on the inquisitorial axis. Pieth, for instance, seeks to distinguish Swiss criminal procedure from that of neighbouring Germany on the basis that it is more inquisitorial:

> *Es muss insbesondere jetzt in die Betrachtung einbezogen werden, dass, anders als etwa in der BRD, in der Schweiz im Wesentlichen noch mittelbare und inquisitorische Strukturelemente überwiegen.*[9]

Inevitably there is often uncertainty and disagreement about the classification of the various systems. Scots criminal procedure, writes Fionda, is 'still theoretically adversarial' despite having 'developed into a quasi-inquisitorial system, reflecting its mainland European neighbours'.[10] Shiels seems to agree: '[i]t is possible... to present a stronger legal argument for the assertion that there is an inquisitorial side to Scots criminal procedure'.[11] Sheehan and Dickson meanwhile take a different view, describing the Scottish system of criminal procedure as an '"accusatorial" as opposed to an inquisitorial system which exists in jurisdictions such as France, Italy and elsewhere'.[12]

The possibility that such classifications are based on modes of procedure which are outdated[13] or irrelevant is ignored. Even where there is recognition that the terms are vague, inconsequent or even perhaps meaningless, none of the authors seems able to resist the temptation to rely on them in order to sustain later arguments and comments. Thus while some, aware of the problematic nature of the categorisation, add caveats to their usage—it is rare for the terms to be entirely rejected. Ellison provides a good example of this. She writes:

> Throughout this article the labels 'inquisitorial' and 'adversarial' are used to denote the criminal justice processes of the Netherlands, and England and Wales, respectively. The appropriateness of the labels 'adversarial' and 'inquisitorial' for contemporary comparative study have been questioned. It has been argued that these terms are outdated and have confusing associations. It is certainly true that no system is an embodiment of either model. Criminal proceedings in England and Wales are however very much within the adversarial mould and the Dutch criminal justice system remains firmly planted within the inquisitorial tradition.[14]

---

[9] M Pieth, *Der Beweisantrag des Beschuldigten im Schweizer Strafprozessrecht* (Basel, Helbing & Lichtenhahn, 1984) at 211: 'it must be acknowledged that in Switzerland, unlike in West Germany, non-immediate and inquisitorial procedure is essentially predominant'.

[10] J Fionda, *Public Prosecutors and Discretion: A Comparative Study* (Oxford, Clarendon Press, 1995).

[11] RS Shiels, 'Inquisitorial Themes' (2005) 23 *Scots Law Times* 133.

[12] AV Sheehan and DJ Dickson, *Scottish Criminal Procedure*, 2nd edn (Edinburgh, Butterworths, 2003) at para 87.

[13] According to some influential writers, there are no subsisting 'inquisitorial' systems in modern Europe: see eg JF Nijboer, 'Common Law Tradition in Evidence Scholarship Observed from a Continental Perspective' (1993) 41 *American Journal of Comparative Law* 299 at 303.

[14] L Ellison, 'The Protection of Vulnerable Witnesses in Court: An Anglo-Dutch Comparison' (1999) 3 *International Journal of Evidence and Proof* 1.

Similarly Gane in his article 'Classifying Scottish Criminal Procedure' notes that the distinction has been subject to increasing criticism in the last 30 years and states that it has been 'recognised that no contemporary system (inquisitorial or adversarial) adheres fully to an ideal type', but nevertheless maintains that 'these terms remain useful analytical tools, not least because they retain a sound empirical foundation'.[15]

These two modes of criminal procedure are often characterised as polar opposites, as 'two broad and divergent Western criminal justice traditions'.[16] A brief examination of the literature, however, makes it very clear that there is little consensus on the meaning of terms such as 'inquisitorial' or 'accusatorial'. So an inquisitorial system is one in which 'the court pursues its own inquiry',[17] or one in which state officials are under an obligation 'to ensure that state policies, both substantive and procedural, are carried out',[18] or even one in which the accused's criminal history is revealed: '[o]ur criminal justice system is adversarial rather than inquisitorial, and admission of uncharged misconduct would change the system into an inquisitorial one'![19]

Some have expanded on the constitutive elements of inquisitorial systems. According to Bradley, 'the norm throughout continental Europe' is 'to a greater or lesser degree' a system where:

> A theoretically neutral judicial officer conducts the criminal investigation and a judge (or panel of judges), who has full access to the investigation file, determines the guilt or the innocence. The trial is a relatively brief and informal affair conducted by a presiding judge without a jury; the accused does not necessarily have a right to testify and, until recently, neither counsel had much of a role.[20]

Duff adopts a similar approach but selects different criteria. In the 'non-adversarial' and '"inquisitorial systems" of continental Europe', he writes:

> There is an official investigation to establish the truth; the parties do not control the presentation of the evidence; there are few restrictive evidentiary rules; the defence is expected to assist in the discovery of the truth; the judge plays an active part in the

---

[15] C Gane, 'Classifying Scottish Criminal Procedure' in P Duff and N Hutton (eds), *Criminal Justice in Scotland* (Aldershot, Ashgate, 1999) at 56.

[16] M Findlay, 'Synthesis in Trial Procedures? The Experience of International Criminal Tribunals' (2001) 50 *International and Comparative Law Quarterly* 26 at 26.

[17] Ludovic Kennedy cited by M Delmas-Marty, 'The Juge d'Instruction: Do the English Really Need Him?' in B Markesins (ed), *The Gradual Convergence: Foreign Ideas, Foreign Influences, and English Law on the Eve of the 21st Century* (Oxford, Clarendon Press, 1994) at 46.

[18] A Goldstein, 'Reflections on Two Models: Inquisitorial Themes in American Criminal Procedure' (1974) 26 *Stanford Law Review* 1009 at 1018. See also Thaman, who suggests that the advocating of the compulsory examination of criminals would mean moving 'in an inquisitorial direction and praising the principle of material truth': S Thaman, 'Miranda in Comparative Law' (2001) 45 *St Louis Law Journal* 581 at 581.

[19] TJ Reed, 'Admitting the Accused's Criminal History: The Trouble with Rule 404(B)' (2005) 78 *Temple Law Review* 201 at 201.

[20] CM Bradley, 'The Convergence of the Continental and the Common Law Model of Criminal Procedure' (1996) 7 *Criminal Law Forum* 471 at 471.

gathering and selection of evidence; and the outcome results from a cumulative administrative process which has built up a case file, or 'dossier' of largely written evidence.[21]

Accusatorial systems get the same treatment. Such a system:

> starts with a police investigation that is openly not neutral but rather, at least after it has focused on a suspect, is aimed at collecting evidence which will prove his guilt. Then an adversarial trial is held before a decision maker, judge or jury who has no prior knowledge of the case. The attorneys conduct the trial, with each side attempting to convince the decision maker of the rectitude of her position.[22]

According to Panzavolta:

> an accusatorial system of criminal procedure allows a judge to make decisions based only on evidence collected in oral form (the principle of orality) in his presence (the principle of immediacy), in a public trial containing adversarial dynamics. In other words, an accusatorial system clearly separates the investigation and trial stages. In an inquisitorial system, the judge's decisions are based on evidence, regardless of whether it was collected in oral form. Inquisitorial systems permit the inclusion of any evidence collected, even if the evidence was obtained in violation of the defendant's or the witnesses' rights.

Mixed procedure systems, he continues, 'are those that provide for an adversarial trial but still allow the judge to make a decision based on evidence collected unilaterally by the judge or prosecutor during the investigation phase. In this sense, mixed procedure is essentially inquisitorial.'[23]

The extent of the involvement of the parties, particularly when compared to the role of the judge, is often a defining factor for commentators in relation to the classification of their system. Pieth, for instance, rejects the idea that the Swiss investigating judge could be seen to be a 'party' to the proceedings, not least because he or she was compelled to 'act objectively and in the best interests of both society and the accused'.[24] Schünemann notes that it is common to read that 'there is no adversarial system in Germany, but rather an inquisitorial system with a purely adversarial façade, in a strict sense there are no parties at all, and both prosecutor and judge theoretically seek objective truth without being opponents of the defendant'. Despite this, '[i]n reality, however, the German

---

[21] P Duff, 'Changing Conceptions of the Scottish Criminal Trial' in A Duff, L Farmer, S Marshall and V Tadros (eds), *The Trial on Trial I: Truth and Due Process* (Oxford, Hart Publishing, 2004) at 30.

[22] CM Bradley, 'The Convergence of the Continental and the Common Law Model of Criminal Procedure' (1996) 7 *Criminal Law Forum* 471 at 471–2.

[23] M Panzavolta, 'Reforms and Counter-Reforms in the Italian Struggle for an Accusatorial Criminal Law System' (2005) 30 *North Carolina Journal of International Law and Commercial Regulation* 577 at 582.

[24] M Pieth, *Der Beweisantrag des Beschuldigten im Schweizer Strafprozessrecht* (Basel, Helbing & Lichtenhahn, 1984) at 211: '[h]ier findet sich der Beschuldigte nicht einer Partei, sondern zwei Repräsentanten der Staatsmacht gegenüber, die beide, wenn auch mit unterschiedlicher Rollendefinition, zur Objektivität verpflichtet sind, also im Grunde nur "das Beste" sowohl für Gesellschaft wie Beschuldigten wollen dürften'.

prosecutor almost always appears as the party opposing the defendant and his counsel'.[25] There is thus considerable uncertainty as to the extent of the control of the parties in the adversarial process, and the extent of the role of neutral officials in the inquisitorial system.[26]

The problematic nature of this approach is confounded by the fact that the methodology dictates the nature of the conclusions which are to be reached. Consequently, the determination of whether the system can be classed as 'accusatorial' or 'inquisitorial', or as moving towards one or other of the procedural forms, often becomes the goal of the study. This is in spite of recognition of the fact that it is highly unlikely that a legal system will fulfil all the attributes of either form.

The framing of the issue in terms of two procedural traditions means that commentators are forced to show developments which signal movement towards 'the other tradition'. As a consequence the issue of whether there are actually significant differences between the systems is left unaddressed. The problems of specific and particular differences are swallowed up by the desire to generalise. 'One recent discernable trend in criminal procedure', writes Smith, 'has been the movement in the direction of the inquisitorial process and away from some of the adversarial practices which have historically characterised English criminal procedure'.[27] A similar conclusion is reached by Shiels who writes, in relation to Scots procedural law, that 'recent developments suggest an expanding quasi-inquisitorial pre-trial procedure',[28] Duff detects in the introduction of a duty to agree uncontroversial evidence 'a move away from an adversarial model of the criminal justice process in an inquisitorial direction',[29] while Hodgson reports on the French scepticism towards the invoking of 'concepts such as "the equality of arms" in a way which might be regarded as moving away from the inquisitorial or mixed system established by the CPP [*Code de procédure pénal*], and to which France is strongly committed, and towards an adversarial procedure—a move which is to be avoided at all costs'.[30] The convergence is not always seen to be a result of 'inquisitorialisation' of accusatorial systems. Carey suggests that the distinction between these two notions has been 'blurred by recent developments

---

[25] B Schünemann, 'Experimentelle Untersuchungen zur Reform der Hauptverhandlung in Straf-sachen' in HJ Kerner, H Kurry and K Sessar (eds), *Deutsche Forschungen zur Kriminalitätsentstehen und Kriminalitätskontrolle* (Cologne, Heymanns, 1983) at 41–2.

[26] See further MR Damaška, *The Faces of Justice and State Authority: A Comparative Approach to the Legal Process* (New Haven, Conn, Yale University Press, 1986) at 3 ff.

[27] AH Smith, 'Criminal Law: The Future' [2004] *Criminal Law Review* 971 at 972.

[28] RS Shiels, 'Preliminary Hearings' (2005) 10 *Scots Law Times* 61.

[29] P Duff, 'Changing Conceptions of the Scottish Criminal Trial' in A Duff, L Farmer, S Marshall and V Tadros (eds), *The Trial on Trial I: Truth and Due Process* (Oxford, Hart Publishing, 2004) at 48.

[30] J Hodgson, 'Codified Criminal Procedure and Human Rights: Some Observations on the French Experience' [2003] *Criminal Law Review* 163 at 175.

in which some European countries have incorporated some adversarial features'.[31] Similarly many writers refer to the Italian reforms as an example of 'a departure from Italy's civil law tradition and a decisive move towards an adversarial model of criminal procedure'.[32]

Within the modern debate on comparative criminal procedure the idea of harmonisation seems to serve as a recurring motif. It is as if the only way to break out of the accusatorial–inquisitorial debate is to show that the procedural systems are coming together. 'Are Inquisitorial and Adversarial Systems Converging?' ask Jörg, Field and Brants, apparently impervious to the difficulties of reconciling this with their earlier assertions that these 'ideal' systems do not in reality exist.[33] Such arguments serve only to reinforce the perception of the existence of two all-important models of criminal procedure.

The focus on the accusatorial and inquisitorial models leads to attention being diverted away from those issues that might otherwise be assumed to be the proper focus of comparative studies. Important issues such as the role of procedural rights, the relationship between procedural fairness and rights, or suggestions for improving the existing procedural rules are, as such, under-developed. It is thus legitimate to question whether there are truly benefits associated with establishing whether a system is more or less 'inquisitorial' or 'adversarial' than another system. Inevitably the use of the terms is loaded—for those brought up in the common law tradition movement towards an 'inquisitorial' system is viewed as a negative development, while those writing from an 'inquisitorial' 'continental European jurisdiction tend to rue 'adversarial' developments as representing the creeping 'Anglo-Americanisation' of the law.

The conceptualisation of the debate on the level of the nation state also encourages the disregarding of divisions within the various legal systems. Instead of a constructive examination of potential improvements to the procedural law, there is a tendency to legitimise the status quo, through highlighting the perceived deficiencies of 'the other system'.[34] The problem with such approaches is that, by ignoring the multi-faceted nature of the various European procedural systems and simply labelling them as 'non-adversarial' or 'inquisitorial', both the

---

[31] J Carey, 'Charles Laughton, Marlene Dietrich and the Prior Inconsistent Statement' (2005) 36 *Loyola University of Chicago Law Journal* 433 at 441.

[32] M Panzavolta, 'Reforms and Counter-Reforms in the Italian Struggle for an Accusatorial Criminal Law System' (2005) 30 *North Carolina Journal of International Law and Commercial Regulation* 577 at 578; WT Pizzi and M Montagna, 'The Battle to Establish an Adversarial Trial System in Italy' (2004) 24 *Michigan Journal of International Law* 429 at 430; E Amodio, 'The Accusatorial System Lost and Regained: Reforming Criminal Procedure in Italy' (2004) 25 *American Journal of Comparative Law* 489.

[33] N Jörg, S Field and C Brants, 'Are Inquisitorial and Adversarial Systems Converging?' in C Harding, P Fennel, N Jörg and B Swart (eds), *Criminal Justice in Europe: A Comparative Study* (Clarendon Press, Oxford, 1995).

[34] That this applies to courts as well as to commentators is demonstrated by the recent Sup Ct judgment in *Crawford v Washington* 124 S Ct 1354 (2004): see S Summers, 'The Right to Confrontation after Crawford v. Washington: A "Continental European" Perspective' (2004) 2 *International Commentary on Evidence* 3.

differences and similarities between the systems are obscured. It therefore becomes difficult not only to establish a basis on which to compare the various systems but also to analyse the procedural values underpinning the various procedural systems.

Damaška's well-known and authoritative works are frequently cited, but often simply in passing and to legitimise the shoehorning of a system into one or other of the models.[35] Yet there seems to be an almost universal complacency towards thinking of new terms of reference for understanding different systems. Damaška's solution was to break down these two models into elements which could then provide the basis for a comparison. There seems to be a certain irony in the fact that his criteria, which he used to develop a deeper critique, have subsequently been liberally used to reinforce the divides which he himself was trying to move away from.[36]

The case law of the Court and of the international criminal tribunals could perhaps have been expected to provide the impetus for new approaches to comparative criminal procedure law. Instead, the response has been framed predominantly in terms of the two traditions approach. International law, write Danner and Martinez:

> seeks to meld two legal systems into a coherent whole; international criminal tribunals combine aspects of the common law adversarial system with the civil law inquisitorial system. In a formal sense, their rules of procedure and evidence draw on both legal traditions; in a practical sense, judges schooled in the common law or the civil law reflect their system of origin in their approach to various legal problems.[37]

Far from ameliorating these tendencies, the case law of the Court and the international tribunals has served to exacerbate reliance among commentators on these stereotypes. This is partly due to the fact that these institutions are in the relatively unusual position, unlike courts within a specific legal system, of not having their own legal tradition to fall back on in the assessment or legitimisation of the criteria for fair criminal proceedings. While they clearly do not operate in a legal vacuum, the member states (and indeed commentators) have jealously guarded their legal practices and traditions, and the case law of the courts has been carefully scrutinised for evidence of bias towards certain countries or traditions. The possibility of a European tradition of procedural principles in criminal proceedings has not been so much rejected as ignored.

---

[35] MR Damaška, *The Faces of Justice and State Authority: A Comparative Approach to the Legal Process* (New Haven, Conn, Yale University Press, 1986); MR Damaška, 'Structures of Authority and Comparative Criminal Procedure' (1975) 84 *Yale Law Journal* 480; MR Damaška, 'Evidentiary Barriers to Conviction and Two Models of Criminal Procedure: A Comparative Study' (1973) 121 *University of Pennsylvania Law Review* 506.

[36] He rejects the adversarial–inquisitorial typology as 'cumbersome and difficult to employ as an instrument of analysis': MR Damaška, *The Faces of Justice and State Authority: A Comparative Approach to the Legal Process* (New Haven, Conn, Yale University Press, 1986) at 5.

[37] AM Danner and JS Martinez, 'Guilty Associations: Joint Criminal Enterprise, Command Responsibility, and the Development of International Criminal Law' (2005) 93 *California Law Review* 75 at 77–8.

B The Connection to Legal Nationalism

One consequence of the reliance on the accusatorial–inquisitorial divide is that it tends to foster a type of legal nationalism. It is perhaps inevitable that criminal law and procedure, which until recently have been situated (trapped?) within the geographical and territorial confines of the nation state, should be closely identified with, and influenced by, that state. Indifference towards and mistrust of other criminal justice systems, which serves to hinder reform in the field—or to protect the identity of the individual systems, depending on how you look at it—can be seen to be a natural consequence of this nationalism.

Commentators who resort to this sort of argument seek to define their systems of criminal procedure through reference to what they are not. Instead of positively identifying those elements that make up their system, they seek to differentiate themselves from the perceived negative aspects of other systems.[38] A good example of this is provided by a leading article from 1863 in *The Times* in which the writer acknowledges the flaws of English criminal proceedings but then, instead of considering alternatives or improvements, cautions against adopting French procedural principles which he sees as being even worse:

> While the deficiencies of our English system are probably overrated, it is impossible to overrate the evils that might arise from transplanting the French criminal procedure into our own company.[39]

This methodology is of questionable value, not least because it obscures the fact that specific legal systems could be better understood if the focus were to be on the nature of the laws of that legal system, rather than on the perceived weaknesses of the other.[40] The persistent recourse to the adversarial and inquisitorial divide has encouraged and contributed to this type of argument, and has as such become part of the problem.

Evidence of legal nationalism pervades much of the work on comparative criminal procedure, but it would be wrong to imagine that this is a novel phenomenon in the European legal forum. Disparaging the criminal justice systems of other countries, and by extension the other countries themselves,

---

[38] There are of course numerous exceptions. The Swiss jurist HF Pfenniger, *Probleme des schweizerischen Strafprozessrechts: Ausgewählte Aufsätze von Prof. Dr. Hans Felix Pfenninger* (Zürich, Schulthess, 1966) and the German jurist G Radbruch, 'Der Geist des englischen Rechts' in *Drei Schriften*, 3rd edn (Göttingen, Hubert & Co, 1956), for instance, were both interested in and enthusiastic about the merits of English criminal law.

[39] *The Times*, 29 Nov 1862, cited in CJW Allen, *The Law of Evidence in Victorian England* (Cambridge, Cambridge University Press, 1997) at 154.

[40] A similar argument is made in the context of the relationship between Scottish and English law in L Farmer, 'Debatable Land: An Essay on the Relationship Between English and Scottish Criminal Law' (1999) 3 *Edinburgh Law Review* 32. Farmer argues that a better understanding of the identity of Scots criminal law can be developed through an analysis of the similarities between English and Scots law rather than by concentrating on the differences.

seems to be a pastime with a considerable heritage. Sometimes the language is direct and absurd, a combination which occasionally achieves an almost comical tone. At other times, the nationalist sentiment is subtly concealed by the rationality of legal argument. Esmein's interesting account of the development of French criminal procedure provides numerous examples that fall neatly into the first category. In the course of debate on procedural reform which occurred in nineteenth century France following the Revolution, he finds several examples which compel him to deduce that 'it is above all on national character which they [various commentators, including representatives of the appeal courts in the context of reforming the law] fasten'.[41] Among Esmein's plentiful examples, perhaps the most amusing are those of the Criminal Courts of Aveyron and Doubs:[42]

> What a different there is between our manners, our customs, and our national character and those of the English nation! Without entering upon the subject in detail and at length... it is sufficient to instance the comparison of Shakespeare's plays and those of other English tragedians with those of Corneille, Racine, and Voltaire... In a word, the sad experience which we have had with the institution of the jury, notwithstanding the various changes to which it has been subjected, proves that it is irreconcilable with the national customs and character, with those feelings of toleration and natural pity in the Frenchman which incline his heart to commiseration.[43]

> The Englishman at the theatre only cares for apparitions, madmen, dreadful criminals, murders long drawn out; he runs to animal fights, and probably regrets those of the gladiators; who knows if he does not seek the functions of a juror for the sake of the pleasure of watching a criminal struggling with his conscience, with the death that awaits him? The Frenchman, on the contrary is delicate in all his tastes; he eagerly flees from any sight which could disagreeably awaken his sensitiveness; could he have any pleasure in wielding the bleeding sword of justice?[44]

Nineteenth century English writers seem to have been equally wary of French criminal proceedings. According to one writer the French judge:

> often passes bounds which the most unscrupulous English barrister would respect in cross-examining a hostile witness. He browbeats the prisoner, he taunts him, he sneers

---

[41] A Esmein, *A History of Continental Criminal Procedure with special reference to France* (trans John Simpson, Boston, Mass, Little Brown & Co, 1913; reprinted Union, NJ, The Lawbook Exchange, 2000) at 472.

[42] Although admittedly there is fierce competition for this title. The Court of Aix writes that, '[w]e do not envy the English their tastes, their habits, their enthusiasm for their laws; we oppose to these declamations the experience and the opinion of one of the greatest magistrates of our time [Séguier], to whom we could add an infinitude of others':, see Esmein, above n41, at 468-9; according to the Court of Nîmes, '[t]he changing picture of crimes of that nation which uses assassination and the plague to repulse an enemy which it has provoked into breaking a solemn treaty hardly signed, ought not to induce us to adopt its system in criminal procedure. The jury has not rendered that people better; and if we recall what travellers have told us, there is no European country where theft, especially upon the highways, is more frequent and better organised than in that island': see Esmein, above n41, at 469.

[43] See *ibid*, at 473

[44] See *ibid*, at 473.

at him, he reproaches him in a voice trembling with suppressed anger, he distorts his answers, he insinuates motives, he glances at the jury and addresses stage 'asides' to them; he makes claptrap moral observations; in short he does everything that is least in accordance with our ideal of the English judge.[45]

Nationalist sentiments are by no means confined to the commentators of the nineteenth century. In his comparison of French and English criminal procedure, Spencer writes that '[t]he two things most Englishmen know about criminal procedure in France is that the French defendant is presumed guilty until he proves that he is innocent, and that the French have something called the Inquisitorial System. The first is false and the second if half true is misleading.'[46] Hodgson meanwhile quotes the former French foreign minister, Madame Guigour, speaking in the Sénat in June 1999 as saying:

> The adversarial system is by its nature unfair and unjust. It favours the strong over the weak. It accentuates social and cultural differences, favouring the rich who are able to engage and pay for the services of one or more lawyers. Our system is better both in terms of efficiency and of the rights of the individual.[47]

This nationalism also encourages insularity through rejecting criticism from 'foreign' commentators not on the basis of the content, but on the basis that those 'outside' the system are not suitably qualified to determine its flaws.[48]

These tendencies are inevitably compounded in Europe by the language barrier. It is difficult enough to comprehend the intricacies of a foreign legal system, but almost impossible to do so without a good understanding of the language or languages of that legal system.[49] The appeal to legal nationalism reduces the potential for debate by imposing constraints on the making of value judgements, while at the same time promoting the use of broad, meaningless categories which become almost impossible to escape. This also serves to prevent analysis of the role and function of procedural rights, and to dissuade commentators from establishing ways in which to assess the appropriateness and desirability of the different procedural structures.

---

[45] *The Times*, 29 Nov 1862, cited in CJW Allen, *The Law of Evidence in Victorian England* (Cambridge, Cambridge University Press, 1997) at 154.

[46] J Spencer, 'French and English Criminal Procedure—a Brief Comparison' in BS Markesinis (ed), *The Gradual Convergence* (Oxford, Oxford University Press, 1994) at 33.

[47] J Hodgson, 'Suspects, Defendants and Victims in the French Criminal Process: The Context of Recent Reform' (2002) 51 *International and Comparative Law Quarterly* 781 at 785.

[48] This sort of argument is of course not restricted to the legal field. Henry James, replying to criticism of his characterisation of some of the English characters in 'An International Episode', complained of 'the bother of being an American'. He noted that 'Trollope, Thackeray, Dickens, even with their big authoritative talents, were free to draw all sorts of unflattering English pictures, by the thousand. But if I make a single one, I am forthwith in danger of being confronted with a criminal conclusion—and sinister rumours reach me as to what I think of English society', cited by C Tóibín, 'At Home: Henry James's New York', 53 *The New York Review of Books*, 9 Feb 2006, at 34.

[49] D Nelken (ed), *Contrasting Criminal Justice: Getting from Here to There* (Aldershot, Ashgate/Dartmouth, 2000) has tried to circumvent this problem by editing a collection of essays written, *inter alia*, by authors who have lived for some time in the systems under examination. For an analysis of the strengths and weaknesses of this project see P Roberts, 'On Method: The Ascent of Comparative Criminal Justice' (2002) 22 *Oxford Journal of Legal Studies* 539.

C Developing a New Approach for Analysing European Criminal Procedure Law

If procedural rights can accurately be described as occupying the space between the application of the substantive criminal law and the authority of the state to enforce this law, then it could be assumed that it would be rather difficult to establish a common European approach to procedural rights. Both the absence of a harmonised or approximated version of European criminal procedure law (or perhaps more accurately procedural laws based on common procedural values) and the existence of justice and state authorities which are differently structured would seem to play against the possibility of the existence of common procedural standards. This is indeed the assumption made by the majority of writers interested in comparative criminal procedure, and consequently these two primary variables have been exhaustively critiqued.

The significance of different procedural priorities is most famously represented by Packer's account of the essentially opposing or competing models of crime control and due process.[50] The crime control model is based on the proposition that the repression of criminal conduct is by far the most important function to be performed by the criminal process, while the due process model highlights the possibility of error, particularly in the context of informal decision making.[51] While as the crime control model emphasises 'at every turn the existence and exercise of official power', the due process model asserts 'limits on the nature of official power and on the modes of its exercise'.[52] According to Packer's theory there is an internal struggle within justice systems between efficiency on the one hand and the rights of the individuals on the other. Consequently the extent of the individual rights will be dependent on the manner in which the state authorities balance these opposing procedural priorities. Critics of this approach have pointed to the fact that crime control and due process are not in fact opposing models and that these are of little use in the comparative context:

---

[50] H Packer, *The Limits of Criminal Sanctions* (Stanford, Cal, Stanford University Press, 1968), in particular ch 8; H Packer, 'Two Models of the Criminal Process' (1964) 113 *University of Pennsylvania Law Review* 1. See also J Griffiths, 'Ideology in Criminal Procedure of a "Third Model" of the Criminal Process' (1970) 79 *Yale Law Journal* 359 who refers to 'family' and 'battle' models, and K Llewellyn, *Jurisprudence: Realism in Theory and Practice* (Chicago, Ill, Chicago University Press, 1962) especially at 444–50, whose opposing models are represented by the terms 'parental' and 'arm's length' respectively.

[51] Packer, above n50, at 163.

[52] *Ibid*, at 173.

this tension (i.e. between due process and crime control) is part and parcel of the dialectics of any criminal process. Any design of criminal procedure, even the extreme inquisitorial one must establish a balance between these two (and some other) inner tendencies.[53]

Perhaps even more problematic is the determination of when this internal balancing act is to take place. This would seem to be dependent on the identification of the essential aspects of each of the procedural values.

The examination of the consequences of differences in the structure and form of the criminal justice systems has also received considerable attention, particularly from scholars working in the field of comparative criminal procedure law. Damaška's important work on the various types of justice and state authorities[54] in which he distinguishes hierarchical and co-ordinate ideals has spawned a vast literature from those seeking to demonstrate the differences between the nature and organisation of state authorities.[55]

Damaška is entirely open about the fact that he starts from the assumption that 'the two evidentiary styles, that of the common and that of the civil law, generate disparate problems of proving guilt'. He attributes these differences to the procedural systems and structures of these two legal traditions and writes that he is convinced that 'distinct common and civil law evidentiary styles' do exist and that they are not 'merely the invention of scholars'.[56] '[I]t is apparent to the most casual observer', he writes, 'that a great divide separates the two systems of criminal procedure devised by Western man over the past eight centuries'.[57] In *Evidentiary Barriers*, he attributes these differences to three predominant factors: first, differences between adversarial and non-adversarial modes of procedure; secondly, differences in the structure of the adjudicating bodies; and, thirdly, the influence of a non-partisan pre-trial investigation.[58] This assumption of the existence of difference also underpins his book on *The Faces of Justice and State Authority* in which he assembles the characteristics of procedural officialdom

---

[53] Eg MR Damaška, 'Evidentiary Barriers to Conviction and Two Models of Criminal Procedure: A Comparative Study' (1973) 121 *University of Pennsylvania Law Review* 506 at 574–9.

[54] MR Damaška, *The Faces of Justice and State Authority: A Comparative Approach to the Legal Process* (New Haven, Conn, Yale University Press, 1986); MR Damaška, 'Evidentiary Barriers to Conviction and Two Models of Criminal Procedure: A Comparative Study' (1973) 121 *University of Pennsylvania Law Review* 506; MR Damaška, 'Structures of Authority and Comparative Criminal Procedure' (1975) 84 *Yale Law Journal* 480 at 481; MR Damaška, *Evidence Law Adrift* (New Haven, Conn, Yale University Press, 1997)

[55] Eg J Hodgson, 'The Police, The Prosecutor and the Juge d'Instruction' (2001) 41 *British Journal of Criminology* 342; J Hodgson, 'Hierarchy, Bureaucracy, and Ideology in French Criminal Justice: Some Empirical Observations' (2002) 29 *Journal of Law and Society* 227; W Perron, 'Funktion und Zusammensetzung des Gerichts im Ermittlungs- und Hauptverfahren' in A Eser and C Rabenstein, *Strafjustiz im Spannungsfeld von Effizienz und Fairness* (Berlin, Duncker & Humblot, 2004).

[56] MR Damaška, 'Evidentiary Barriers to Conviction and Two Models of Criminal Procedure: A Comparative Study' (1973) 121 *University of Pennsylvania Law Review* 506 at 508–10.

[57] MR Damaška, 'Structures of Authority and Comparative Criminal Procedure' (1975) 84 *Yale Law Journal* 480 at 481.

[58] Damaška, above n56, at 510–11.

which seem to him to be relevant for the forms of justice. He then constructs 'two models from [the] major features that seem to distinguish the machinery of justice on the Continent and in the lands of the Anglo-American tradition'.[59] This starting point obviously has a considerable impact on both the scope of his work and the conclusions that he reaches. He is not interested in questioning this notion of difference, but rather sets out to explain how such divergence can be explained by differences in the structure and nature of state authority. Inherent in this approach is the conviction that there is a connection between the nature of state authority and the type of procedural laws within the criminal justice system.

The two models ideology that Damaška develops is not entirely unproblematic, not least because these are idealised forms which do not exist in reality. He acknowledges this point in his 'Afterword' to *The Faces of Justice and State Authority*:

> This book sought to discern and to define distinctive styles in the tangled mass of procedures through which justice is variously administered around the world. The reason for this effort was the belief that, without a suitable typology, comparative studies of procedural form cannot even begin. But as my scheme was applied to existing systems, most of them were found to be pastiches of the pure styles I have identified. If the real world is one of mixtures, the reader must have wondered, what is the point in developing pure styles?[60]

He accepts that his analysis offers little information about the individual systems, but maintains that it is possible to examine individuality only after the 'conceptual instruments with which to see and discuss individuality in terms of generic notions' have been obtained.[61] Damaška's approach is broad and ambitious in that he seeks to develop a global conceptual framework. But this breadth necessarily excludes recourse to the content of the criminal law or the social and historical background of the various legal systems.

Unlike Damaška's methodology, which focuses on broad theoretical possibilities, the approach adopted here aims to develop an understanding of European criminal proceedings by examining the ideas influencing and justifications for their development. It can be characterised by its scepticism towards arguments which emphasise the extent of the differences between the various European procedural systems. Instead of explaining why and where the criminal justice systems diverge, it seeks to question the basis of this divergence. Instead of asking: how can we explain differences in criminal justice systems?, it asks: do differences really exist between the European criminal justice systems and are they significant? This methodology is inspired, to a certain extent, by the relative ease with which the European Court of Human Rights has assumed the mantle of the regulator of European procedural rights in criminal proceedings.

---

[59] MR Damaška, *The Faces of Justice and State Authority: A Comparative Approach to the Legal Process* (New Haven, Conn, Yale University Press, 1986) at 10.

[60] *Ibid*, at 241.

[61] *Ibid*, at 242.

The existence of differences between procedural systems, and particularly those pertaining to the nature of state authority, has been assumed to preclude a common approach to, or conception of, procedural rights. This view, however, has been somewhat disrupted by the work of the Court, which has purported to apply one notion of 'procedural fairness' to a politically, religiously and geographically divergent group of member states. It is perhaps inevitable that the response of the comparative criminal law scholarship to the case law of the Court has been to examine the developments within the context of the existing 'two traditions' framework. This has resulted once more in the reduction of the analytical potential of comparative law to the determination of whether the Court is applying a more accusatorial (read Anglo-Saxon) or more inquisitorial ('continental European') conception of procedural law. The main concern is with divergence and, of course, convergence between these two traditions. But the case law of the Court—not through its ability (or perhaps inability) to reconcile procedural differences but by simple virtue of its existence—offers something more; for its existence hints at the possibility of pre-existing common, underlying values in the field of criminal procedure law.

The successful application of common procedural rights does not cast doubt on the existence of differences between the state authorities of the various jurisdictions (for these have been exhaustively shown). But it does call into question the importance of these differences in terms of their impact on the formation of procedural standards or rights. Is it possible, in spite of all evidence to the contrary, that there are in fact procedural standards common to all European systems? And can these common standards be situated within one European criminal procedural tradition?

In order to answer these questions it is necessary to determine whether there can be said to be fundamental legal principles on which all, or a majority of, European criminal procedural systems rely. Central both to the identification and appreciation of these fundamental principles and to the explanation of the reasons for their neglect in modern comparative criminal procedural discourse is an understanding of their development. In order to explore the prospect of common European procedural values it is essential to have an understanding of the historical basis of procedural rights in criminal proceedings. This historical slant is vital to the uncovering of a European criminal procedural tradition. An examination of the development of those principles deemed to be central to the taking place of criminal proceedings enables an assessment of the main similarities and differences in the European criminal justice systems. The identification of the values underpinning the procedural rights should allow an evaluation of the sufficiency and purpose of these standards.

The approach is not comparative in the sense of a direct examination and comparison of the provisions of the various legal procedural laws in criminal proceedings: the aim here is not to compare or contrast the European procedural systems,[62] but rather to strive for a better understanding of procedural values through an examination of those principles which have influenced the development of the law in the various European legal systems. The identification of these principles not only permits system analyses against this benchmark, but also enables scrutiny of those areas which cannot yet be said to be governed by common procedural standards or values. This should provide a basis on which the nature of procedural values in Europe can be identified and evaluated.

This in turn will provide the basis on which to assess the role of the Court in the application of the fair trial guarantees of the ECHR. Has the Court contributed significantly to the creation or enhancement of procedural values? Or should its role be seen rather in the context of a restatement, albeit an authoritative and a high profile one, of pre-existing procedural norms and values? Only through an examination of the degree of procedural similarity between the systems before the involvement of the ECHR is it possible to gauge the measure of convergence and to analyse the importance of the Strasbourg authorities. This will then provide a foundation on which to build a critique of the Court's standards and to assess whether there can be said to be a theoretical coherence and consistency to its case law. Further, it will allow for an examination of the areas where the Court has encountered difficulties and for the identification of possible solutions to these problems.

Finally the examination of the development of criminal proceedings in Europe enables not just a better understanding of the European criminal procedural tradition but also provides a basis on which to examine the relationship between procedural fairness and procedural rights. The framing of the definition of procedural fairness in terms of defence rights is closely connected to the notion that 'the criminal justice system is not merely about convicting the guilty and ensuring the protection of the innocent from conviction' but is also orientated toward promoting the 'moral integrity of the criminal trial process'.[63] Although this is a substantial and broad concept that potentially demands the imposition of 'fair trial type' constraints on the authorities both at trial and during the investigation, it is also related to an understanding of criminal proceedings as part of the criminal law's 'conceptual structure of blame, conviction, stigma and punishment'.[64] There are distinct parallels here with the theory of 'orthodox subjectivism'[65] and with according citizens the 'status of autonomous moral agents with an entitlement to freedom of action and the ability to exercise

---

[62] Various studies like this already exist: eg M Delmas-Marty (ed), *Comparative Criminal Procedures* (Cambridge, Cambridge University Press, 2002); C van den Wyngaert (ed), *Criminal Procedure Systems in the European Community* (London, Butterworths, 1993).

[63] N Taylor and D Ormerod, 'Mind the Gaps: Safety, Fairness and Moral Legitimacy' [2004] *Criminal Law Review* 266 at 267, citing R Dworkin, *A Matter of Principle* (Cambridge, Mass, Harvard University Press, 1986) at 72.

[64] IH Dennis, 'The Critical Condition of Criminal Law' [1997] *Current Legal Problems* 213 at 241.

[65] RA Duff, *Agency and Criminal Liability* (Oxford, Oxford University Press, 1990).

self-determination in their choice of actions'.[66] This means in turn that they can 'fairly be held accountable and punishable for the rational choices of wrongdoing that they make'.[67]

It is no coincidence therefore that the majority of analyses of the development of criminal proceedings and indeed the Court in its case law concentrate on the rights of the defence, and specifically on the right to be heard.[68] The increasing emphasis in the course of the nineteenth century on the importance of communication with the accused is seen as corresponding ideally to theories of 'individual responsibility' and the 'rise of individualism'.[69] The right to be heard thus becomes a natural consequence of the developing understanding of the accused as a 'rational and responsible agent', whereby 'the absence of that right would entail a refusal by the court to recognise the accused's status as a participant at trial'.[70] Such accounts place the rights of the defence in the middle of the picture and relegate the institutional structure of the proceedings to the background. This allows notions such as 'communication' to take centre stage, thereby reinforcing notions of fairness as based on the rights of the accused. The emphasis is firmly on the effect of these rights on the procedural form of the proceedings, not on the ways in which the procedural forms dictate the extent of the participatory rights. This is highlighted, for instance, by Cairns, who writes that '[t]he influence of advocacy on the shape of the procedure and the development of the law in this way makes it a proper and long overdue subject for jurisprudential study'.[71]

An examination of the development of criminal proceedings in the nineteenth century will enable an analysis of the strength of arguments emphasising the importance of individual rights during this period. The focus of this evaluation will not lie in the challenging of the idea that participatory rights can be of value to the accused, but rather in examining the ways in which these rights were

[66] IH Dennis, 'Reconstructing the Law of Criminal Evidence' [1989] *Current Legal Problems* 21 at 35; see also H Packer, *The Limits of Criminal Sanctions* (Stanford, Cal, Stanford University Press, 1968) at 74 ff.

[67] IH Dennis, 'The Critical Condition of Criminal Law' [1997] *Current Legal Problems* 213; HLA Hart, *Punishment and Responsibility* (Oxford, Oxford University Press, 1968) especially ch 1.

[68] JH Langbein, 'The Criminal Trial Before The Lawyers' (1978) 45 *University of Chicago Law Review* 263; JH Langbein, 'The Prosecutorial Origins of Defence Counsel in the Eighteenth Century: The Appearance of Solicitors' (1999) 58 *Cambridge Law Journal* 314; JM Beattie, 'Scales of Justice: Defense Counsel and the English Criminal Trial in the Eighteenth and Nineteenth Centuries' (1991) 9 *Law and History Review* 221; DJA Cairns, *Advocacy and the Making of the Adversarial Criminal Trial 1800–1865* (Oxford, Clarendon Press, 1998).

[69] Eg CJW Allen, *The Law of Evidence in Victorian England* (Cambridge, Cambridge University Press, 1997) at 173: the extension of competency to all accused persons may have been more readily achieved because this reform was consistent with the emphasis placed on individual responsibility by much nineteenth century political theory. Between the paternalistic relationships of the eighteenth century state and the administrative state, which was largely in place by the 1870s, came a period in which individualism was valued in social and political reform.

[70] *Ibid*, at 175.

[71] DJA Cairns, *Advocacy and the Making of the Adversarial Criminal Trial 1800–1865* (Oxford, Clarendon Press, 1998) at 179.

fundamentally influenced and indeed constrained by the institutional structure of criminal proceedings which was developing during this period.

It will be argued that the focus on inquisitorial and accusatorial models of procedure has led to the neglect of the nineteenth century procedural tradition and has as such significantly restrained the development of the fair trial protections set out in Article 6. An examination of the traditional values underlying the form of the proceedings and acknowledgement of their importance will highlight the potential for a more coherent development of the fair trial principles in Article 6. This will further provide the basis for an evaluation of the limitations of an understanding of procedural fairness conceived solely or primarily in terms of individual procedural rights.

2

The Origins of the European Criminal Procedural Tradition

The trend of the trial procedure in the various European countries is shown rather by common characteristics than by essential differences.[1]

A The Importance of the Developments of the Nineteenth Century

THE ORIGINS OF the European criminal procedural tradition are to be found in the developments of the nineteenth century. This is a bold claim, but it should not be misunderstood as being more ambitious than it is. It is not a claim about the unification of nineteenth century procedural laws across the continent, nor should it be regarded as implying that there were no pre-nineteenth century procedural principles or that any pre-nineteenth century developments were entirely irrelevant. It would certainly be an exaggeration to claim that the nineteenth century had a monopoly on criminal procedural developments. Many of the principles that will be examined here pre-date this period, and several important writers began analysing these concepts well before this time.[2] Nevertheless, it cannot be denied that this was an extremely significant period in the development of European criminal procedure law. It was not until the nineteenth century that the principles that are now associated with criminal proceedings began to be articulated and justified in such a way as to be recognisable in the modern context.

---

[1] A Esmein, *A History of Continental Criminal Procedure with Special Reference to France* (trans J Simpson, Boston, Mass, Little Brown & Co, 1913; reprinted Union, NJ, The Lawbook Exchange, 2000) at 604.

[2] Eg E Coke, *The Third Part of the Institutes of the Laws of England* (New York, Garland Publishing, 1979, reprint of the 1644 edn); C Beccaria, *Dei delitti e delle pene* (1764), translated into English as *On Crimes and Punishments* by E D Ingraham (Philadelphia, Penn, H Nicklin, 1819); W Blackstone, *Commentaries on the Laws of England* (Oxford, Clarendon Press, 1765); G Filangieri, *Scienza della legislazione* (Filadelfia, Nella Stamperia delle provincie unite, 1800), translated into English as *The Science of Legislation* by Sir R Clayton (Bristol, T Ostell 1806).

The importance of this period rests on two predominant factors. First, in the wake of the French Revolution there was a desire for substantial change and for a complete overhaul of criminal procedure. There is some suggestion that the jurists writing around this time believed that, through expressing and explaining the need for the adoption of a number of procedural values, they could interrupt the injustices of the unsatisfactory procedures of the inquisition.[3] Both their demands for reform and the reasons given to justify the necessity of these reforms are thus of potential relevance in the search for common European procedural values in criminal proceedings.

The second important factor concerns the evidence in the works of the important European jurists and writers of this time of an emerging European discourse.[4] Stephen writes that 'it is difficult to criticise the system [of English criminal law] properly or to enter into its spirit except by comparing it with what may be described as the great rival system,—that which is contained in the French and German penal codes'.[5] The jurists writing during this period unashamedly sought inspiration for the justification and the development of their own procedural principles in the laws of other jurisdictions.[6] Mittermaier, for instance, examines the criminal procedure laws of Scotland, England, France, Austria and the various Swiss Cantons before going on to develop his own critique of German criminal procedure law.[7] Similarly in his book on the role and rights of the defence, the Austrian jurist Vargha writes chapters on everything from the law of the Greeks and the Romans to that of England and France. Glaser in his work on the law of evidence frequently refers to Best, Greenleaf, Stephen and Bentham and to the French jurist Bonnier,[8] while Hélie cites Bentham and Mittermaier,[9] and Zachariä and Stephen both refer to Hélie.[10] There are numerous cross-references throughout all of these works to the writings of the other

---

[3] It is important to note that their demands for reform were made in the belief that they could interrupt the smooth working of the procedure of the inquisition and thereby abolish, or at least limit, the abuses of this procedure. According to Glaser, '*Die Umgestaltung einzelner Räder im Mechanismus des (Inquisitions-) Prozesses können einzelne Umstände beheben, mancherlei Missbräuche beiseitigen oder doch einschränken*', cited in K Geppert, *Der Grundsatz der Unmittelbarkeit im deutschen Strafverfahren* (Berlin, Walter de Gruyter, 1979) at 68.

[4] The jurists whose works are examined here have been selected not only on the basis of their reputation but also for their longevity and their continued importance in the modern literature on criminal procedure law. Their selection is intended to illustrate the opinions of the time rather than to enable an exhaustive historical study of the work of 19th century European jurists.

[5] JF Stephen, *A History of the Criminal Law of England* (London, Macmillan, 1883), i, at 544.

[6] See K Geppert, *Der Grundsatz der Unmittelbarkeit im deutschen Strafverfahren* (Berlin, Walter de Gruyter, 1979) at 68: '*[s]ehr bald setzte sich hier jedoch die Erkenntnis durch, dass eine prinzipielle Neugestaltung erforderlich und ohne Heranziehung ausländischer Vorbilder nicht möglich war*'.

[7] CJA Mittermaier, *Die Gesetzgebung und Rechtsübung über Strafverfahren nach ihrer neusten Fortbildung* (Erlangen, Ferdinand Enke, 1856)

[8] Eg J Glaser, *Beiträge zur Lehre vom Beweis im Strafprozeß* (Leipzig, Duncker & Humblot, 1883) at 34–5.

[9] Eg F Hélie, *Traité de l'Instruction Criminelle*, 2nd edn (Paris, Henri Plon, 1866–7), iv, at 330–5.

[10] Eg HA Zachariä, *Handbuch des deutschen Strafprozesses* (Göttingen, Verlag der Dieterichschen Buchhandlung, 1861 & 1868), i, at 421–5; JF Stephen, *A History of the Criminal Law of England* (London, Macmillan, 1883), i, at 544.

important European jurists, regardless of their nationality. There is a distinct sense in many of the works of this time that the European procedural systems were, if not converging, then developing according to common principles.[11] The works of the nineteenth century jurists therefore provide an ideal foundation for the identification of underlying procedural principles common to the various European jurisdictions. This in turn will allow an examination of whether these reforms can be said to have laid the foundations for a common European approach to criminal procedure law, while simultaneously casting doubt on the validity of the modern accusatorial–inquisitorial classifications.

The nineteenth century is often portrayed as an era in which the liberal ethos of the Enlightenment was finally accepted as applicable in the context of criminal proceedings. According to such arguments, the reforms were primarily orientated towards providing an understanding of the accused as a citizen, and as a participant in the proceedings rather than merely an object of an investigation conducted by state officials. The fairness of the proceedings is thus connected directly to vague political conceptions of liberal reform:

> The early nineteenth century had seen the introduction of considerably fairer trials than in previous centuries when the gentry, judges, and the Crown had generally used the criminal law to keep lower orders in their place.[12]

The procedural developments, and in particular those relating to the 'rights' of the accused, are thereby seen as representative of an era of 'individualism' and of an 'intellectual climate that recognised the principle of individual responsibility'.[13] But despite the prevalence of such theories, there is also evidence which casts serious doubts on their accuracy. Alvarez, for instance, in his informative essay on the dominant legal influences of the second half of the nineteenth century, points on one hand to the enormous increase in civil liability during this period and to the limited extent of the criminal law on the other. He explains the limited use of the criminal law on the basis that:

> jurists, with the results of these sciences [referring to psychology and psychiatry] (and also public sentiment) before them, have been more and more convinced that the criminal is not morally culpable, and that he has acted as a result of more or less apparent forces. The problem of crime is, then, not the punishment of the guilty for an act for which he was never wholly responsible, but his redemption by appropriate means.[14]

---

[11] A Esmein, *A History of Continental Criminal Procedure with Special Reference to France* (trans J Simpson, Boston, Mass, Little Brown & Co, 1913; reprinted Union, NJ, The Lawbook Exchange, 2000) at 604.

[12] J Hostettler, *The Politics of Criminal Law Reform in the Nineteenth Century* (Chichester, Barry Rose, 1992) at 149.

[13] CJW Allen, *The Law of Evidence in Victorian England* (Cambridge, Cambridge University Press, 1997) at 175.

[14] A Alvarez, 'Dominant Legal Influences on the Second Half of the Century' in A Alvarez, L Duguit *et al* (eds), *The Progress of Continental Law in the Nineteenth Century* (London, John Murray, 1918) at 60.

Alvarez is by no means alone in casting doubt on claims that emphasise the link between the fair trial rights of the accused, the 'moral' conception of criminal law and the political climate of 'individualism'. Others have portrayed the development of criminal proceedings in the nineteenth century as being closely connected to the emergence of the 'disciplinary society' and to improvements in the administration and organisation of the prosecution.[15] By focusing on the justifications and principles underlying the form of criminal proceedings, it should be possible to obtain a better understanding of the role of criminal proceedings. The nineteenth century provides the ideal setting for an examination of '[t]he fluidity of criminal procedure and the occasionally close relationship between fairness and efficiency'.[16]

As the objective of this study is to look for influences that have had an impact on the development of the modern criminal procedure law and not to examine the development of the individual criminal procedure laws of the countries themselves, the focus will be on the major institutional principles developed in the works of the jurists. While the study will be concentrated primarily on the largest and most influential of the European legal systems, namely England, France and Germany, the laws of, and developments in, many other countries including Austria, Belgium, Italy, Scotland and Switzerland will also be considered. In the course of this examination it is hoped that it will be possible to demonstrate both that many European legal systems were influenced by the principles advocated and discussed by these 'liberal' reformers and that the institutional developments were not designed solely to ensure that the accused had a forum in which to exercise participatory rights.

B The Development of the 'Accusatorial Trinity'[17]

Das Criterium des Anklageprocesses ist die accusatorische Trinität von Richter, Anklage- und Vertheidigungspartei.[18]

One of the most important moments in the development of European criminal procedure law occurred in 1808 with the enactment of the French *Code*

---

[15] See eg M Foucault, *Power: Essential Works of Foucault 1954–1984* (London, Penguin Books, 2002) at 52 ff; L Farmer, *Criminal Law, Tradition and Legal Order: Crime and the Genius of Scots Law 1747 to the Present* (Cambridge, Cambridge University Press, 1998).

[16] WW Pue, 'The Criminal Twilight Zone: Pre-trial Procedures in the 1840s' (1983) 21 *Alberta Law Review* 335 at 349.

[17] This term, which is a direct translation of that used by Vargha, will be used throughout this ch; although its religious undertones may be seen as inappropriate, it is nevertheless preferable to alternative translations such as the 'accusatorial threesome'!

[18] J Vargha, *Die Vertheidigung in Strafsachen* (Vienna, Manz'sche k k Hof-Verlag und Univ Buchhandlung, 1879) at 288: '[t]he decisive characteristic of criminal proceeding is the accusatorial trinity which is made up of the judge and the prosecuting and defence parties'.

d'instruction criminelle. The institutional structure of French criminal proceedings became the subject of considerable controversy during the drafting of the Code, as supporters of the revolutionary laws of the intermediary period, which had been heavily influenced by English procedural principles, clashed with traditionalists who favoured a return to the principles of the Ordinance of 1670.[19] The principal concerns involved the division of powers between the authorities of the criminal process and the nature of the division between the trial and pre-trial proceedings.

Hélie, writing almost 60 years later, characterised the debate as concerning two possible procedural forms: the accusatorial (*la forme accusatoire*) and the inquisitorial (*la forme inquisitoriale*). In the pure accusatorial model, there was no public prosecution authority, the claimant and the accused were responsible for the collection of their own evidence and the charge was to be determined by an independent judge. In the inquisitorial system the judge was a public official and instituted the prosecution with or without the agreement of the parties; he secretly conducted an examination of the evidence and determined the truth of the facts.[20] Hélie notes that neither of these procedural forms was 'sufficient, taken alone, to protect the diverse interests which it was required to safeguard'.[21] In their pure forms, both models were, as their respective histories demonstrated, deeply flawed, and thus it was essential to develop *'un mode d'instruction qui puisse protéger avec plus d'efficacité, les droits de la société et les droits de l'individu'.*[22] For him, the solution was clear: *'[o]n voit qu'il s'agit d'établir une procédure mixte'.*[23]

The inquisitorial form was seen to be ideal for the investigation. A neutral state authority in the form of an investigating judge with responsibility for gathering the evidence was seen to be the best way of ensuring that the procedural system was not overly reliant on individual interests. This guarded not just against over-enthusiastic prosecutors but also against the potential for those accused of criminal offences or their representatives to interfere with the evidence. On the other hand, Hélie was equally convinced that the inquisitorial form was not the ideal model for the determination of the charge. The investigating judge was to be able to search, to examine and to analyse, but not to judge: the judgment, he

---

[19] For an overview of these developments see A Esmein, *A History of Continental Criminal Procedure with Special Reference to France* (trans J Simpson, Boston, Mass, Little Brown & Co, 1913; reprinted Union, NJ, The Lawbook Exchange, 2000) especially at 462–81.

[20] F Hélie, *Traité de L'instruction Criminelle*, 2nd edn (Paris, Henri Plon, 1866–7), iv, at 38.

[21] *Ibid,* at 40: '*ni la procédure accusatoire, ni la procédure inquisitoriale, n'est suffisante, prise exclusivement, pour la protection des intérêts divers qu'elle doit sauvegarder'.*

[22] *Ibid,* at 41: 'a type of proceedings which could most effectively protect the rights of society and those of the individual'.

[23] *Ibid,* at 42: 'it is a question of establishing a mixed procedural system'; see also F Carrara, *Opuscoli di Diritto Criminali*, 5th edn (Lucca, Tip. Giusti, 1877), ii, at 372; J Glaser, *Handbuch des Strafprozesses* (Leipzig, Duncker & Humblot, 1883 & 1885), i, at 211: One could see that it was essential to establish a mixed procedural system.

writes, was 'the product of personal conviction, not of science', and this conviction could arise 'only in the course of the trial'.[24] Essentially, the trial was to involve 'the interrogation and defence of the accused, the hearing and discussion of the evidence of witnesses, the examination of all of the facts and the assessment of the evidence'. Further, it was necessary that 'the judge, magistrate or jury be present during the debating of these facts and statements', in order to be able to examine and assess the arguments of the prosecution and the defence, and to deliver the verdict.[25]

The procedural reforms adopted in France[26] led to considerable debate on these principles in other European jurisdictions including in Germany and Austria. As in France, the focus of the reform movement was on the trial. The publication of Feuerbach's *Betrachtungen über die Öffentlichkeit und Mündlichkeit der Gerechtigkeitspflege* in 1813 drew attention to the need for reform in Germany, and by the middle of the century a number of influential jurists[27] had published books urging reform. The first significant sign[28] of reform came in 1849 with the publication of the *Reichsverfassung,* in which it was stated both that '*[i]n Strafsachen gilt der Anklageprocess*'[29] and that '*[d]as Gerichtsverfahren soll öffentlich und mündlich sein*'.[30] Although the majority of German regions accepted these principles, which were strongly influenced by the French reforms, they did not gain unanimous acceptance until the enactment of the first German

---

[24] F Hélie, *Traité de L'instruction Criminelle,* 2nd edn (Paris, Henri Plon, 1866–7), iv, at 44: '*le jugement est l'oeuvre de la conviction et non de la science, et une méthode, quelque savante qu'elle soit, peut conduire à former le jugement, mais ne le forme pas. La conviction, ce sentiment intime de la vérité, ne peut naître que dans le débat*'.

[25] *Ibid:* '*[l]a conviction, ce sentiment intime de la vérité, ne peut naître que dans le débat. En effet, ses éléments sont l'interrogatoire et la défense de l'accusé, l'audition et la discussion des témoignages, l'examen de tous les faits, l'appréciation de toutes les preuves. Il faut que le juge, magistrat ou juré, soit présent au débat contradictoire de ces faits et de ces déclarations; que, placé au milieu des allégations contraires de l'accusation et de la défense, qui se heurtent sans cesse, il examine, il apprécie, il arrête son opinion. Les preuves les plus palpables n'ont de valeur que lorsqu'elles ont été soumises à cette épreuve; c'est dans la lutte qu'il soulève que se manifeste la vérité. Et c'est par ce motif que, parmi toutes les formes qui ont pour objet d'affermir la justice humaine, il n'en est aucune qui apporte les garanties de la forme accusatoire*'.

[26] See especially Arts 22, 47, 61 and 70 of the *Code d'instruction criminelle* of 1808; for further comment see Hélie, above n24, iv, at 114 ff.

[27] Notably CJA Mittermaier, *Die Mündlichkeit, das Anklageprinzip, die Öffentlichkeit und das Geschworenengericht in ihrer Durchführung in den verschiedenen Gesetzgebungen dargestellt und nach den Forderungen des Rechts und der Zweckmäßigkeit mit Rücksicht auf die Erfahrung der verschiedenen Länder* (Stuttgart and Tubingen, Cotta, 1845).

[28] It is notable, though, that several German regions had adopted the principle of oral trials before this time: K Geppert, *Der Grundsatz der Unmittelbarkeit im deutschen Strafverfahren* (Berlin, Walter de Gruyter, 1979) at 77.

[29] See para 179 of the *Reichsverfassung* (constitution) of 1849: 'criminal cases shall be accusatorial'. This principle was first set out in the Proclamation of the Frankfurter Nationalversammlung on the fundamental rights of the German nation (*Grundrechten des Deutschen Volkes*) of 21 Dec 1848. A similar provision was adopted in Austria in Art 10 of the *Staatsgrundgesetzes über die Richterlichen Gewalt* of 21 Dec 1867, no 144 of the RGBI: see J Glaser, *Handbuch des Strafprozesses* (Leipzig, Duncker & Humblot, 1883 & 1885), i, at 217.

[30] See para 178 of the *Reichsverfassung* (constitution) of 1849: 'court hearings shall be public and oral'.

federal Code of Criminal Procedure in 1877. These reforms were orientated towards ensuring that an oral hearing could take place at which the judge had the opportunity to observe the examination of the evidence and was intended to move away from a system in which the judge had to reach a verdict on the basis of written evidence provided by a third party.

But if there was a growing consensus as to the idea that the trials should be impartially adjudicated and that both the defence and the prosecution ought to have the opportunity to convince the court of their position, a constellation that Vargha rather poetically refers to as the 'accusatorial trinity',[31] there was considerably less agreement as to the role of the investigation phase (*Voruntersuchung*). Certainly the reforms did not result in its abolition; rather it was reorganised and re-orientated.[32] Whereas in earlier times the investigation phase had been the essence of the proceedings and the forum for the examination of the evidence, in the reformed criminal process it was to be limited to providing for the determination of the necessity or dispensability of the trial (*Hauptverhandlung*), and for securing any evidence which was likely not to be available during the trial. This is clearly set out, for instance, in the 1864 criminal procedure code of Baden[33] and in the German federal Code of Criminal Procedure of 1877:

> *Die Voruntersuchung ist nicht weiter auszudenen, als erforderlich ist, um eine Entscheidung darüber zu begründen, ob das Hauptverfahren zu eröffnen oder der Angeschuldigte ausser Verfolgung zu setzen sei. Auch sei Beweise, deren Verlust für die Hauptverhandlung zu besorgen steht, oder deren Aufnahme zur Vorberitung der Vertheidigung des Angeschuldigten erforderlich erscheint in der Voruntersuchung zu erheben.*[34]

The acceptance of the oral trial as the correct forum for the examination of the evidence and the diminished importance of the pre-trial phase may explain why there were fewer calls in France for reform of the pre-trial phase. Indeed the continuing dominance of the investigating judge in this phase and the strictly limited role afforded to the defence (and the prosecution) seem to have been

---

[31] J Vargha, *Die Verteidigung in Strafsachen* (Vienna, Manz'sche k k Hof-Verlag und Univ Buchhandlung, 1879) at 288.

[32] See J Glaser, *Handbuch des Strafprozesses* (Leipzig, Duncker & Humblot, 1883 & 1885), i, at 211: '*der alte Untersuchungsprozess ward nicht abgeschafft, sondern als Glied eines Prozesses beibehalten, der in einem anderen seiner Bestandtheile unter die Formen des alten mündlich-öffentlichen Anklageprozesses sich unterordnet*'.

[33] Para 65(2) of the criminal procedure code of Baden of 1864 states '*[d]ie Beweise, die in der Hauptverhandlung noch erhoben werden können, sind in der Voruntersuchung nur insoweit zu erheben, als erforderlich ist, um zu beurtheilen, ob die Hauptverhandlung anzuordnen oder das Verfahren einzustellen ist*'.

[34] Para 188 of the German criminal procedural code (StPO) of 1877: 'the investigation phase is not to be more wide-ranging than is required in order to make a decision whether to send the case for trial or to drop the prosecution. Moreover any evidence which may be unavailable at trial or which is required to enable the accused to prepare his defence is to be secured during this phase'. See also J Vargha, *Die Verteidigung in Strafsachen* (Vienna, Manz'sche k k Hof-Verlag und Univ Buchhandlung, 1879) at 390, n 4; J Glaser, *Handbuch des Strafprozesses* (Leipzig, Duncker & Humblot, 1883 & 1885), ii, at 315.

widely accepted.[35] In Germany too, the investigation phase was to remain under the control of the investigating judge with little room for the involvement of the parties.[36] This however found little support among the German jurists who—perhaps also with the advantage of having had the opportunity to witness the developments of the French reforms—maintained that it was essential for the consistent application of the *Anklageprinzip* that it also be applied to the investigation phase.[37] They argued that an impartial authority should be responsible for conducting the investigation proceedings, and that both the prosecution and the defence ought to have certain opportunities to participate.

In view of the fact that the parties were in any event to be given the opportunity to challenge the evidence at an oral and public hearing before an impartial judge, participatory opportunities in the investigation phase might have been expected to be of secondary importance. But there seems to have been widespread realisation among Austrian and German jurists in particular that, in spite of the reforms, the examination of the evidence did not always occur at trial and that this meant that it was essential that the investigation phase was similarly regulated. According to Vargha the fact that the investigation continued to play a dominant role in the criminal process was the result of two main factors. On the one hand investigating judges continued to investigate too much, and on the other there was often considerable reliance at trial on written evidence gathered during the investigation.[38] This necessarily lessened the benefits of the oral and public trial, as much of the evidence was principally examined during the secret investigation phase.

It is important to note therefore that these developments, while essentially resulting in the splitting of the proceedings into an investigative pre-trial phase and a determinative trial, did not restrict judicial involvement to the trial phase.

---

[35] F Hélie, *Traité de L'instruction Criminelle*, 2nd edn (Paris, Henri Plon, 1866–7), iv, ch 4.

[36] According to the Commission responsible for drafting the 1877 Act, the involvement of the parties in the investigation phase could not be reconciled with its 'inquisitorial' character. According to K Geppert, *Der Grundsatz der Unmittelbarkeit im deutschen Strafverfahren* (Berlin, Walter de Gruyter, 1979) at 104: '[d]ie Mehrzahl der Kommission entschied sich jedoch eindeutig für die strenge Fassung des Entwurfs III: weitergehende Parteiöffentlichkeit sei mit der inquisitorischen Natur des Vorverfahrens unvereinbar und führte "auf die Spitze getrieben zu den verderblichsten Konsequenzen", kurz: sei "wissenschaftliche Theorie" und in der Praxis nicht brauchbar' (footnotes omitted).

[37] HA Zachariä, *Die Gebrechen und die Reform des deutschen Strafverfahrens, dargestellt auf der Basis einer consequenten Entwicklung des inquisitorischen und des accusatorischen Prinzips* (Göttingen, Dieterichschen Buchhandlung, 1846) at 64, 73; CJA Mittermaier, *Die Gesetzgebung und Rechtsübung über Strafverfahren nach ihrer neusten Fortbildung* (Erlangen, Ferdinand Enke, 1856) at 272.

[38] J Vargha, *Die Verteidigung in Strafsachen* (Vienna, Manz'sche k k Hof-Verlag und Univ Buchhandlung, 1879) at 391: '[w]er sich diesen verschiedenen Charakter und Zweck des Voruntersuchungsverfahrens der beiden Processe lebhaft vor Augen hält und die Praxis des heutigen österreichischen Anklageprocesses zu beobachten Gelegenheit hatte, wird auch wohl nicht im Zweifel darüber geblieben sein können, dass denselben auch hierin die noch nicht genug bekämpften Reminiscenzen und Einflüsse des abgethanen Inquisitionsprocesses stets noch allzu sehr beherrschen. Es wird einerseits noch immer zu viel "voruntersucht", anderseits aber in der Hauptverhandlung auf das Untersuchungsprotokoll, auch wo es bloss summarische Aufzeichnungen enthält, noch ein allzu grosses Gewicht gelegt'.

In both France and Germany the investigating judge was responsible for supervising the investigation, at least in relation to certain categories of crime.[39] Although they were no longer responsible for the determination of the charge, they had responsibility for overseeing the examination, and in some cases examining the evidence through questioning the accused and witnesses. In the course of the nineteenth century, then, a conception of the structure of the trial as involving opposing sides (the defence and the prosecution) and an impartial judge with responsibility for determining the charge was accepted in England,[40] France and Germany and became the dominant procedural model across Europe. The uncertain role of the investigation phase particularly with regard to its influence on the trial led however to continuing tensions and the relationship between the trial and the investigation was subject to considerable scrutiny by the nineteenth century commentators. Three distinct issues can be marked out as having caught their attention, and are thus of particular interest in the examination of the origins of European criminal procedure: the character of various judicial officers and their relationship in particular to the prosecution; the importance of public hearings; and the requirement that the trial proceedings be oral and immediate.

C Judicial Impartiality

The interpretation of the notion of judicial impartiality[41] had a considerable impact on the development of the form and function of European criminal proceedings. The elucidation of the judicial role necessitated the identification of those parts of the proceedings that required the supervision of an impartial authority as well as regulation of the acceptable extent of the judicial role in relation to the examination of the evidence. The impartiality requirement can be

[39] Following the enactment of the German procedure code of 1877, the investigating judge took part in the investigation of only serious crimes.

[40] On the development of the English adversarial criminal trial see notably JH Langbein, *The Origins of the Adversary Criminal Trial* (Oxford, Oxford University Press, 2002). See also DJA Cairns, *Advocacy and the Making of the Adversarial Criminal Trial 1800–1865* (Oxford, Clarendon Press, 1998); JM Beattie, 'Scales of Justice: Defense Counsel and the English Criminal Trial in the Eighteenth and Nineteenth Centuries' (1991) 9 *Law and History Review* 221.

[41] Impartiality differs from independence in that it prohibits bias towards any of the people involved in the criminal proceedings rather than independence from the other organs of the state: see S Trechsel, *Human Rights in Criminal Proceedings* (Oxford, Oxford University Press, 2005) at 49. On the importance of judicial impartiality see eg L Solum, 'Equity and the Rule of Law' in I Shapiro (ed), *The Rule of Law* (New York, New York University Press, 1994) at 132; B Barry, *Justice as Impartiality* (Oxford, Oxford University Press, 1995); A Schedler, 'Arguing and Observing: Internal and External Critiques of Judicial Impartiality' (2004) 12 *Journal of Political Philosophy* at 248; J Rawls, *A Theory of Justice* (Cambridge, Mass, Harvard University Press, 1971) at 58.

seen to be made up of two principal elements: first that judges be free from personal involvement in or bias towards the case at issue, and secondly that they be institutionally impartial.[42]

The requirement that the judge responsible for determining the charge be personally impartial was accepted during the course of the nineteenth century by many jurisdictions as a prerequisite of criminal proceedings. Perhaps the most common expression of this principle was to be found in provisions preventing judges from ruling on matters directly affecting either their own interests or those of their direct relatives. There are many examples of such rules. The German federal Code of Criminal Procedure of 1877, for instance, prevented judges ruling on a matter in which they, or their close relatives, were personally involved.[43] This provision required that judges be disqualified from ruling in the case if they were the spouse or guardian of the accused or the victim, if they were directly related to the accused or the victim by blood, marriage or adoption, or if they had already been heard in the case as witnesses.[44] Similarly, according to *Archbold's Pleading and Evidence*, a principal challenge to the array could be made in England where the sheriff was 'the actual prosecutor or party aggrieved',[45] where 'he was actual affinity to either party' or if he returned 'any jurors at the request of the prosecutor or defendant', or any person whom he believed 'to be more favourable to the one side than to the other'.[46] Hume suggests that analogous rules applied to the Scottish jury: '[i]n the case of a prosecution at private instance, it is a good objection to any juryman, that he is near of kin to the accuser'.[47]

The relatively uncontroversial nature of the personal impartiality requirement stands in direct contrast to the position with regard to the obligation to ensure institutional impartiality. The difficulties in defining an acceptable notion of

[42] B Barry, *Justice as Impartiality* (Oxford, Oxford University Press, 1995).

[43] According to para 22(1), (2), (3) and (5). Further, para 22(4), *'[e]in Richter ist von der Ausübung des Richteramts kraft Gesetzes ausgeschlossen . . .: 4. wenn er in der Sache als Beamter der Staatsanwaltschaft, als Polizeibeamter, als Anwalt des Verletzten oder als Vertheidiger thätig gewesen ist . . .'* provides that a judge is not competent to act if he has already been involved in the case in his capacity as an officer of the prosecuting authorities, as a police officer or as the lawyer for either the victim or the accused. Para 23 meanwhile provides that a judge who has sat at first instance is not competent to take part in any appeals, while an investigation judge is prohibited from sitting as a judge at first instance.

[44] HA Zachariä, *Handbuch des deutschen Strafprozesses* (Göttingen, Verlag der Dieterichschen Buchhandlung, 1861 & 1868), i, at 334 ff suggests that the idea that *'niemand Richter in eigener Sach sehn und dass der verdächtige Richter recusirt werden könne'* had a considerable history in German customary law.

[45] *R v Sheppard*, 1 Leach 101; *R v Edmonds*, 4 B & Ald 471.

[46] J Jervis (ed), *Archbold's Pleading & Evidence in Criminal Cases* (London, H Sweet, 1878) at 164.

[47] D Hume, *Commentaries on the Law of Scotland, Respecting Crimes* (Edinburgh, Bell & Bradfute, 1844), ii, at 311. In Scotland the procurator fiscal had had responsibility for composing the list of jurors. As such 'dependence on the pursuer' was a legitimate ground for objecting to a member of the jury. According to Hume, '[i]t was nothing unusual formerly, to have an assizer rejected, (ordained to *stand aside*, as the style for it was,) because he, or perhaps his wife, was second or third cousin, *seconds and thirds* as they called it, to the prosecutor', citing the cases of *Hew Crosbie*, 20 July 1616 and *George Mylne*, 27 Feb 1618.

institutional impartiality reflected the lack of unanimity as to the role of judges in the proceedings, particularly with regard to their relationship to the prosecution. In jurisdictions such as France and Germany, the controversy was mainly the result of unresolved tension involving the distribution of functions between the trial and investigative phases of the proceedings. In England on the other hand, the difficulties were predominantly tied to the frequent absence of prosecuting counsel at trial which gave rise to concerns that, in the course of examining the evidence, the judge was forced into assuming the mantle of the prosecutor.[48]

(i)   The Separation of the Functions of 'Judging' and 'Prosecuting' in France and Germany

> From the nature of the institution the public prosecutor is a party; from his title it belongs to him to prosecute, but for that very reason it would be contrary to justice to allow him to conduct the examination proceedings.[49]

Prior to the nineteenth century it was quite common to find, in both France and in the various German regions, one authority (often known as an 'investigating judge' or an 'examining magistrate') with responsibility for overseeing the investigation, conducting the hearings in which the evidence was examined and for determining the charge. By the end of the eighteenth century this 'inquisitorial' system was increasingly viewed as unacceptable, and it was effectively abolished in the wide-ranging criminal procedural reforms that followed the French Revolution. The 'main crime' of the inquisitorial system, according to Zachariä, was not the lack of procedural opportunities of the defence but rather the fact that the same authority had been responsible both for prosecuting and examining. Many writers marked out this duality of functions as the most pressing institutional aspect of the system that had to be reformed.[50] Mittermaier agreed with this, and noted that 'as soon as investigating judges were also required to act as prosecutors', their 'objectivity and impartiality' were 'endangered'.[51] The separation of the functions of prosecuting and examining' provided, in Hélie's

---

[48]   D Bentley, *English Criminal Justice in the Nineteenth Century* (London, Hambledon Press, 1998) at 65.

[49]   Minister of Religion, Locré vol XXV at 124, cited by A Esmein, *A History of Continental Criminal Procedure with Special Reference to France* (trans J Simpson, Boston, Mass, Little Brown & Co, 1913; reprinted Union, NJ, The Lawbook Exchange, 2000) at 502.

[50]   HA Zachariä, *Handbuch des deutschen Strafprozesses* (Göttingen, Verlag der Dieterichschen Buchhandlung, 1861 & 1868), i, at 421: '[d]ie Vermischung beider Functionen im Inquisitionsprocess war das Hauptgebrechen desselben und der Gewinn eines besondern Organs für die gerichtliche Verfolgung des Verbrechens eine der dringendsten reformatorischen Forderungen'.

[51]   CJA Mittermaier, *Die Gesetzgebung und Rechtsübung über Strafverfahren nach ihrer neusten Fortbildung* (Erlangen, Ferdinand Enke, 1856) at 273: '[s]obald man den Untersuchungsrichter zum Ankläger machte, musste seine Unparteilichkeit gefährdet [werden]'.

opinion, the best way of safeguarding the investigation proceedings as it allowed investigating judges, by virtue of their institutional independence, to concentrate solely on the interests of justice.[52]

These developments seem to have been influenced not just by the rights of the accused but also by a strengthened understanding of the criminal procedural system as constructed around the notion of the interests of society. The public prosecutor was to be responsible for representing the interest of the state in the prosecuting of crime and the instituting of proceedings against the accused.[53] This task, however, could not be reconciled with the impartiality required of the judiciary and of the investigating judge. Although until the introduction of these reforms the prosecution of crime had been a matter for the state organs, there was no one institution responsible for representing the interests of the state in the prosecution of crime.

Despite having responsibility for preparing the case against the accused, investigating judges were supposed, in theory, to be neutral agents of the state, who were charged with the neutral task of uncovering the truth. Consequently, in the course of gathering and examining the evidence they were expected to represent both the interests of the accused and the interests of society in the prosecution of crime. Even after the acceptance of the form of the trial as based on the accusatorial trinity of trial judge,[54] prosecution and defence, the continued dominance of investigating judges in the proceedings meant that their role was subject to considerable scrutiny. According to Mittermaier the debate concerning the desirability of dividing the functions of prosecution and investigation had been raging since the middle of the eighteenth century.[55] The procedural reforms did not begin however until around the time of the drafting of the French Code of Criminal Examination 1808, when the issue became the subject of considerable debate. Both the pre-revolutionary laws and the laws of the intermediary period (which had instituted a number of reforms including notably improved defence 'rights' and jury trials) had allowed for the same authority to receive denunciations and complaints, hear the witnesses, issue the

---

[52] F Hélie, *Traité de L'instruction Criminelle*, 2nd edn (Paris, Henri Plon, 1866–7), iv, at 114: '[c]ette division des pouvoirs, qui maintient exclusivement entre les mains du juge toute la procédure, est la plus forte garantie de l'instruction, puisque le juge, par l'indépendance même de ses functions, ne peut avoir d'autres intérêts que les intérêts de la justice'.

[53] HA Zachariä, *Handbuch des deutschen Strafprozesses* (Göttingen, Verlag der Dieterichschen Buchhandlung, 1861 & 1868), i, at 421: '[d]er Character der Staatsanwaltschaft in ihrer Beziehung zur Strafrechtspflege wird im Allgemeinen richtig dahin bezeichnet, dass sie den in seiner rechtlichen Ordnung durch das Verbrechen verletzten Staat zu vertreten hat'.

[54] The term 'trial judge' is used here (rather in the sense of the 'erkennende Richter') to distinguish the judge whose task it is to determine the verdict from the investigating judge, and is without prejudice to the manner and form of the criminal proceedings.

[55] CJA Mittermaier, *Die Gesetzgebung und Rechtsübung über Strafverfahren nach ihrer neusten Fortbildung* (Erlangen, Ferdinand Enke, 1856) at 269: '[s]eit der Mitte des vorigen Jahrhunderts wurde in Bezug auf die Strafprozessgesetzgebung der Streit über den Vorzug des Anklage- und des Untersuchungsprozesses lebhaft verhandelt'.

warrant to bring the accused before the court and interrogate the accused.[56] Similarly, the initial draft of the 1808 Act made provision for one authority to be trusted with investigating and examining the evidence. Many, including the French Minister of Religion and the Archchancellor, viewed this as unacceptable. The concern was expressed in the following terms:

> From the nature of the institution the public prosecutor is a party; from his title it belongs to him to prosecute, but for that very reason it would be contrary to justice to allow him to conduct the examination proceedings.[57]

Their apprehensions were thus primarily orientated towards the fact that the investigating judge (or as Esmein—or at least his translator—puts it, public prosecutor) was responsible for conducting the examination of the evidence:

> functions have been transferred to the public prosecutor which formerly belonged exclusively to the judge. This is a return it is true to the existing system where the magistrate of the police takes the double function of public prosecutor and examiner; but the old system had the advantage of putting two officials in action in such a way that the inaction of a single official was not sufficient to stay the course of justice.[58]

Those opposing the drafts appealed to the French criminal legal 'tradition' and to the situation in other European criminal justice systems. Recourse to the historical or traditional procedural roots was particularly evident and frequent reference was made to the Ordinance of 1670, which had provided for a separation of the functions of prosecuting and examining. This allowed those challenging the draft to argue that the difficulties associated with combining the functions of prosecuting and examining had earlier been recognised in French law, and that the reforms were in keeping with the French tradition:

> The old system also gave more safeguards to the accused; the public prosecutor claimed, the judge pronounced; so that the authority was not concentrated in the same hands. It was impossible to see without consternation the same official receiving the complaint or the denunciation, hearing the witnesses, and disposing of the liberty of the accused.[59]

The opponents of the draft succeeded in their opposition and the 1808 Code provided for the separation of the roles of the prosecutor and the investigating judge.[60] The French reforms did not go unnoticed elsewhere in Europe. The

---

[56] A Esmein, *A History of Continental Criminal Procedure with Special Reference to France* (trans J Simpson, Boston, Mass, Little Brown & Co, 1913; reprinted Union, NJ, The Lawbook Exchange, 2000) at 500.

[57] Cited in Esmein, above n56, at 502.

[58] The then Archchancellor, cited in *ibid.*

[59] M. Defermon, locré vol XXIV, 552, cited in Esmein, above n58; see generally F Hélie, *Traité de L'instruction Criminelle*, 2nd edn (Paris, Henri Plon, 1866–7), iv, at 112 ff: '*[l]'une des règles fondamentales de notre procédure criminelle est la séperation de la poursuite et de l'instruction*'.

[60] A Esmein, *A History of Continental Criminal Procedure with Special Reference to France* (trans J Simpson, Boston, Mass, Little Brown & Co, 1913; reprinted Union, NJ, The Lawbook Exchange, 2000) at 504. See Arts 22, 53 and 54 of the *Code d'instruction criminelle* 1808.

duality of functions of the investigating judge was also recognised as problematic in many of the German regions. That the French reforms did not have an immediate impact in all of the German regions is highlighted however by the fact that in 1813 legislation was still being enacted which, like the former French system, invested complete control of the examination proceedings in investigating judges.[61] But a number of regions in Germany were sufficiently influenced by the French reforms to enact similar principles requiring the separation of the functions of prosecuting and investigating,[62] and following the enactment of the federal Code of Criminal Procedure in 1877 the separation of the investigating judge from the prosecuting authorities had been completed, at least in relation to serious crimes.

The insistence on the importance of the impartiality of the investigating judge from the parties to the proceedings, despite the acceptance of the idea that the trial had to be conducted orally before the judge responsible for determining the charge, is of particular interest. In part it seems to have been influenced by the recognition of the continuing importance of the investigation phase. But the insistence on the existence of impartial investigation authorities also allowed legislators to restrict the role of the accused and their representatives in this phase of the proceedings. The impartiality of the investigating judge was deemed sufficient to uphold the legitimacy and fairness of the proceedings, and crucially without recourse to defence 'rights'. Mittermaier had argued that the well-intentioned but ultimately flawed principle, which required the 'investigating judge' to investigate the accused person's guilt as well as his or her innocence, compromised the legitimacy of the investigation hearings. This principle meant that the investigating judge was expected to take on the role of the accused person's defence counsel, a function that, in view of his or her role in prosecuting the accused, was impossible to fulfil, but which nevertheless justified the refusal to allow the accused to appoint a 'real' defence counsel during the investigation phase.[63] Freeing investigating judges of their responsibility to prosecute, however, meant that there was no longer the same need to ensure that the accused was permitted a participatory role in the proceedings.

---

[61] Bavarian procedural code of 1813, especially Arts 157 and 158. See also W Breithaupt, *Die Strafe des Staupenschlags und ihre Abschaffung im Gemeinen Recht* (Jena, Diss, 1938) and RJ Evans, *Tales from the German Underworld: Crime and Punishment in the Nineteenth Century* (New Haven, Conn, Yale University Press, 1998) at 97.

[62] CJA Mittermaier, *Die Gesetzgebung und Rechtsübung über Strafverfahren nach ihrer neusten Fortbildung* (Erlangen, Ferdinand Enke, 1856) at 355, referring, *inter alia*, to Hannover, Saxony and Brunswick.

[63] *Ibid*, at 273.

(ii) Impassivity or Activity: The Role of the English Judge in the Examination of the Evidence

> It is a disgrace to the county to impose on the judge the necessity to act as counsel against the prisoners.[64]

> The duty most appropriate to the office and character of a judge is that of an attentive listener to all that is to be said on both sides, not that of an investigator.[65]

In England where the focus of the proceedings was the accusatorial trial there was less interest in the role of the investigation proceedings, but this does not mean that the issue of judicial impartiality was entirely uncontroversial. In pre-nineteenth century English criminal law, 'the private vengeance of the person wronged by a crime was the principal source to which men trusted for the administration of criminal justice'. Indeed this was taken by Stephen to be the 'principal distinctive peculiarity' of the English criminal justice system and explained 'the degree to which a criminal trial resembles private litigation'.[66] The absence of a centralised system of prosecution meant that victims (or their relatives in cases involving homicide) usually served as the 'prosecutors' in the case, although, according to Stephen, English procedure law permitted 'any one to take upon himself that office, whether or not he is aggrieved by the crime'.[67] This was also reflected in the inefficiency of the criminal trial, not least because prosecutors seldom appeared. It was not until the end of the nineteenth century that counsel for the prosecution appeared in the majority of cases.[68] The absence of prosecuting counsel at trial resulted not only in inefficiency and difficulties securing convictions, but was also seen as problematic because it forced judges into 'acting as prosecutors'. In *R v Anon*, for instance, Coleridge J held that 'prosecutors should always instruct counsel, and in every case a brief for the prosecution will be allowed. *A judge ought never to prosecute.*'[69] The 'acting as a prosecutor' here seems to refer to the judicial involvement in 'examining the prosecution witnesses'.[70]

This idea is more clearly expressed in *R v Hezell* where the judge held that '[t]here has been a great deal of neglect of duty somewhere. In a case of this

---

[64]   Patteson J in *R v Anon*, reported in *Bedford Mercury*, 23 Mar 1844; see D Bentley, *English Criminal Justice in the Nineteenth Century* (London, Hambledon Press, 1998) at 65.

[65]   JF Stephen, *A History of the Criminal Law of England* (London: Macmillan, 1883), i, at 544.

[66]   *Ibid*, at 245.

[67]   *Ibid*, at 154.

[68]   See eg D Bentley, *English Criminal Justice in the Nineteenth Century* (London, Hambledon Press, 1998) at 71. It is worth noting here that Langbein has pointed to the emergence of a role for solicitors for the prosecution in the early decades of the 18th century as a pivotal moment in the development of English criminal proceedings. As these 'prosecutors' were often prohibited from appearing in court at trial, their principal activities took place in the context of the pre-trial phase and involved the collection of evidence: JH Langbein, 'The Prosecutorial Origins of Defence Counsel in the Eighteenth Century: The Appearance of Solicitors' (1999) 58 *Cambridge Law Journal* 314 at 360.

[69]   *R v Anon* (1843) 1 Cox 48 (Western Circuit: Devon Summer Assizes, Exeter, 29 July).

[70]   Eg D Bentley, *English Criminal Justice in the Nineteenth Century* (London, Hambledon Press, 1998) at 71.

magnitude a judge ought not to be required to prosecute. It is most unseemly for a judge to be called to act as a prosecutor, instead of holding the scales between the parties.' In summing up he continued, '[t]here was imposed on me the disagreeable and *improper*—if such an expression may be allowed—I say, *improper* task of prosecuting, owing to which I have been unable to take notes of evidence'.[71] Similar disquiet was expressed by Maule J in *R v Page*:

> The fiction of law in criminal cases is, that the judge is counsel for the prisoner, but here it is sought, not only to upset and to reverse that doctrine, and make me counsel for the prosecution, but to throw the whole burden of the prosecution on me, and to leave me to make out the best case I can against the prisoner by a careful and diligent perusal of the dispositions. But I will not do it. It is indecent. I will be counsel for the prisoner, and let the depositions be handed to some counsel to conduct the prosecution.[72]

Bentley writes that

> from the accused's point of view, the obvious objections to judges prosecuting was the look of the thing and the potential for unfairness. If there was no prosecuting counsel, and Crown witnesses went back on what they had said in their depositions, it was the judge who had the task of cross-examining them about the inconsistency. If the accused called witnesses or gave evidence himself (as he could do after 1885 in most cases of sexual assault) it was the judge who had to cross-examine. This descent of the judge into the arena looked unfair. When done in a partisan spirit (an ever-present danger where counsel appeared for the prisoner), it could actually work injustice.[73]

This observation, though, seems to be aimed at the potential for unfairness rather than being based on any particular model of fairness.

There are clear parallels here with the concerns of the nineteenth century French and German jurists in relation to the succession of functions of the investigating judge. The requirement that English trial judges question and challenge the accused and the witnesses meant that, like their continental counterparts, they were forced into the dual roles of investigating and prosecuting, the only difference being that this occurred in the course of a public hearing and not in the context of the secret investigation hearings. In neither case did it make a difference that a separate authority (the 'trial judge' in France and Germany and the jury in England) was ultimately responsible for determining the verdict, because there was a realisation that the succession of functions on the part of the judicial authorities nevertheless negatively impacted on the fairness of the proceedings.

The precise relationship between judicial impartiality and the requirement that the judge refrain from involvement in questioning witnesses remains somewhat unclear. Although the notion of judicial impartiality seems (and indeed is often held to be) closely tied to the principle that the judge should not take an active

---

[71] *R v Hezell* (1844) 1 Cox 348 (Western Circuit: Exeter Lent Assizes, 18 Mar).
[72] *R v Henry J Page* (1847) 2 Cox 221
[73] *Ibid*, at 74.

role in examining the evidence, these cases, particularly when viewed in the broader European context and from an historical perspective, suggest that the major concern was not the issue whether the judge should be permitted to ask questions, but rather the point that the judge should not assume the role or even the attitude of a prosecutor. This view appears to receive support from Stephen who writes that it was acceptable for the judge and jury to ask 'such questions as they may think necessary'.[74] This seems to suggest that it was not the judicial activity in asking questions per se that was undesirable, but rather the idea that in the absence of the prosecutor the judge was forced to construct a case for the prosecution, thereby assuming mentally the role of a prosecutor, and it was this element that was irreconcilable with the principle of judicial impartiality.

This is also supported by Stephen's comparison of English and French trial procedure where he refers to the questioning of the accused by the judge as 'the weakest and most objectionable part of the whole system of French criminal procedure except parts of the law as to the functions of the jury'.[75] His objections seemed to have been principally directed towards the manner in which the accused was examined:

> The accused is cross-examined with the utmost severity, and with continual rebukes, sarcasms, and exhortations, which no counsel in an English court would be permitted by any judge who knew and did his duty to address to any witness… It cannot but make the judge a party—and what is more, a party adverse to the prisoner—and it appears to me, apart from this, to place him in a position essentially undignified and inconsistent with his other functions… The duty most appropriate to the office and character of the judge is that of an attentive listener to all that is to be said on both sides, not that of an investigator. After performing that duty patiently and fully, he is in a position to give a jury the full benefit of his thoughts on the subject, but if he takes the leading and principal part in the conflict—and every criminal trial is as essentially a conflict and struggle for life, liberty from imprisonment, or character, as the ancient trials by combat were—he cannot possibly perform properly his own special duty. He is, and of necessity must be, powerfully biased against the prisoner.[76]

It would be inaccurate to conclude that the English notion of judicial impartiality was principally dependent on the idea of judicial passivity. The nineteenth century judicial revolt seems to have been related to broader institutional concerns, and principally to the absence of the prosecutor which, by impinging on the judicial role, was seen as unbalancing the proceedings and thereby negatively affecting the position of the accused. But it would be wrong to see the introduction of prosecuting counsel as being solely, or even primarily, to protect the position of the accused; the chaotic nature of prosecutions was equally relevant. The system of 'reward-based prosecutions' which had been introduced in an attempt to increase the number of criminal prosecutions had given rise in

---

[74] JF Stephen, *A History of the Criminal Law of England* (London, Macmillan, 1883), i, at 430.
[75] *Ibid,* at 543.
[76] *Ibid,* at 544.

turn to serious concerns about the potential of solicitors to 'falsify or to tamper with evidence in ways that judge and jury might be unable to detect at trial'. Latterly these payments were so successfully contested by defence counsel that there was some suggestion that 'many notorious offenders' were commonly escaping justice.[77] The judicial refusal to 'prosecute' and the subsequent introduction of prosecuting counsel must also be seen as orientated towards increasing the efficiency and effectiveness of prosecutions.

(iii)   Institutional Impartiality

The extent of the judicial impartiality requirement can be seen to have had a considerable effect on the form of the proceedings. In England at the beginning of the nineteenth century the prosecutorial system, if indeed it can be classed as a system, was in disarray. The growing judicial disquiet with this and the requirement that the judiciary take on the roles of judging, prosecuting and defending mirrored societal disquiet with the inefficiency of prosecutions. The decision to insist on the appearance of counsel for the prosecution at trial and the consequent change of emphasis from the relationship between the judge and the prosecution to the relationship between the prosecution and the defence must also be seen as an institutional reform designed to increase the efficiency of criminal prosecutions. In France and Germany meanwhile, where the increasing the role of the defence in the investigation hearings was perceived as having the potential seriously to compromise the efficiency of the investigation, the creation of the institution of the impartial investigating judge was seen by the legislatures (although not by the majority of jurists) as an ideal alternative able to uphold the legitimacy of the proceedings without interfering too much with the effectiveness of prosecutions. The evolution of the defence's role was thus contingent across Europe on the definition of judicial impartiality. It would of course be disingenuous to suggest that judicial impartiality was orientated only towards facilitating the prosecution; but equally it would be inaccurate to characterise it solely in terms of defence rights. Crucially it enabled, as part of the accusatorial trinity, the construction of a system of criminal proceedings that could be presented as both efficient and fair.

D   The Public Hearing Requirement

The requirement that criminal trials take place in public was the subject of considerable debate in many European countries during the nineteenth century,

---

[77] See L Radzinowicz, *A History of English Criminal Law and Its Administration from 1750* (London, Stevens & Sons, 1948–68), ii, at 57–137; P Colquhoun, *A Treatise on the Police of the Metropolis*, 7th edn (London, J Mawman, 1806) at 222.

and it had, by the end of the century, become a feature of the majority of European legal systems.[78] Before this time, the principle that criminal proceedings be conducted in public had been established in only a limited number of jurisdictions—among them Scotland and England. The Scottish writer Hume refers in his *Commentaries* to the statute of 1693 c 27, which stated:

> That after the debate concerning the relevancy of criminal libels, dittays, or exculpations made by the parties or their prosecutors are closed, the Commissioners of Justiciary, and other criminal Judges, shall advise the same with open doors, in presence of the pannel, the assize and all others.[79]

He makes reference to just one exception, in cases of 'rape, adultery and the like', and even this seems to have been relatively narrowly defined. In *Granville Sharp Pattison and others, surgeons,* where the crime involved 'raising a corpse from the grave, and dissecting it', the court held that the case did not come 'within the exception of the act of Parliament', and that, because the Act was 'otherwise imperative on the Court', the trial was 'to proceed with open doors, in the usual form'. Hume explains this in the following way:

> The judges were of the opinion, that the exception in the act relates to those cases only, where the evidence is of such a kind as may vitiate the minds, or endanger the morals of the hearers; which is not true of *anatomical* details.[80]

This approach is confirmed by MacDonald, who writes:

> The trial of a crime takes place with open doors. It is illegal to exclude the public except in case of indecent and unnatural offences, or in cases where the Court has been cleared in consequence of disorderly conduct or intimidation.[81] Where the Court is cleared to try cases of an indecent description, the doors should be opened before the jury return their verdict.[82]

---

[78] This principle is also widely considered to be of importance in modern criminal procedure law. According to the German High Court the principle, '*zählt zu den Grundlagen des Strafverfahrens*', and to '*den grundlegenden Einrichtungen des Rechtsstaates*' ('is considered to be a fundamental principle of criminal procedure law and one of the fundamental requirements of the rule of law'), BGHSt 1, 335; 2, 57; 9, 281. See too M-T Fögen, *Der Kampf um die Gerichtsöffentlichkeit* (Berlin, Duncker & Humblot, 1974). On the importance of the publicity principle in Switzerland see F Bommer, 'Öffentlichkeit der Hauptverhandlung zwischen Individualgrundrecht und rechtsstaatlich-demokratischem Strukturprinzip' in A Donatsch, M Forster and C Schwarzenegger (eds), *Strafrecht, Strafprozessrecht und Menschenrecht: Festschrift für Stefan Trechsel zum 65. Geburtstag* (Zurich, Schulthess, 2002) and F Clerc, 'Réflections sur la publicité des débats' (1961) 77 *Schweizerische Zeitschrift für Strafrecht* 233.

[79] D Hume, *Commentaries on the Law of Scotland, Respecting Crimes* (Edinburgh, Bell & Bradfute, 1844) at 304.

[80] *Ibid*, referring to *Granville Sharp Pattison and others, surgeons*, judgment of 6 June 1814.

[81] Referring to the Act of 1693, c 27; and to *Finnie v Gilmour*, HC, 11 June 1850, J Shaw 368; *Orr v McCallum*, HC, 25 June 1855, 2 Irv 183 and 27 SJ 500.

[82] JHA MacDonald, *A Practical Treatise on the Criminal Law of Scotland* (Edinburgh, William Green & Son, 1894) at 426. It is interesting to note that Art 6(1) is significantly more restrictive in this respect in that it does not require absolutely that the verdict be pronounced publicly: see eg S Trechsel, *Human Rights in Criminal Proceedings* (Oxford, Oxford University Press, 2005) at 131.

In England there was little discussion in the works of nineteenth century writers of the importance of the principle that trials be public, precisely because publicity was seen as an integral characteristic of the English trial, its significance so obvious and self-explanatory as not to warrant further explanation. Stephen does underline in passing the importance of the principle when considering the possibility (and desirability) of excluding the public in cases of indecency, suggesting that '[a]ll necessary publicity might be secured, and all possibility of perversions of justice by reason of the exclusion of the public opinion might be avoided, by providing that persons having business in court, and particularly reporters for newspapers, should not be excluded'.[83]

In other jurisdictions where a culture of secrecy had dominated criminal proceedings in the seventeenth and eighteenth centuries there was considerable discussion of the value of the public hearing requirement. Until the reforms around the turn of the nineteenth century, French criminal proceedings were based on the principle of secrecy set out in the Ordinance of 1670 which was, according to Esmein, 'rigorously followed':[84] '[t]he witnesses shall be heard secretly and separately'.[85] It is of little surprise therefore that the public trial requirement was not recognised in France until after the revolutionary reforms of the late eighteenth century.[86] The secrecy of the trial was one of the mains reasons cited by commentators in support of their demands for reform. Among the important eighteenth century writers Voltaire was a particularly vocal advocate for public trials and, aware no doubt of the significance of the nationalistic sentiment at this time, referred not just to the English law but also to the Roman law in support of his claims. Thus:

> Among the Romans the witnesses were heard publicly, in the presence of the accused, who could reply to them himself, or employ an advocate to do so. That procedure was noble and frank; it breathed Roman magnanimity.[87]

But Voltaire's main source of reference and inspiration was undoubtedly England. 'Voltaire constantly refers to what passes on the other side of the Channel', writes Esmein, and his support for the public nature of the English trial is evident:

---

[83]   JF Stephen, *A History of the Criminal Law of England* (London, Macmillan, 1883), i, at 516.

[84]   A Esmein, *A History of Continental Criminal Procedure with Special Reference to France* (trans J Simpson, Boston, Mass, Little Brown & Co, 1913; reprinted Union, NJ, The Lawbook Exchange, 2000) at 220.

[85]   Title VI, Art 1 of the Ordinance of 1670.

[86]   On the possibility that many of these reforms mirrored the earlier French law as set out in the Ordinance of 1670 see A Esmein, *A History of Continental Criminal Procedure with Special Reference to France* (trans J Simpson, Boston, Mass, Little Brown & Co, 1913; reprinted Union, NJ, The Lawbook Exchange, 2000) at 500–27.

[87]   Volatire, quoted in *ibid*, at 360.

Fortunately in England no trial is secret, because the chastisement of crimes is intended to be a public lesson to the people and not a private vengeance; the examinations are made with open doors and accounts of all the trials of interest are published in the newspapers.[88]

Montesquieu's 'disciple' Beccaria, whose *On Crimes and Punishments* was translated in 1766 from Italian into French,[89] was also hugely influential, perhaps even more so in France than in his native Italy.[90] 'Let the judgments be public', he writes, 'let the proofs of the crime be public, and public opinion, which can be the only social restraint, will keep violence and passion in check'.[91]

The principle that trials be public was adopted, for both civil and criminal cases, in the French laws of the late eighteenth and early nineteenth centuries,[92] and was included in the *Code d'instruction criminelle* of 1808. That it was held to be of considerable importance was reflected in the fact that proceedings—which were to be taken to include the hearing (*l'audience*) as well as the debates (*les débats*)—not held in public were to be deemed null and void.[93] The principle of public hearings thus became not just part of the French procedural system, but also *'l'une des premières règles posées par l'Asemblée constituante'.*[94]

The influence of the French reforms on the other European jurisdictions was considerable. In neighbouring Germany, there were even some calls for the French principles to be adopted in their entirety.[95] Writing in 1821, Feuerbach however cautioned against such an approach, arguing instead for careful consideration of the essence of concepts such as public and oral proceedings.[96] His pioneering work was subsequently taken up by a number of jurists including, in

---

[88] Quoted in *ibid*, at 361.

[89] Quoted in *ibid*, at 362.

[90] *Ibid*, at 362–4.

[91] C Beccaria, *Dei delitti e delle pene* (1764), translated into English as *On Crimes and Punishments* by ED Ingraham (Philadelphia, Penn, H Nicklin, 1819) ch VII.

[92] See, *inter alia*, the Law of 8–9 Oct 1789; Arts 14 and 15, Title II, of the Law of 16–24 Aug 1790; Art 203 of the Constitution of 5 fructidor; Art 81 of the Charter of 1814; Art 55 of the Charter of 1830; Art 81 of the Constitution of 1848; Art 153 of the *Code d'Instruction Criminelle* 1808 (des Tribunaux de Simple Police); Art 190 (des Tribunaux en Matière Correctionelle); and Art 309 (Cours d'Assises), cited in F Hélie, *Traité de L'instruction Criminelle*, 2nd edn (Paris, Henri Plon, 1866–7), vii, at 474; see also J-E Boitard, *Leçons sur les Code Pénal et d'Instruction Criminelle*, 3rd edn (Paris, Gustave Thorel, 1844); A Esmein, *A History of Continental Criminal Procedure with Special Reference to France* (trans J Simpson, Boston, Mass, Little Brown & Co, 1913; reprinted Union, NJ, The Lawbook Exchange, 2000) at 510–11.

[93] Art 7 of the Law of 10 Apr 1810. See also the judgment in Cass, 17 May 1810 (JP, tome VIII, 312) cited by F Hélie, *Traité de L'instruction Criminelle*, 2nd edn (Paris, Henri Plon, 1866–7), vii, at 475. There were some exceptions to this rule: see *ibid*, at 478.

[94] *Ibid*, at 474: 'one of the first rules laid down by the Constituent Assembly'.

[95] On the influence of the French reforms see K Geppert, *Der Grundsatz der Unmittelbarkeit im deutschen Strafverfahren* (Berlin, Walter de Gruyter, 1979) at 67 ff; on the suggestion that the reforms be adopted and the rejection of this suggestion see A von Feuerbach, *Betrachtung über die Öffentlichkeit und Mündlichkeit der Gerechtigkeitspflege* (Gießen, Heyer, 1821 & 1825), i, at 12.

[96] *Ibid*, at 14.

particular, Mittermaier[97] and Zachariä.[98] By the middle of the nineteenth century a number of the German procedural codes[99] had introduced the general requirement that trials be public, although—as in France and Scotland—a number of exceptions were permitted. The principle received German-wide recognition in 1849 when it was enshrined in the Constitution (*Reichsverfassung*): *das Gerichtsverfahren soll öffentlich und mündlich sein.*[100]

By 1860 some writers were confident enough to declare that the requirement that proceedings be conducted in public had been widely accepted. According to Zachariä, the:

> *lange und lebhaft für und gegen die Oeffentlichkeit des Strafverfahrens geführte Streit, kann gegenwärtig zu den im Wesentlichen erledigten Controversen gerechnet werden.*[101]

In order to have a better understanding of the public trial requirement it is valuable to take a closer look at the reasons provided in support of its existence. Feuerbach's writings provide a useful starting point for an examination of reasons for the significance of the principle. In his work on oral and public proceedings, he sets out to examine in depth the many facets of the public hearing requirement. He is not just concerned with the presence of the general public (*'volkstümliche Öffentlichkeit'*, ie *Publikumsöffentlichkeit*) but identifies the presence of the parties (*'parteiliche Öffentlichkeit'*, ie *Parteiöffentlichkeit*) as integral to the notion of public proceedings:

> *Diese Öffentlichsehn der Gerichte für die Betheiligten, also die persönliche Gegenwart der Partheien oder ihrer Vertreter, ist zugleich der Mittelpunkt in welchem gleichsam alle*

---

[97] See, *inter alia*, CJA Mittermaier, *Die Gesetzgebung und Rechtsübung über Strafverfahren nach ihrer neusten Fortbildung* (Erlangen, Ferdinand Enke, 1856); CJA Mittermaier, *Die Mündlichkeit, das Anklageprinzip, die Öffentlichkeit und das Geschworenengericht in ihrer Durchführung in den verschiedenen Gesetzgebungen dargestellt und nach den Forderungen des Rechts und der Zweckmäßigkeit mit Rücksicht auf die Erfahrung der verschiedenen Länder* (Stuttgart und Tubingen, Cotta, 1845); CJA Mittermaier, *Das deutsche Strafverfahren in der Fortbildung durch Gerichts-Gebrauch und Particular-Gesetzbücher und in genauer Vergleichung mit dem englischen und französischen Straf-Processe* (Heidelberg, JCB Mohr, 1840); CJA Mittermaier, *Die Lehre vom Beweis im deutschen Strafprozesse nach der Fortbildung durch Gerichtsgebrauch und deutsche Gesetzbücher in Vergleichung mit den Ansichten des englischen und französischen Strafverfahrens* (Darmstadt, Heyer's Verlag, 1834)

[98] See eg HA Zachariä, *Handbuch des deutschen Strafprozesses* (Göttingen, Verlag der Dieterichschen Buchhandlung, 1861 & 1868); HA Zachariä, *Die Gebrechen und die Reform des deutschen Strafverfahrens, dargestellt auf der Basis einer consequenten Entwicklung des inquisitorischen und des accusatorischen Prinzips* (Göttingen, Dieterichschen Buchhandlung, 1846)

[99] Eg The Prussian Decree of 1846, para 15; See further CJA Mittermaier, *Die Gesetzgebung und Rechtsübung über Strafverfahren nach ihrer neusten Fortbildung* (Erlangen, Ferdinand Enke, 1856) at 317. Until 1877 and the creation of the first German federal Code of Criminal Procedure, criminal procedure was regulated on the regional level.

[100] According to para 178 of the *Reichsverfassung* of 28 Mar 1849: '[c]ourt proceedings shall be public and oral'.

[101] HA Zachariä, *Handbuch des deutschen Strafprozesses* (Göttingen, Verlag der Dieterichschen Buchhandlung, 1861 & 1868), i, at 60: 'the long and lively argument as to the pros and cons of the public nature of the proceedings can now be counted among those controversies which have been essentially resolved'.

Strahlen einer vernünftigen Vorstellung von der gerichtlichen Öffentlichkeit sich vereinigen und durch welchen alles übrige erst seine volle Kraft und Bedeutung erhält.[102]

This statement is interesting because the reference to the importance of the presence of the parties at the trial seems to be an attempt to address the question *how* the trial should look, rather than *why* the trial should be public. In linking these two issues he seems to imply that publicity demands a certain type of hearing. Indeed Feuerbach is not alone in looking beyond the constraints of publicity to the issue of what form the trial should take. Many jurists, when faced with the task of justifying the public nature of the proceedings, linked the public element of the trial to the form or nature of the trial itself.

Mittermaier suggests that one of the reasons justifying the public hearing requirement was that it served to increase the pressure on witnesses to tell the truth as they would have to fear that others present at the hearing could discover their lies.[103] He seems therefore to link the public trial requirement to the importance that witnesses be present. Similarly Volatire's explanation that '[w]e do not make the witnesses testify in secret; that would breed informers. The proceedings are public; secret trials are the invention of tyrants'[104] expressly connects the publicity of the trial to the requirement that the witnesses testify in public. Zachariä provides us with the clearest interpretation of this standpoint and makes an express claim for the mutual dependence of the oral and public hearing requirements. He writes that while it would be possible to have public proceedings in cases where the procedure followed was written, this would render the principle of publicity absolutely useless (*sehr nuztlos*) and fruitless (*unesprisesslich*).[105] Although he does not expand on why this is the case, it seems that he views publicity and immediacy as providing optimum restraints on the examination of evidence, in a way that would not be achievable, say, through making a written record of the evidence public. The manner in which the evidence was obtained would presumably be less evident in a written record of the evidence, which would not provide evidence of the behaviour of the authorities in securing

---

[102] A von Feuerbach, *Betrachtung über die Öffentlichkeit und Mündlichkeit der Gerechtigkeitspflege* (Gießen, Heyer, 1821 & 1825), i, at 96: this requirement that the court be open to the parties, in the sense of ensuring the personal presence of the parties or their representatives, is the focal point at which all the strands of a sensible conception of the public hearing requirement come together and from which all the other aspects derive their full power and meaning.

[103] CJA Mittermaier, *Die Gesetzgebung und Rechtsübung über Strafverfahren nach ihrer neusten Fortbildung* (Erlangen, Ferdinand Enke, 1856) at 320: '[d]urch sie (dh die Öffentlichkeit) kann die Entdeckung der Wahrheit in zweifacher Hinsicht besser gesichert werden, indem theils oft manche neue wichtige Beweise durch die Zuhörer in der Sitzung entdeckt werden, theils die Antriebe volle Wahrheit auszusagen, bei den Zeugen verstärkt werden, die fürchten müssen, dass ihre Lügen durch gegenwärtige Personen entdeckt werden können' (footnotes omitted).

[104] Voltaire, '*Histoire d'Elisabeth Canning et de Calas*', cited in A Esmein, *A History of Continental Criminal Procedure with Special Reference to France* (trans J Simpson, Boston, Mass, Little Brown & Co, 1913; reprinted Union, NJ, The Lawbook Exchange, 2000) at 361.

[105] HA Zachariä, *Handbuch des deutschen Strafprozesses* (Göttingen, Verlag der Dieterichschen Buchhandlung, 1861 & 1868), i, at 59.

the evidence or for the authenticity of the testimony.[106] It must be questioned however whether the public hearing requirement can really be seen to require that the proceedings take on a certain form. It is perhaps inevitable that the reasons given to justify the public trial requirement were associated with the justifications of other principles such as orality and immediacy. Notwithstanding this, only by understanding the scope and demands of the individual principles is it possible to ascertain whether they rest on a legitimate basis and to assess whether they are being correctly applied.[107]

It is clear that several writers including Feuerbach, Mittermaier, Zachariä and Beccaria share a conception of the public trial as fundamentally related to the presentation of the evidence. For them the hearing of the evidence in court was essential in order to provide the accused with the opportunity to challenge the evidence, and to enable the judge to monitor the work of the investigation and prosecution authorities during the earlier phases of the proceedings. In this way it also served to reinforce the position of the judge as the main figure of authority in the criminal process.[108] It must be questioned, however, whether this potential for restraint can be attributed to the notion of publicity. It would seem rather that any restraint in this sense is provided by the judicial supervision. Crucially the relationship here is not between the investigating authorities and the public, but rather between the investigating authorities and the trial judge. In view of this, these suggestions seem to be more closely connected to the immediacy principle than to the publicity requirement.[109]

The most convincing explanations of the importance of public proceedings relate to their connection to the conception of criminal prosecutions as a public exercise rather than a private matter. Many commentators highlight the role played by the public trial in publicising the effectiveness of public prosecutions. Mittermaier writes that public trials can be justified, *inter alia*,[110] by the fact that they demonstrate the effectiveness of the criminal justice system and thereby bolster public confidence in the abilities of the authorities to bring offenders to justice:

---

[106] A von Feuerbach, *Betrachtung über die Öffentlichkeit und Mündlichkeit der Gerechtigkeitspflege* (Gießen, Heyer, 1821 & 1825), i, at 165.

[107] S Maas, *Der Grundsatz der Unmittelbarkeit in der Reichsstrafprozessordnung* (Breslau, Schletter, 1907).

[108] HA Zachariä, *Handbuch des deutschen Strafprozesses* (Göttingen, Verlag der Dieterichschen Buchhandlung, 1861 & 1868), i, at 61.

[109] See below for an analysis of the immediacy principle.

[110] CJA Mittermaier, *Die Gesetzgebung und Rechtsübung über Strafverfahren nach ihrer neusten Fortbildung* (Erlangen, Ferdinand Enke, 1856) at 319: '*[d]ie Würdigung der Bedeutung der Öffentlichkeit und zwar in dem Hauptverfahren ergiebt sich am besten durch den Zweck des Strafverfahrens. Erkennt man an, dass dasjenige Verfahren am meisten diesem Zweck entspricht, durch welches am sichersten die Wahrheit erforscht, die Wirksamkeit der Strafjustiz gesichert und das allgemeine Vertrauen zur Gerechtigkeit der Urtheile in Strafsachen begründet werden kann, so erscheint die Oeffentlichkeit, als eines der Mittel durch welches diese Vortheile erreicht werden können*'.

Ein Vortheil der Öffentlichkeit ist der grosse moralische Eindruck, der dadurch bewirkt wird, dass die Zuhörer sehen, dass alle Schlauheit des Angeklagten alle kluge Zurückhaltung des Zeugen nicht vermögen, das noch so schlau verhüllte Verbrechen von der gesetzlichen Strafe zu befreien.[111]

Similarly for Zachariä, the public hearing requirement was best explained through its connection to the principle of public prosecution (*causa publica*) and by its role in gaining the trust of the public by demonstrating the seriousness of the proceedings and the independence of the judge. This was achieved moreover by guaranteeing the accused freedom from illegal treatment and through strengthening the impression that the court was to be regarded as the primary authority.[112]

The explanation of the importance of the principle of publicity as relating essentially to its role in highlighting the functions of the criminal justice system is also evident in Hélie's work. Public hearings, he writes, 'were an essential part of criminal procedure, perhaps the most essential part, because they served to clarify all the actions of the judge; to restrain judicial excesses; to reassure those subject to trial; and to emphasise the functions of the justice system'.[113] Only through allowing the public access to criminal trials was a citizen able to recognise the criminal justice system:

als ein Stück seines eigenen Lebens, als eine wohltätige, von jedem nach Kräften zu unterstüztende öffentliche Einrichtung.[114]

In this sense, the essence of the requirement that the trial take place in public cannot accurately be characterised as either a right of the accused or a restraint on the state authorities. Instead the publicity of the trial can be seen exclusively as 'a means of displaying the legitimate consequences of a criminal act, the representation of punishment as an idea'.[115] The scope of the trial, and in particular the determination of whether or not the evidence has to be led in open court, does not turn on the notion of publicity, but is rather dependent on those values from which the proceedings, and the consequent acceptance of these proceedings by the public, derive.

---

[111] *Ibid*, at 321: ' [o]ne advantage of public trials is the significant moral impression that they convey, which allows those watching to see that all the cleverness of the accused, all the cautiousness of the witnesses will not spare the accused, and his slyly concealed crime, from criminal sanction'.

[112] HA Zachariä, *Handbuch des deutschen Strafprozesses* (Göttingen, Verlag der Dieterichschen Buchhandlung, 1861 & 1868), i, at 60–1.

[113] F Hélie, *Traité de L'instruction Criminelle*, 2nd edn (Paris, Henri Plon, 1866–7), vii, at 474–5: '*une forme essentielle de la procédure, la plus essentielle peut-être, car elle éclaire tous les actes du juge; elle les défère, à mesure qu'ils s'accomplissent à l'examen et au contrôle du public; elle contient tous les excès en permettant de juger tous les jugements; elle rassure les justiciables; elle rehausse enfin les fonctions de la justice en y attachant plus de considération et d'éclat.*

[114] HA Zachariä, *Die Gebrechen und die Reformen des deutschen Strafverfahrens* (1846) at 310 et seq, cited by H Henkel, *Strafverfahrensrecht* (Stuttgart, Kohlhammer, 1968): 'as a piece of his own life, as a beneficial public institution to be supported by everyone to the best of his or her ability'.

[115] L Farmer, 'Criminal Responsibility and Proof of Guilt' in M Dubber and L Farmer (eds), *Modern Histories of Crime and Punishment* (Stanford, Cal, Stanford University Press, 2007).

In view of this, one could be forgiven for expecting that the public trial requirement would have had minimal affect on the form of the criminal process. But the nineteenth century debate can be seen by virtue of one important distinction as to what should (and therefore what should not) be public to have substantially influenced the form of the criminal process. Although there are clear differences in the works of the nineteenth century jurists in relation to the underlying conception of the nature and form of the trial—it was commonly accepted that only the trial (irrespective of its form) should take place in public. There was however no corresponding movement in favour of a public investigative phase. Mittermaier writes:

> In Bezug auf die Oeffentlichkeit der Voruntersuchung muss bemerkt werden, dass in Frankreich und Deutschland fortdauernd viele Stimmen sich dagegen erklären.[116]

A number of reasons are put forward in support of this reluctance, including the fear that publicity at this stage could interfere with the discovery of evidence or impede the honesty of the testimony of witnesses or the accused.[117] Another concern frequently voiced was that of the implications for innocent people who would be suffer unnecessary public scrutiny were the investigations to be made public.[118] The importance of the secrecy of the preliminary investigations seems to have been upheld throughout the whole century. Esmein cites the committee responsible for examining the possibilities for reforming the French procedural code as stating in 1880:

> Our temperament is no less repugnant to the régime of publicity; not to speak of the difficulties which might result therefrom in regard to the detection of guilty persons and notably of accomplices remaining at liberty, informed by the progress of the examination of the moment when flight or the destruction of the 'corpus delicti' would become necessary.[119]

There are thus clear indications of the emergence of a nineteenth century consensus that characterises trial hearings as public and investigation proceedings as secret. This in turn necessarily strengthens the conception of the criminal

---

[116] CJA Mittermaier, *Die Gesetzgebung und Rechtsübung über Strafverfahren nach ihrer neusten Fortbildung* (Erlangen, Ferdinand Enke, 1856) at 323: 'in relation to the public nature of the pre-trial, it must be noted that in both France and German many voices continue to speak against it'.

[117] Eg F Hélie, *Traité de L'instruction Criminelle*, 2nd edn (Paris, Henri Plon, 1866–7), v, at 529. There is an obvious link between this issue and the subject of pre-trial publicity more generally. For an interesting overview of the English approach to pre-trial publicity in the 19th century see D Bentley, *English Criminal Justice in the Nineteenth Century* (London, Hambledon Press, 1998) at 43–9.

[118] Eg CJA Mittermaier, *Die Gesetzgebung und Rechtsübung über Strafverfahren nach ihrer neusten Fortbildung* (Erlangen, Ferdinand Enke, 1856) at 323: '[s]elbst der Nachtheil, dass nach Umständen in dem ersten Abschnitt der Voruntersuchung so oft auch Unschuldige verdächtig werden und durch Oeffentlichkeit leicht empfindlich leiden könnten, wird für die Nothwendigkeit geheimer Voruntersuchung geltend gemacht'. See also D Bentley, *English Criminal Justice in the Nineteenth Century* (London, Hambledon Press, 1998) at 43–9.

[119] Committee Report, Official Journal of 14 Jan 1880, 302, col 3, cited in A Esmein, *A History of Continental Criminal Procedure with Special Reference to France* (trans J Simpson, Boston, Mass, Little Brown & Co, 1913; reprinted Union, NJ, The Lawbook Exchange, 2000) at 548.

process as comprising two distinct phases. The public hearing becomes the symbol of the criminal justice system, the point in the process against which the legitimacy of the whole system falls to be measured, while the secret investigation phase is relegated to a position of relative obscurity. These developments did not, however, meet everywhere with the same level of success. In those jurisdictions, such as Malta and Zurich, where the confrontation hearings involving witnesses took place in the investigation phase, provision had been made in the criminal procedure codes for the presence at this stage of the parties.[120] The strict distinction between the pre-trial (non-public) and trial (public) meant that evidence was no longer examined in their presence, and thus led to the introduction of a less public system of procedure in these legal systems.[121]

The preoccupation with the regulation of the trial, at the expense of controls at the investigative stages of the process, can be attributed, at least in part, to the interpretation of the public trial requirement. It is difficult to construe it as being a 'right' or a 'restraint', and it does not seem in itself to demand that the trial take on a certain form. Rather it seems to dictate that whatever type of procedure is chosen as representing the best way to regulate the application of the substantive law, it must be able to withstand public scrutiny and engender public acceptance. In view of the fact that it seems to turn exclusively on the importance of demonstrating to the public the efficiency and legitimacy of the process, and thus to encourage their participation in the criminal justice system, the requirement can be seen through the interpretation of its extent (ie the differentiation between the trial and pre-trial phases) to have had a greater effect on the form of criminal proceedings than might otherwise have been expected.

E Immediate and Oral Proceedings

Although there seem to be clear deficiencies in the reliance on the public hearing requirement to uphold a particular conception of the trial hearing, this was in any case of little relevance as the nineteenth century writers also focused on two other principles, namely that trials be oral and immediate, to support their vision of the correct forum for the determination of the evidence. The term 'immediacy' (*Unmittelbarkeit*) is most commonly referred to in the context of German

---

[120] CJA Mittermaier, *Die Gesetzgebung und Rechtsübung über Strafverfahren nach ihrer neusten Fortbildung* (Erlangen, Ferdinand Enke, 1856) at 323. According to Art 121 of the Zurich Criminal Procedure Code, the court was free to determine whether to allow the presence of the parties during the hearing of the witnesses. Rüttimann, in his commentary, was of the opinion that the investigation hearings ought to be public: JJ Rüttimann, *Zur Geschichte und Fortbildung der zürcherischen Rechtspflege* (Zurich, Höhr, 1855) at 129.

[121] See for instance the Criminal Procedure Code of the Canton of Schaffhausen of 1909 which expressly rules out the presence of the accused/parties during the pre-trial investigation and confrontation hearings.

procedural law and was coined by German jurists in the nineteenth century. For this reason, the principle is not commonly referred to, for instance, in the British literature on criminal procedure law. In spite of this, the essence of the principle—the requirement that all evidence be led directly before the judge or fact-finder—was analysed by the majority of the jurists of the time.

The definition of immediacy was complicated by its connection to the requirement that the proceedings take place orally.[122] Amidst the nineteenth century procedural reforms, commentators seized upon the notions of oral and immediate procedure as integral to the establishment of the reformed procedural system, and immediacy was seen by some to be '*eine unabweisbare Forderung der Gerichtigkeit*'.[123] Holtzendorff considers the requirement that the proceedings be 'oral, or perhaps more accurately immediate' to be more important than the public hearing requirement,[124] and thereby draws attention to the close relationship between orality and immediacy. In much of the literature the exact relationship between these principles is unclear. Holtzendorff's explanation of the scope of the principle seems to suggest that they guarantee the same concept:

> *Man versteht darunter die Vernehmung des Angeklagten und die Vorführung des gesammten Beweismaterials in einer Anklagesache, sowohl der belastenden, als der entlastenden Thatsachen unmittelbar vor dem erkennenden Richter in der Art, dass er den Angeklagten und die Zeugen selbst hört und aus ihrem Munde, nicht durch Vermittlung schriftlicher Aufzeichnungen, ihre Behauptungen und ihre Wahrnehmungen sich vortragen lässt.*[125]

The terms are frequently referred to together or interchangeably, and it is not uncommon for reference to be made to only one of the principles. Feuerbach, for instance, in his famous work on public and oral trials does not refer to the immediacy principle—although it is clear that it is incorporated within his conception of the principle that the trial take place orally.[126] Similarly Mittermaier refers to the 'oral (immediate)' procedure requirement as necessitating that 'the entire determination of the charge, the hearing and use of the various pieces

---

[122] For an excellent historical overview of the distinctions between these principles in German criminal procedural law see S Maas, *Der Grundsatz der Unmittelbarkeit in der Reichsstrafprozessordnung* (Breslau, Schletter, 1907).

[123] A von Hye, *Die Leitenden Grundsätze der österreichischen Strafprozessordnung* (Vienna, F Manz, 1854) at 26: 'an irrefutable requirement of justice'.

[124] F von Holtzendorff (ed), *Handbuch des Deutschen Strafprozessrechts* (Berlin, Carl Habel, 1879), ii, at 63: '[e]ine noch wichtigere und bedeutungsvollere Gewähr als die Oeffentlichkeit für unparteiische Rechtspflege und für Erzielung einer möglichst genauen Übereinstimmung des richterlichen Urtheils im Strafverfahren mit der materiellen Wahrheit, ist die Mündlichkeit, oder, wie richtiger gesagt wird, die Unmittelbarkeit des Verfahrens'.

[125] *Ibid*: 'these principles mean that the hearing of the accused and of all the evidence relevant to the charge, including both incriminating and exculpatory facts, are to be led immediately before the trial judge in such a way as to enable him himself to hear the live testimony of the accused and the witnesses and not to experience them through reading written protocols through which their claims and insights are conveyed by others'.

[126] See further K Geppert, *Der Grundsatz der Unmittelbarkeit im deutschen Strafverfahren* (Berlin, Walter de Gruyter, 1979); M Stüber, *Die Entwicklung des Prinzips der Unmittelbarkeit im deutschen Strafverfahren* (Frankfurt, Peter Lang, 2005).

of evidence on which the judgment should be based, and the arguments of the prosecution and the defence should take place in front of the judge with the responsibility for determining the case'.[127]

Although the concepts are closely connected, only through distinguishing the scope of each principle is it possible to understand the full extent of the reasons for their existence and the nature of the guarantees provided by them. Perhaps the best elucidation of the two principles is made by Glaser, who suggests that while they were connected each principle was charged with the regulation of a different aspect of the proceedings. While the primary role of the immediacy principle concerned the regulation of the hearing of the evidence, the requirement that the hearings be conducted orally was connected to the importance of enabling discussion and challenging of the evidence.[128] Thus the principles can be seen to be a response to two separate issues: first the judicial role in the supervision of the determination of the evidence and, secondly, the adequacy of the opportunity of the accused to challenge the evidence.

By 1861 some writers suggested that the long-discussed argument whether the trial should be conducted orally or in writing could be regarded as settled.[129] According to Zachariä it was generally accepted that the oral procedure was the most fundamental and irrefutable guarantee for the establishment of the material truth,[130] especially in the context of criminal procedure law where the crime could not be divorced from the accused himself. Consequently, there could be no exception to the principle and it was certainly unacceptable for oral procedure to be replaced by a written process, at least in relation to the main hearing (*Hauptverhandlung*).[131] On this basis 'the court should ground its judgment only

---

[127] CJA Mittermaier, *Die Gesetzgebung und Rechtsübung über Strafverfahren nach ihrer neusten Fortbildung* (Erlangen, Ferdinand Enke, 1856) at 307: '*[d]as Wesen der Mündlichkeit (Unmittelbarkeit) liegt darin, dass die gesammte Verhandlung der Anklage, die Erhebung und Benützung der verschiedenen Beweise, auf welche das Urteil gebaut werden soll, die Anträge und Vorträge zur Begründung der Anklage und Vertheidigung vor den urtheilenden Richtern vorgehen, dass sie nicht blos davon, welche Aussagen von den vorgerufenen Personen abgelegt wurden, sondern auch von den zur Erhebung gebrauchten Mitteln und der Art der Ablegung der Aussagen sich überzeugen und selbst die nöthigen Mittel anwenden können, um die zuverlässigste Wahrheit sich zu verschaffen*'.

[128] J Glaser, *Handbuch des Strafprozesses* (Leipzig, Duncker & Humblot, 1883 & 1885), i, at 247: '*Mann muss sich vor allem klar machen, dass es sich sowohl was das Mittel, als auch was den Zweck anbelangt, um zweierlei handelt, nämlich einerseits um die Unmittelbarkeit und Mündlichkeit und anderseits um die Aufnahme des Beweises und um die Erörterung des hieraus sich ergebenden Folgerungen. Für die Erhebung der Beweise ist mehr die Unmittelbarkeit, für deren Erörterung mehr die mündliche Form des Vortrages von Bedeutung*'.

[129] HA Zachariä, *Handbuch des deutschen Strafprozesses* (Göttingen, Verlag der Dieterichschen Buchhandlung, 1861 & 1868), i, at 50: '*[d]er, besonders in Deutschland unter der Herrschaft des schriftlichen Untersuchungsprocesses, lange geführte Streit über die Frage, ob das mündliche oder das schriftliche Verfahren den Vorzog verdiene? ist gegenwärtig als erledigt zu betrachten*'.

[130] A view shared in relation to civil procedure law by RF von Canstein, *Die rationellen Grundlagen des Zivilprocesses* (Vienna, privately published, 1877) at 78–96.

[131] HA Zachariä, *Handbuch des deutschen Strafprozesses* (Göttingen, Verlag der Dieterichschen Buchhandlung, 1861 & 1868), i, at 50–1: '*Man ist allgemein zu der Ueberzeugung gelangt, dass das mündliche Verfahren als die wesentlichste und unabweisbarste Garantie für die Herstellung materieller Wahrheit betrachtet werden müsse . . .*'.

on evidential sources which it had actually heard, and not on inquiries or conclusions drawn from another time, place or person'. Importantly he expressly states that this meant that 'the judgment must not be based on the files of the written preliminary investigation'.[132] Furthermore, the judgment had to contain a summary of all the conclusions taken directly from the evidence which had been heard (*unmittelbare Beweisaufnahme*).[133]

(i) Immediate and Oral Examination of the Evidence at Trial

The requirement that the trial be conducted orally was set out in Article 317 of the French *Code d'instruction criminelle* of 1808. According to Hélie the principle that the evidence be examined orally and in front of the decision maker was a fundamental procedural principle of French criminal law.[134] Oral discussions in which the accused and witnesses were confronted with each other were the best way of providing for the uncovering of the truth and were far preferable to written alternatives.[135] Further, only oral proceedings could be considered compatible with the principle of '*conviction intime*', which required the decision maker to take personal responsibility for determining the accuracy of the charge.[136]

In 1877 the principles of orality and immediacy were included in the German federal Code of Criminal Procedure.[137] According to this code, the examination of evidence was to occur at two distinct stages in the proceedings. First, in all cases which would be the responsibility of the *Reichsgericht* or the *Schwurgericht*, and also in some cases the *Landesgericht* or the *Schöffengericht*, an investigation (*Voruntersuchung*) had to take place.[138] As noted above, the purpose of the investigation was not to be determinative, in the sense of involving a determination of the guilt or innocence of the accused, but rather was to further the

---

[132] *Ibid*, at 52: '[d]as Gericht darf sein Urtheil nur auf die vor ihm selbstlich eröffnenden und ergießenden Beweisquellen stützen, nicht auf thatsächliche Erhebungen und Feststellungen, die zu anderer Zeit, an anderem Orte, von andern Personen gemacht worden sind; also insbesondere nicht auf den Inhalt der schriftlichen Voruntersuchung'.

[133] *Ibid*, at 52.

[134] F Hélie, *Traité de L'instruction Criminelle*, 2nd edn (Paris, Henri Plon, 1866–7), vii, at 487: '[l]'instruction qui se fait à l'audience doit être exclusivement orale. C'est là l'une règle fondamentale de notre procédure criminelle'.

[135] *Ibid*: '[l]a discussion orale est la seule qui puisse faire jaillir la vérité d'un débat: elle place les accusés et les témoins en face les uns des autres; elle provoque les explications et les révélations, les dénégations ou les aveux; elle dépouille les faits de leurs premières apparences et les livre aux yeux dans leur nudité. La discussion écrite, plus froide et plus réservée, n'a ni ces épanchements, ni ces chocs qui font briller l'éclair; elle est parfaitement propre à recueillir les éléments du débat; mais le débat, c'est-à-dire la discussion de toutes les preuves, l'examen de tous les éléments du procès, ne peut se faire qu'oralement à l'audience'.

[136] *Ibid*, at 488.

[137] For a brief summary, which also examines the influence of the French Revolution on the reformed German procedure, see C Roxin, *Strafverfahrensrecht*, 25th edn (Munich, Beck, 1998) at 481.

[138] Para 176 StPO (1877).

investigation; its function, as expressly stated in paragraph 188 of the Code, was to enable a decision to be made whether or not there was enough evidence for the case to proceed to trial.

These examinations were to be presided over by an investigating judge (who was to be separate from the prosecutor). In those cases that were to be heard in the *Reichsgericht*, the investigating judge was to be appointed by the trial judge.[139] The preliminary examinations of the accused, witnesses and experts were to be led by the investigating judge in the presence of a court writer with the responsibility for recording all evidence heard.[140] While the accused was to be questioned in the absence of both the prosecutor and defence counsel, the examination of witnesses or experts was to take place in the presence of both the prosecution and defence counsel.[141] The presence of the accused could however be restricted if the investigating judge thought that his or her presence would prevent the witness telling the truth.[142] In the event that the investigating judge decided that there was enough evidence to prosecute, the case was to proceed to trial. The trial was to take place in the uninterrupted presence of the judge, the prosecution and the accused,[143] and the accused was to be entitled to have the assistance of counsel, not just at trial but also at every stage of the procedure.[144] The presiding judge was to be responsible for leading the proceedings, for questioning the accused and hearing the evidence.[145] Witnesses and experts led by the prosecution were to be questioned first by them and then by the defence; while the defence was to have the right to question its witnesses first, the judge was then entitled to ask any supplementary questions.[146]

The requirement that all the evidence be led directly at trial was a relatively uncontroversial feature of Scottish and English law.[147] In Scotland it was usual for witnesses to be examined in front of a judge at trial. Before trial, the accused was served with a list of the witnesses and their addresses in order to enable him to 'learn who the witness was, and where to be found, and all circumstances concerning his character and situation'.[148] According to Hume, the witnesses were brought successively into court and the accused had the chance to voice any objections to them. In the event that there were no objections the witnesses had to take the oath, purge himself of all malice to the accused, and state that no one had instructed him how to depone (give evidence). Each of the witnesses was

---

[139]   *Ibid*, para 184.
[140]   *Ibid*, para 185.
[141]   *Ibid*, paras 190 and 191.
[142]   *Ibid*, para 192. See further Ch 3.
[143]   See *ibid*, paras 225–235.
[144]   *Ibid*, para 137.
[145]   *Ibid*, para 237.
[146]   *Ibid*, para 238.
[147]   With the important exception of the accused, who was deemed incompetent to testify (and thus unable to be heard by the court) until 1898.
[148]   *MacDonald and Williamson Black*, 7 June 1812, cited in D Hume, *Commentaries on the Law of Scotland, Respecting Crimes* (Edinburgh, Bell & Bradfute, 1844), ii, at 372, n 2.

then separately examined. Moreover the law required that the witnesses were precognosced separately. Before giving evidence the witness had the opportunity to revoke any earlier declarations. Hume notes:

> even if the declaration should not be cancelled, yet certainly it can never be employed, in any manner of way, to the prejudice of the witness; nor can it be produced in the trial, to discredit his evidence, by showing that he had given a different account on some former occasion.[149]

Hume's commentaries demonstrate that Scots law at that time required that all evidence be presented not only before those determining the charge but also before the accused:

> First of all, no evidence is lawful or competent on either side, but that which is taken (as we say) in the face of judgment,—in open court, before the parties, and the assize who are charged with the panel....[150]

This was based on the principle set out in the statute of 1587 cc 91 and 92 that each witness had to present his or her evidence in the presence of the assize in order that the accused:

> has the like protection against the producing of any testimonies to the assize, though in his presence, and with his knowledge, which are not emitted by the witnesses in the face of the Court, and to and before the persons of the assize themselves.[151]

The emphasis in the English literature was on cross-examination and hearsay rather than on the manner in which the witness statements were taken, and this means that few writers expand on the reasons for the requirement that the evidence be heard at trial.[152] There is however some authority for the proposition that objections to out-of-court statements were not related just to the accuracy of the statements but also to the manner in which they were taken. Gilbert, for instance, writes:

> [T]he Credit of Dispositions ceteris paribus falls much below the Credibility of a present Examination viva voce, for the Examiners and Commissioners in such Cases do often dress up secret Examinations, and set up a quite different Air upon them from they would seem if the same Testimony had been plainly delivered under the strict and open Examination of the Judge of the Assizes.[153]

---

[149]   *Ibid*, at 381.
[150]   *Ibid.*
[151]   *Ibid*, at 405.
[152]   JH Wigmore, *Evidence in Trials at Common Law*, 4th edn (rev JH Chadbourne, Boston, Mass, Little Brown, 1974) at 158, for instance, is often quoted by those seeking to stress the evidential rather than procedural side of the rule as stating that there was no such thing as a confrontation per se in England, as the emphasis was on the right to cross-examination: '[t]here was never at common law any recognized right to an indispensable thing called confrontation as distinguished from cross-examination'.
[153]   G Gilbert, *The Law of Evidence* (London, 1754, reprinted London, Garland Publishers, 1979).

(ii)   Consideration at Trial of Evidence Collected Before the Trial and Submitted in Writing

In England it was a firm rule that evidence collected during pre-trial investigations (such as in the course of magistrates' hearings) could not be introduced in written form at trial.[154] That this was also the case in Scotland is evidenced by Hume's comment that it was not permissible for the prosecution to try and gain an advantage by supplying written statements of what witnesses are supposed to have said;[155] 'mere hearsay evidence' was therefore rejected as insufficient to meet the procedural requirements. The witnesses had to be 'produced to tell their own story themselves and say what they know concerning those matters, of their own proper knowledge'. The only legitimate exceptions to the rule concerned the statements of witnesses who had died before trial or who had given their testimony while dying (dying declarations).[156]

Despite this strong requirement that the proof be presented in the presence of the assize, these principles were not always applied in practice. Hume mentions, and is critical of, several cases where depositions were taken in advance and later only read out at trial with 'some trifling additions before the assize'. These however 'were not the only nor the worst irregularities'. Hume reserves this label for cases in which the assize never saw the witnesses, who had previously testified before 'some inferior magistrate'.[157] This practice was almost entirely abolished with the introduction of the Supreme Court, and the only case cited by Hume from the modern procedure was *Duncan McGregor alias Drummond*, in which, on the consent of both parties, facts relating to the trial of the accused's brother for the same facts were read out.[158]

In Germany too, following the introduction of the Code of 1877, it was determined that the live presentation of the evidence was not to be replaced by the reading out in court of earlier statements or written explanations.[159] Exceptions to this principle related, as in other countries, to cases where the expert or witness had died, become mentally ill or could no longer be traced.[160] The testimony of a witness who refused to testify at trial could not be read out in

---

[154]   JF Stephen, *A History of the Criminal Law of England* (London, Macmillan, 1883), i, at 232 ff.

[155]   D Hume, *Commentaries on the Law of Scotland, Respecting Crimes* (Edinburgh, Bell & Bradfute, 1844), ii, at 408.

[156]   *Ibid*, at 406–10.

[157]   *Ibid*, at 406 referring to the cases of *Alexander Gylour* judgment of 2 Feb 1642 and *Jamie Macrie* judgment of 20 Feb 20 1650.

[158]   Judgment of 22 Jan 1753; see D Hume, *Commentaries on the Law of Scotland, Respecting Crimes* (Edinburgh, Bell & Bradfute, 1844) at 406.

[159]   Para 249 StPO: '*[b]eruht der Beweise einer Thatsache auf der Wahrnehmung einer Person, so ist die letztere in der Hauptverhandlung zu vernehmen. Die Vernehmung darf nicht durch Vorlesung des über eine frühere Vernehmung aufgenommenen Protokolls oder einer schriftlichen Erklärung ersetzt werden*'.

[160]   *Ibid*, para 222.

court,[161] but where the witness had merely forgotten a part of his or her earlier testimony it was permissible for part of the earlier statement to be read out in order to aid his or her memory.[162] Importantly, following the testimony of an expert, witness or co-accused, the accused was to be given the chance to add his or her explanations.[163]

In France the situation was slightly different. The principal distinction between France and countries like England, Germany and Scotland was contained in Articles 318 and 341 of the French *Code d'Instruction Criminelle* of 1808 and concerned the use of written evidence collected during the secret, pre-trial, examination hearings. According to Article 318:

> The president shall cause a note to be taken by the clerk of the court of the additions, changes, or variations which may exist between a witness's deposition and his previous statements. The attorney-general and the accused may require the president to have notes take on these changes, additions, and variations.

According to Article 341:

> The president puts the written issues before the jury in the presence of the foreman of the jury; he adds thereto the indictment, the official reports establishing the offences, and the documents of the action other than the written depositions of the witnesses.

Thus the French procedure allowed for the written statements of witnesses collected during the secret, pre-trial investigations to be conveyed in writing to the judge or fact-finder.[164]

(iii) Immediate and Oral Proceedings as Fundamental to the Accusatorial System

The introduction of the transcripts of statements made during the investigation hearings was the subject of considerable concern among the nineteenth century jurists. If evidence gathered in the course of the investigation was to be submitted in the form of written transcripts at trial as a substitute for live evidence, how could the public and oral trial be seen as anything other than '*eine die treuherzige Einfalt täuschende Maskerade*'?[165] Although the nineteenth century developments had led to the acceptance across the continent of oral and public hearings at which the accused was entitled to be represented by a lawyer, to produce his or

---

[161] *Ibid*, para 250.
[162] *Ibid*, para 252.
[163] *Ibid*, para 256.
[164] F Hélie, *Traité de L'instruction Criminelle*, 2nd edn (Paris, Henri Plon, 1866–7), vii.
[165] A von Feuerbach, *Betrachtung über die Öffentlichkeit und Mündlichkeit der Gerechtigkeitspflege* (Gießen, Heyer, 1821 & 1825), ii, at 383: 'a deceptive masquerade'.

her own witnesses and to confront those of the prosecution,[166] the introduction of evidence from the investigation phase was seen as having the potential seriously to compromise the essence of these reforms. Discussions involving the importance of immediacy are therefore not merely confined to the benefits of the principle itself but also relate to the importance of the reformed system of procedure, which had been developed in the course of the nineteenth century. Failure to uphold the immediacy principle necessarily contributed to the undoing of this system.

In discussing the importance of the oral proceedings requirement, Feuerbach concentrates on the problems associated with the use of evidence collected in earlier phases of the proceedings, which was then conveyed by way of written protocols to the court responsible for determining the charge. He reserves special criticism for the French procedure law of the time[167] which, despite its apparent endorsement of oral and public hearings, was in his view too reliant on the statements taken from the preliminary investigation:

von dem Protocollen der geheimen polizeylichen Voruntersuchung auch bei den öffentlichen Hauptverhandlungen so oft Gebrauch gemacht (wird), . . . so dass nicht blos dasjenige, was in dem öffentlichen Gerichte selbst mündlich vorgekommen ist, was Richter und Geschworene selbst gesehen und gehört haben, sondern auch die geheimen, vielleicht erschlichenen order erpressten schriftlichen Geständnisse, die geheimen, vielleicht halb untergeschoben, dem Zeugen in den Mund gelegten, falsch oder unvollständig niedergeschriebenen Zeugenaussagen, auf das Urtheil über die Schuld mit einwirken, dieses oft ganz allein entscheiden.[168]

Und was jene Akten betrifft, so sind zwar diese selbst Handlungen des Gerichts zeigen doch aber weiter nichts als—sich selbst. Wie sie geworden, was hinter ihnen liegt, was ihnen vorausging, was nebenbei geschah oder nicht geschah, als sie angefertigt wurden: von allem dem erscheint an ihnen mehr nicht, als sie selbst davon zu melden für gut fanden.[169]

---

[166] A Esmein, *A History of Continental Criminal Procedure with Special Reference to France* (trans J Simpson, Boston, Mass, Little Brown & Co, 1913; reprinted Union, NJ, The Lawbook Exchange, 2000) at 514.

[167] A von Feuerbach, *Betrachtung über die Öffentlichkeit und Mündlichkeit der Gerechtigkeitspflege* (Gießen, Heyer, 1821 & 1825). On the importance of Feuerbach's work see H Henkel, *Strafverfahrensrecht* (Stuttgart, Kohlhammer, 1968) at 53.

[168] A von Feuerbach, *Betrachtung über die Öffentlichkeit und Mündlichkeit der Gerechtigkeitspflege* (Gießen, Heyer, 1821 & 1825), ii, at 374: 'the written protocols of secret police investigations are so often used in trial proceedings that the evidence which is taken orally in open court and which the judge and the jury have personally seen and heard is not the only evidence which is used to determine the verdict; rather it is accompanied by the secret, written confessions which have perhaps been obtained by devious means or under compulsion, and the secret, incompletely recorded or false witness evidence obtained on the basis of leading questions, and suggestions placed in the witness' mouth, and this evidence not only influences the verdict, but often is the sole basis for it'.

[169] *Ibid*: 'And with regard to the files, while these are produced by the court, they show nothing more—than themselves. How they came about, what lay behind them, what was assumed, what happened or did not happen in the process of their creation: from all this appears nothing more than that which the authorities wanted to show'.

Protokolle legen wenigstens wider sich selbst kein Zeugniss ab. Klagt aber der Anges-
chuldigte das Protokoll und den Richter an; so können die stummen Wände für ihn kein
Zeugniß geben.[170]

His concerns were thus based on several different but ultimately connected
issues. Although the trial hearing took place in public in the presence of a judge
(and sometimes a jury), the determination of the charge was primarily based on
evidence taken during the secret preliminary investigations. The problem was not
so much the secrecy of these preliminary investigations but rather that the verdict
was ultimately based on evidence which had been examined and challenged in
secret. Consequently, the accused was unable to challenge the content of the
evidence or the manner in which it had been obtained. Moreover despite the
impartiality of the investigating judge there were no restraints (such as publicity
or involvement of the parties) regulating the investigation phase. For Feuerbach,
the only way to resolve this was to demand that the evidence be presented orally
to the court and in the presence of the accused in order that he or she be
presented with an adequate opportunity to challenge it. Mittermaier was similarly concerned with the relationship between the judge and the evidence and the
requirement that the judge be able to see and hear both the accused and any
witnesses.

[I]n einer solchen Einrichtung des Verfahrens, dass alle Verhandlungen, auf deren Grund
verurtheilt werden kann, daher die Anklage, alle Beweise, die Begründung derselben von
den Richtern, welche das Urtheil fällen sollen, selbst geführt werden und zwar so, dass die
Richter ebenso wie der Ankläger und der Angeklagte die Benützung und Erhebung der
Beweise beobachten und darauf wirken können.[171]

For him the essential point was that the judge responsible for determining the
charge be able to see and hear the witnesses in order to be able to ask
supplementary questions and to get a better impression of the reliability of the
witnesses' testimony. Consequently the use of statements obtained during the
investigative phase constituted a violation both of the notion of immediacy and
of the requirement that the proceedings take place orally. In order to rectify this
he favoured a solution whereby the evidence collected during the preliminary
phase could be used only to assist in the decision whether or not to prosecute.[172]

---

[170] *Ibid*, i, at 165: 'the written protocols cannot take on the role of a witness. If the accused disputes
the record of the evidence and challenges the judge, the mute walls cannot testify for him'.
[171] CJA Mittermaier, *Die Mündlichkeit, das Anklageprinzip, die Öffentlichkeit und das Gesch-*
worenengericht in ihrer Durchführung in den verschiedenen Gesetzgebungen dargestellt und nach den
Forderungen des Rechts und der Zweckmäßigkeit mit Rücksicht auf die Erfahrung der verschiedenen
Länder (Stuttgart and Tubingen, Cotta, 1845) at 246: 'in such proceedings, all hearings which could
provide the basis for the accused's conviction, ie the indictment, the evidence, the reasoning of the
judges responsible for determining the charge, were to be conducted in such a way as to allow the
judge, the prosecution and the accused to observe and participate in the use and hearing of the
evidence'.
[172] *Ibid*, at 70.

Both Mittermaier and Feuerbach can be seen to be arguing for the imposition of limits on the powers of investigation authorities, while simultaneously strengthening their understanding of the criminal process as split between a determinative and public trial phase and a non-determinative secret investigation phase,[173] with the trial judge standing as the ultimate authority. This is also visible in Hume's commentaries on the procedure adopted in Scottish criminal cases. He describes the rule that only evidence taken in open court before the parties and the decision makers could be considered lawful as:

> A rule which is grounded in the soundest reason, and most substantial justice. Not only because it would be iniquitous, that either party should privily communicate any thing to the assize; but because it is only by observing the words, manner, nay aspect and countenance of the several witnesses, that the assize can fully judge of the credit that is due to them: Not to mention, that it is fit that those who are to decide on the case have an opportunity of eliciting the truth from witnesses on either part, by questions of their own.[174]

He thus makes several claims for the necessity of the principle. The first relates to a reassurance to the accused that the determination of the charge is based on evidence which he or she knows of, and that there is no ground to fear the possibility of the prosecution conveying, by some other secret means, incriminating evidence to the court. This argument is emphasised later when he refers to a solemn ordinance of 1587, c 91, which draws attention to the potential of the prosecutor to prejudice the case against the accused by addressing the jury in his or her absence. To guard against such happenings and to ensure the 'fair and open taking of all evidence' it held:

> That in all tyme cuming, the haill accusatioun, ressoning, writtis, witnessis, and uthir probatioun and instructioun quhatsumever of the cryme, sall be allegit, resonit, and deducit, to the assize, in the presence of the apartie accusit, in the fact of judgment, and na uthirwayes.[175]

Hume's justifications seem to express the importance of oral communication between those involved in the proceedings in the assessment of the evidence. There seems to be a suggestion that the responsibility for the determination of the evidence can be satisfactorily realised only through giving the decision maker the opportunity to ask questions of the witnesses and the accused. The oral and immediate hearing requirements can therefore be seen to be based on the principle that the examination and determination of the evidence must take

---

[173] A von Feuerbach, *Betrachtung über die Öffentlichkeit und Mündlichkeit der Gerechtigkeitspflege* (Gießen, Heyer, 1821 & 1825), i, at 54; CJA Mittermaier, *Die Gesetzgebung und Rechtsübung über Strafverfahren nach ihrer neusten Fortbildung* (Erlangen, Ferdinand Enke, 1856) at 308: '[d]ie Durchführung des Prinzips der Mündlichkeit steht in Zusammenhang mit der Unterscheidung der Voruntersuchung und Hauptverhandlung'.

[174] D Hume, *Commentaries on the Law of Scotland, Respecting Crimes* (Edinburgh, Bell & Bradfute, 1844), ii, at 404.

[175] *Ibid.*

place not only in the presence of the parties but also in the presence of the judge. This is also visible in Stephen's comment that, while cross-examination was an 'indispensable instrument for the discovery of truth', it was also 'the part of the whole system which is most liable to abuse' and thus 'had to be kept most carefully and jealously under control by the judge'.[176] Decision makers had to be able to observe those testifying in order make their own decision as to their credibility. Importantly, this is more than simply an argument about the ability of people correctly to interpret witness evidence by examining their demeanour while testifying. The vital issue here relates to the determination of *who* is to have the responsibility for determining the credibility of the witnesses and their testimony. Hume implies that this is the responsibility of the fact-finder/decision maker, not of the prosecution or investigation authorities, and this suggestion is strengthened by his express reference to the requirement that those responsible for determining the outcome of the case be provided with the opportunity to ask their own questions.

These issues are important as they demonstrate both that it was *the examination of the evidence* that was the subject of the oral procedure requirement and that there was firm acceptance of the principle that the 'accusatorial trinity' represented the only satisfactory procedural setting for the determination of the charge. Acceptance of the adversarial conception of truth meant that the accusatorial structure had to be considered as the only satisfactory procedural structure: In the words of Mittermaier:

> *Man fühlte, dass das Strafverfahren eine Art des rechtlichen Verfahrens ist, das in einem Kampfe von zwei Parteien besteht, von welchen Eine gegen die Andere Behauptungen aufstellt, aus diesen gewisse Folgerungen und Anträge ableitet und sich bemüht, diejenigen, von denen die Entscheidung über die Anträge abhängt, von dem Dasein der Behauptung und der Richtigkeit der Folgerungen zu überzeugen.*[177]

F Conclusions

In their examinations of the ideal structural form of European criminal proceedings nineteenth century jurists on both sides of the channel focused on the accusatorial trial as the point in the process which was to carry the legitimacy of the system by providing a carefully regulated forum for the 'adversarial' examination of the evidence and the determination of the charge. This led, though, to the

---

[176] JF Stephen, *A History of the Criminal Law of England* (London, Macmillan, 1883), i, at 431.

[177] CJA Mittermaier, *Die Gesetzgebung und Rechtsübung über Strafverfahren nach ihrer neusten Fortbildung* (Erlangen, Ferdinand Enke, 1856) at 285: '[o]ne felt that criminal proceedings were a type of legal proceedings which consisted of a dispute between two parties, in the course of which each side put forward arguments against the other, drew certain conclusions, proposed motions and endeavoured to convince the person charged with determining these motions of the reality of these arguments and the accuracy of the conclusions'.

development of a conception, fostered by notions like the public hearing require-ment, of criminal proceedings as comprising two distinct elements: the public and oral 'trial' hearing and the secret investigation phase. It was precisely this emphasis on the trial, however, which allowed for the regulation of the investiga-tion phase to be neglected. There was little enthusiasm outside the scholarly books for accusatorial regulation of the investigation phase, but this did not hinder the portrayal of criminal proceedings—supported by the accusatorial trial—as a fair and effective means of determining criminal charges. In spite of this, the investigation phase continued to exercise considerable influence on the criminal proceedings. The neutrality of the investigation authorities and the subsequent control exercised by the trial authorities were deemed sufficient for the regulation of this phase. In order to determine the effect of this regulatory structure on the theoretical concept of the trial developed by nineteenth century writers, it is essential to examine the role and rights of the defence.

3

The Rights of the Defence: Lessons from the Nineteenth Century

A The Institutional Nature of the 'Rights of the Accused'

D EFENCE RIGHTS ARE inevitably associated with 'fairness' and, more often than not, with conceptions of individual responsibility and autonomy. On this basis their development in the course of the second half of the nineteenth century is often portrayed as a natural consequence of the influence of the individualistic philosophy of the Enlightenment. An examination of the correspondence between the institutional form of the proceedings developed by nineteenth century jurists and the nature and extent of the defence rights afforded to the accused will however provide the basis for an understanding of defence rights as 'institutional' rather than as 'individual' in character. It will be argued here that the changing nature of the rights of the defence reflected the institutional and procedural changes that had occurred in the course of the nineteenth century. These reforms had less to do with improving the position or increasing the autonomy of the accused in the proceedings and more to do with the creation of an effective system of criminal justice, which could also be presented as legitimate and fair.

It was the rights of the 'defence' and not of 'the accused' that were seen as important in the works of the nineteenth century writers. The nature of the 'defence' was seen as dependent on the other institutional elements of the proceedings.[1] Mittermaier, writing in 1840, devotes much of the section on the 'conditions of the defence in criminal proceedings'[2] in his textbook on German criminal procedure to the inadequacies of the institutional set up, highlighting

---

[1] CJA Mittermaier, *Das deutsche Strafverfahren in der Fortbildung durch Gerichts-Gebrauch und Particular-Gesetzbücher und in genauer Vergleichung mit dem englischen und französischen Straf-Processe* (Heidelberg, 1840), ii, at 186: '[a]ber auch die Grundform des Processes, je nachdem die der Anklage oder die der Untersuchung Grundlage ist, ändert das Institut der Vertheidigung'.

[2] *Ibid*, at 184: '*Verhältniß der Vertheidigung im Strafprocesse*'.

the fact that investigating judges were responsible for both investigating and prosecuting, and noting that this meant that it could not really be expected that they would exert the same energy with regard to both the incriminating and the exculpatory evidence.[3] This meant not only that the report of the investigating judge was likely to be a 'one-sided' affair but that this would also compromise the verdict because the judges could base their decisions only on these files.[4] His description of the importance of strengthening the rights of the defence in terms of an attempt to balance the position of the defence and that of the prosecution is firmly based on a broader procedural understanding of the defence rights.[5] This is further emphasised by his comments on the importance of oral and public proceedings and the belief that, while it was important to grant the accused the right to counsel, this would not be sufficient to correct the deficiencies inherent in the structure of the proceedings.[6]

The development of the principles of judicial independence and partisan public prosecutions meant that the institutional form of criminal proceedings was principally shaped by the relationship between the judiciary and the prosecution. Although the rights of the defence were not of great significance in relation to these institutional developments, once the new procedural structure had been finalised it was necessary to re-evaluate the role of the defence. As the judge was no longer to take responsibility for the defence of those accused of criminal offences, the latter had to be afforded other opportunities to take on this role themselves. The primary focus was therefore on ensuring that they had sufficient freedom to organise their defence. This involved guaranteeing both the active and the passive aspects of the right to be heard in order that they were able both to understand the proceedings and to make themselves understood.[7]

---

[3] *Ibid*, at 185: '[i]m Inquisitionsprocesse, wo der Inquirent ohnehin zwei nicht wohl zu vereinigende Rollen, die des Anklägers und Inquirenten, vereinigen soll, kann von diesem Untersuchungsbeamten noch weniger erwartet werden, daß er mit gleich angestrengter Thätigkeit und Umsicht den Entschuldigungs-beweis führe'.

[4] *Ibid*: 'und eine gewisse Einseitigkeit ist daher eben so leicht in Bezug auf diesen Beweis zu befürchten, als sie von Seite der urtheilenden Gerichte besorgt werden muß, die vorzüglich im geheimen schriftlichen Processe nur an den Acteneinhalt sich halten müssen, kein Mittel, sich selbst durch zweckmäßige Fragen Aufklärung zu verschaffen, haben, und die Acten nur auszugsweise durch das oft nicht sehr treue Medium des Referenten erfahren' (footnotes omitted).

[5] *Ibid*, at 185–6: '[f]ür das beste Mittel der Herstellung des rechtlichen Gleichgewichts zwischen Ankläger und Angeklagten hat man von jeher die Aufstellung eines rechtsgelehrten Defendors gehalten, welcher dem Angeklagten zur Seite steht, unabhängig und kräftig jeden Fehler in den Verhandlungen rügt, die geeigneten Anträge wegen Führung des Entschuldigungsbeweises macht, und die Summe der Verhandlungsgründe vollständig, klar und zweckmäßig den urtheilenden Richtern darstellt'.

[6] *Ibid*, at 185–91.

[7] J Vargha, *Die Verteidigung in Strafsachen* (Vienna, Manz'sche k k Hof-Verlag und Univ Buchhan-dlung, 1879) at 286: '[d]as reformierte Strafverfahren, das den Beschuldigten als Processsubject aner-kannt und principiell die möglichst Freiheit der Vertheidigung anstrebt, erheischt unfraglich eine consequente Realisirung des rechtlichen Gehörs in activer wie Passiver Richtung'; '[d]er processuale Grundsatz: "Respondere nemo cogitur in judicio, nisi prius quae proponuntur intelligat", legt dem Gericht vor Allem die Pflicht auf, für die materielle Möglichkeit Vorsorge zu treffen, dass die Vertheidigungspartei verstehen und sich verständlich machen könne'.

These issues will be the focus of the next section which will contain an examination of the development of the principal aspects of the right to be heard, namely the presence and participation of the accused and his or her right to the assistance of a lawyer. In view of the close relationship between the defence rights and the form of the proceedings, particular attention will be focused on the stages at which the defence was able to participate and why this participation was permitted or prohibited. In this regard the relationship between the trial and the investigation phases will be of particular interest. This will enable us to achieve a better understanding of the relationship between defence rights and procedural forms, and will facilitate an evaluation of the extent of these rights. It will be suggested that the 'dangers of the pre-trial process' were instrumental in the success of the 'adversarial' trial, not because they led to its development but because they maintained the 'effectiveness' of criminal prosecutions while allowing the trial to carrying the weight through the equality of arms of legitimating the criminal process.[8]

B   The Rights of the Defence at Trial

(i)   The Presence of the Accused

The notions of the presence and the participation of the accused in criminal proceedings are closely related but ultimately separate principles. In modern times the presence requirement is inevitably connected to the benefits that the accused is said to derive from having the opportunity to participate in the proceedings, and consequently it is often subsumed by notions of participation. In the context of the nineteenth century procedural principles, the presence of the defence at the public and oral trial was a prerequisite to any participatory role. 'The personal presence of the panel [ie the accused] in every step, from first to last, of the trial' was seen as an important aspect of criminal proceedings in the nineteenth century in both England and Scotland.[9] The Scottish jurist Hume writes:

> With one exception, which was introduced in evil times, in cases of treason, it has been our invariable custom, that no sort of proceeding can here [ie in the absence of the accused] take place, as for trial of the crime libelled.[10]

---

[8]   Cf JH Langbein, *The Origins of the Adversary Criminal Trial* (Oxford, Oxford University Press, 2002) at 4.
[9]   D Hume, *Commentaries on the Law of Scotland, Respecting Crimes* (Edinburgh, Bell & Bradfute, 1844), ii, at 269.
[10]   *Ibid*, ii, at 269–70; JHA MacDonald, *A Practical Treatise on the Criminal Law of Scotland* (Edinburgh, William Green & Son, 1894) at 429.

The absence of the accused meant that there could be no 'security for doing justice to the case' because it denied the accused the opportunity to defend him- or herself and seriously interfered with the possibility of enforcing the verdict. But some legal systems were less disturbed by these issues, and in several jurisdictions, including France, provision was made even in the reformed nineteenth century procedural codes for trials to take place notwithstanding the absence of the accused. The French system employed different approaches depending on the nature of the crime. In cases before the *Tribunaux de police* and the *Tribunaux correctionnels* the court applied, in the event of the accused's failure to appear, a *jugement par défaut*:

> *Si la personne citée ne comparait pas au jour et à l'heure fixé par la citation, elle sera jugée par défaut.*[11]

> *lorsque le prévenue ne comparait pas, il sera jugé par défaut.*[12]

There was no question of sending the accused a repeat citation for his or her appearance. The trial could go ahead notwithstanding the accused's absence and, providing that there was sufficient evidence, it was permissible for the court to find the accused guilty. The accused was then given five days to appeal against the verdict.[13] In cases before the *Assises* a different procedure, known as *jugement de la contumace,* applied.[14] Here the failure of those accused of criminal offences to appear for trial led to a pronouncement declaring them rebels against the law,[15] to the suspension of their civil and political rights and to the sequestration of their property. After the expiry of another time limit, the court ruled *in contumaciam*—a procedure which the accused's lawyer was not permitted to attend. In the event that the accused was later arrested or turned him- or herself in, the judgment was revoked and a new trial followed in accordance with the normal procedural principles.

The *jugement de la contumace,* which was also followed in several of the German jurisdictions before the enactment of the federal Code of Criminal Procedure 1877,[16] was criticised by several German commentators. Zachariä was

---

[11] Art 149 of the Code d'instruction criminelle 1808 (Tribunaux de police): 'if the person cited to appear does not appear on the day and time arranged, he or she will be judged by default'.

[12] Art 186 of the Code d'instruction criminelle 1808 (Tribunaux correctionnelles): 'if the accused does not appear, he will be judged by default'.

[13] See generally F Hélie, *Traité de L'instruction Criminelle,* 2nd edn (Paris, Henri Plon, 1866–7), vi, at 393–6 and 696–719; J-E Boitard, *Leçons sur les Code Pénal et d'Instruction Criminelle,* 3rd edn (Paris, Gustave Thorel, 1844) at 437–8 and 472–5; see further HA Zachariä, *Handbuch des deutschen Strafprozesses* (Göttingen, Verlag der Dieterichschen Buchhandlung, 1861 & 1868), ii, at 382.

[14] A Esmein, A *History of Continental Criminal Procedure with Special Reference to France* (trans J Simpson, Boston, Mass, Little Brown & Co, 1913; reprinted Union, NJ, The Lawbook Exchange, 2000) at 515–16.

[15] '[E]in Rebellen gegen das Gesetz': see HA Zachariä, *Handbuch des deutschen Strafprozesses* (Göttingen, Verlag der Dieterichschen Buchhandlung, 1861 & 1868), ii, at 382.

[16] See eg SH Meyer, *Das Strafverfahren gegen Abwesende: geschichtliche dargestellt und vom Standpunkt des heutigen rechts geprüft* (Berlin, Verlag von Georg Reimer, 1869).

notably scathing about the process, writing that there could be no doubt that the procedure was not compatible with the fundamental principles of reformed accusatorial criminal procedure law and maintaining that proceedings which took place in the absence of the accused could be considered only as totally reprehensible.[17] For him it was self-evident that the presence of the accused before the judges responsible for determining the charge had to be considered an indispensable condition of a complete and just verdict, which obviously could not be replaced by statutory fiction or legal presumption.[18]

Although provision was made in several German regional procedural codes for trials *in absentia*[19] these were superseded in 1877 by the federal Code of Criminal Procedure, which stated that as a general rule the trial could take place only in the presence of the accused.[20] In spite of this, it is fair to say that before the introduction of the Code of 1877 the prevailing opinion was not supportive of a ban on trials *in absentia* and many influential commentators were in favour of the retention of contumacial-type proceedings.[21] Meyer attributes the acceptance of the abolition of such proceedings to the recognition that this was needed in order to meet the new procedural requirements of oral proceedings and the conception of criminal proceedings as regulated by the accusatorial trinity.[22] Here there is thus evidence of the defence 'rights' developing primarily in order to accord with the stipulated procedural form, and not primarily in order to

---

[17] Zachariä, above n14, at 391–2: '[e]s kann keinem begründeten Zweifel unterliegen, dass bei einer consequenten Festhaltung des Grundprinzips des Strafprocesses ein Contumacial-Verfahren im . . . Sinne der modernen Gesetzgebungen, unter Verurtheilung des in der Hauptverhandlung nicht gegenwärtigen Angeklagten, als durchaus verwerflich bretrachtet werden muss'.

[18] Ibid, at 392: '[f]ür alle Criminalsachen . . . muß die persönliche Gegenwart des Angeklagten vor dem das Urtheil findenden Richter und die dadurch bedingte Möglichkeit seiner Verantwortung gegen den Schuldbeweis im Ganzen und im Einzelnen als unentberliche Voraussetzung einer materiell vollständigen und gerechten Urtheilsfällung betrachtet werden, die selbstverständlich durch keine gesetzliche Fiction oder juristische Präsumtion erstzt werden kann'.

[19] It was included for instance in the Prussian draft procedural code of 1865: see T Goldtdammer, 'Das Kontumazialverfahren nach Preußischen Rechte' (1863) 11 Archiv für Preußisches Strafrecht 450 at 450 ff; HA Zachariä, Handbuch des deutschen Strafprozesses (Göttingen, Verlag der Dieterichschen Buchhandlung, 1861 & 1868), ii, at 383.

[20] Para 229 of the StPO of 1877; see further F von Holtzendorff (ed), Handbuch des Deutschen Strafprozessrechts (Berlin, Carl Habel, 1879), ii, at 221–3 and J Glaser, Handbuch des Strafprozesses (Leipzig, Duncker & Humblot, 1883 & 1885), i, at 181–2.

[21] See eg A Buchner, 'Das Strafverfahren gegen Abwesende' (1857) 9 Der Gerichtssaal 81 at 81 ff; H Ortloff, 'Das Strafverfahren gegen Abwesende und Flüchtige' (1871) 19 Archiv für Preußisches Strafrecht 492; T Goldtdammer, 'Das Kontumazialverfahren nach Preußischen Rechte' (1863) 11 Archiv für Preußisches Strafrecht 450.

[22] F von Holtzendorff (ed), Handbuch des Deutschen Strafprozessrechts (Berlin, Carl Habel, 1879), ii, at 222: '[d]en Grund, weßhalb es richtig ist, in beiden Fällen auf die Aburtheilung zu verzichten, vermögen wir in Uebereinstimmung mit unserer vorgenannten Schrift nur darin zu erblicken, daß der auf das Anklageprinzip und auf den Grundsatz der Mündlichkeit des Verfahrens gebaute Straprozeß die Gegenwart des Angeklagten bei der Hauptverhandlung erfordert'.

enhance the accused's autonomy. While trials *in absentia* were effectively out-lawed in Germany, Scotland and England, they were retained in Italy and France.[23]

Although it might be tempting to link the importance of the presence of the accused to the concern of the new procedural system with the importance of protecting his or her participatory rights, this would not be entirely accurate. It is important to note in this regard that the presence of the accused was not just a right, but also an obligation. While in France the response of the state to the decision of an accused not to appear for trial was to continue with the proceedings regardless, the other European jurisdictions resorted to other measures in order to ensure that the accused appeared for trial. In many jurisdictions, the failure to appear for trial led to the imposition of sanctions on the accused. Zachariä, for instance, while condemning trials *in absentia* saw no reason for opposing measures such as sequestration of property and the suspension of the accused's civil and political rights as punishment for his or her disobedience in failing to appear for trial.[24] Thus it is interesting that the commentators take issue with the taking place of a trial in the absence of the accused, but not with the imposition of a (often very substantial) punishment for his or her failure to attend.

There seems to be some tension between explanations such as those of Hume, in which the importance of the participation of the accused is emphasised and implicitly linked to notions of autonomy, and the consequences of a refusal to appear for trial. Lest the reader think that the requirement that the accused be present was somehow linked to a belief in the innocence of those who did not appear for trial, Hume adds this qualification:

> But although our law justly refuses to take any step towards the trial of any one in his absence, it is however, very necessary on the other hand, that we have some means of compelling to appear, or of driving out of the country those wicked and dangerous persons, who abscond owing to consciousness of their guilt. Our expedient for this purpose is sentence of fugitation or outlawry, which passes against the accused, on his absence at the diet of his libel, and is attended with the forfeiture of his person in law,

---

[23] It is interesting to note that trials *in absentia* have been found not to be incompatible per se with Art 6 ECHR, although the Strasbourg authorities have held that such proceedings must, inter alia, entitle an accused who is tried and sentenced *in absentia* to a re-trial in event of his or her reappearance. See eg *Colozza v Italy*, judgment of 12 Feb 1985, Series A no 89, (1985) EHRR 516; *Poitrimol v France*, judgment of 23 Nov 1993, Series A no 227-A, (1994) 18 EHRR 130. For an overview of the regulatory structure see S Trechsel, *Human Rights in Criminal Proceedings* (Oxford, Oxford University Press, 2005) at 253–61. See also the judgment of the Human Rights Committee of the United Nations interpreting the ICCPR in *Daniel Monguya Mbenga v Zaire*, Communication no 16/1977 (1990) para 76, in which it was held that Art 14 'cannot be construed as invariably rendering proceedings in absentia inadmissible irrespective of the reasons for the accused person's absence'.

[24] HA Zachariä, *Handbuch des deutschen Strafprozesses* (Göttingen, Verlag der Dieterichschen Buchhandlung, 1861 & 1868), ii, at 395: '*[n]iemals darf aber dazu in Criminalsachen die Annahme eines Geständnisses des angeschuldigten Verbrechens gerechnet werden; wogegen die Verhängung einer Sequestration der Güter und der Suspension der staatsbürgerlichen Rechte, als Nachtheilen des Ungehorsams, prinzipmäßig nichts im Wege steht*'.

(*amittit legem terrae*): So that he cannot bear testimony on any occasion, or hold any place of trust or even pursue or defend in any process, civil or criminal, or claim any personal privilege or benefit whatsoever of the law.[25]

He continues:

This sentence is a warrant also for denouncing him a rebel, or putting him to the horn, as it is called, whereby his moveable substance escheats to his Majesty; and if he remain a year in this condition, the profits also of his heritable estate are forfeited to his superior, for his lifetime. These consequences do not in anywise ensue, on a presumption of his being guilty of what is laid to his charge, (for the penalty would then be various, according to the degree of the crime); but as a punishment of his contumacy and rebellion (so it is construed) in disobeying the will of the King's letters, which order him to appear and underlie the law. In contemning this injunction, he is held to have cast off his allegiance as a subject, and to have entered into a state of rebellion to the law, and the Sovereign of the land.[26]

In England too the *judgment of outlawry* was used to compel the appearance of the accused who failed to appear after five citations.[27] It was finally abolished in 1879 by which time it appears in any case to have become obsolete. This may explain why the Commission of 1879 did not believe it necessary to substitute outlawry with another procedure, thereby rejecting Stephen's recommendation that outlawry be replaced with a power enabling the courts to make a 'fugitive from justice' bankrupt.[28] Interestingly Stephen is critical of this decision, writing that:

It is true that under the provisions of the extradition treaties offenders may be brought back to England, but I do not see why, if a wealthy man committed treason or treasonable felony, he should be able to live in France with no other inconvenience than that of being unable to return to England. If a man will not answer to the laws of his country, I think he ought to forfeit the property which he holds under their protection…. The process of outlawry is obsolete, but bankruptcy is well understood; and if flying from justice were made an act of bankruptcy, it would operate as a severe check upon wealthy persons disposed to avoid justice.[29]

The use of other mechanisms to compel the accused to appear at trial, such as detaining them on remand, left the accused with even less autonomy to decide whether or not to appear at trial, and it is perhaps no coincidence that the improving provision for detention on remand coincided with the abolition of procedures such as outlawry.[30]

---

[25] D Hume, *Commentaries on the Law of Scotland, Respecting Crimes* (Edinburgh, Bell & Bradfute, 1844), ii, at 270.

[26] *Ibid*, at 271.

[27] W Blackstone, *Commentaries on the Laws of England* (Oxford, Clarendon Press, 1765), iv, ch 24.

[28] JF Stephen, *A History of the Criminal Law of England* (London, Macmillan, 1883), i, at 515.

[29] *Ibid.*

[30] See eg F von Holtzendorff (ed), *Handbuch des Deutschen Strafprozessrechts* (Berlin, Carl Habel, 1879) at 339–62; CJA Mittermaier, *Die Gesetzgebung und Rechtsübung über Strafverfahren nach ihrer*

It is obvious therefore that there are difficulties with construing the requirement that the accused be present at trial solely in terms of defence rights. 'Rights' imply that the person possessing them can choose whether or not to exercise them. Here, however, the accused person has no choice, no option not to exercise the right. Failure to attend trial often resulted in the imposition of severe sanctions and thus it would seem that the attendance requirement was as much an obligation as a right. The historical evidence seems to suggest that the requirement that the accused be present at trial ought to be viewed at least in part as a means of compelling those accused of crimes to submit to the might of the criminal justice system and to accept the court's jurisdiction to try them. Failure to co-operate and to accept the courts' legitimacy to determine the charge leads to the imposition of draconian sanctions in the form of the withdrawal of the legal (and sometimes also political) rights of the accused and/or the sequestration of his or her property. It is impossible to disregard the institutional importance of the accused's presence. As trials become seen as a dispute to be conducted between two parties, the absence of the accused leads to a serious imbalance, which in turn creates something of a legitimacy crisis for the accusatorial system.

Despite the fact that the presence requirement seems to have been something of an obligation rather than offering the accused substantive rights, both its development and the movement against trials *in absentia* in the second half of the nineteenth century are nevertheless of interest, because they can be seen to be connected to a particular conception of criminal proceedings involving oral and public hearings. Moreover it cannot be ruled out that it did play a significant role in facilitating defence rights through laying the foundations for the accused to be afforded the opportunity to participate in the proceedings.

(ii) Participatory Rights of the Accused

(a) *The Developing Conception of the Accused as a 'Party'*

The justification most frequently employed during the nineteenth century to explain the importance of the presence of the accused was the fact that it provided him or her with an opportunity to participate in the proceedings. An 'essential prerequisite of the reformed criminal procedure law', writes Glaser, 'is the presence and potential for participation of the person who is the subject of

---

neusten Fortbildung (Erlangen, Ferdinand Enke, 1856) at 340 ff; F Hélie, *Traité de L'instruction Criminelle*, 2nd edn (Paris, Henri Plon, 1866–7), iii, paras 1514–1523; J Paterson, *Commentaries on the Liberty of the Subject* (London, MacMillan, 1877).

the criminal charge'.[31] The absence of the accused impedes the criminal proceedings because he or she is unable to defend him- or herself, and thus it would not be legitimate for there to be a conviction.[32] Hélie refers to 'the right to be heard' as a principle of natural justice[33] and notes that it was upheld in Roman law, which dictated that 'no one, not even a slave, could be convicted without first having the chance to defend him- or herself' (*si non habebunt advocatum, ego dabo*).[34] Although the principle was expressly set out in the intermediary laws of the revolutionary period in France, it was not included in the *Code d'instruction criminelle* 1808. Hélie writes however that it was applied in practice and served to protect both the interests of the accused and those of society.

The right to participate was principally orientated towards the public and oral trial. It was at this point in the proceedings that those accused of criminal offences were to have the opportunity to 'defend themselves' during the hearing and challenging of the evidence. This is apparent in the set up of the English trial, which was quite clearly designed to enable the defence to challenge the evidence against it.[35] This seems also to have been the case in Scotland. According to Hume:

> It is considered, that unless the accused is present to take charge of his own interest, there can be no security for doing full justice to his case; for pleading all his defences, bringing forward all his evidence, stating all objections to the evidence on the other part, and still less for taking advantage of all those pleas and grounds of challenge, which may arise in the course of the proceedings in the trial.[36]

Vargha too expresses this idea clearly when he writes that the presence of the accused and his or her defence counsel at trial was essential in order to guarantee the defence the opportunity to observe and to influence the taking and hearing of evidence.[37]

---

[31] J Glaser, *Handbuch des Strafprozesses* (Leipzig, Duncker & Humblot, 1883 & 1885), ii, at 194: '[e]ine wesentliche Voraussetzung des eigentlichen Strafprozesses... ist das Vorhandsein und die Möglichkeit der Mitwirkung derjenigen Person, wider welche die Strafklage erhoben wird...'.

[32] *Ibid*, at 202: '[a]uch Abwesenheit des Beschuldigten ist ein Hinderniss des Strafverfahrens, weil grundsätzlich daran festgehalten wird, dass der Abwesende, weil er sich nicht vertheidigen kann, auch nicht verurtheilt werden darf'.

[33] F Hélie, *Traité de L'instruction Criminelle*, 2nd edn (Paris, Henri Plon, 1866–7), vii, at 383.

[34] *Ibid*, at 382: '[l]a jurisprudence romaine n'admettait pas qu'une personne, même un esclave, pût être traduite en justice sans être défendue'.

[35] JF Stephen, *A History of the Criminal Law of England* (London, Macmillan, 1883), i, at 429: '[t]he opening speech for the prosecution is followed by the examination of the witnesses, who are first examined in chief by the counsel for the Crown, then cross-examined by the counsel for the prisoner if he is defended by counsel, or by the prisoner himself if he is not, and then re-examined by counsel for the Crown'.

[36] D Hume, *Commentaries on the Law of Scotland, Respecting Crimes* (Edinburgh, Bell & Bradfute, 1844), ii, at 269–70; JHA MacDonald, *A Practical Treatise on the Criminal Law of Scotland* (Edinburgh, William Green & Son, 1894) at 429.

[37] J Vargha, *Die Verteidigung in Strafsachen* (Vienna, Manz'sche k k Hof-Verlag und Univ Buchhandlung, 1879) at 393: '[d]ie Anwesenheit des Angeklagten und seines Vertheidigers in der Hauptverhandlung gewährt ihnen die Möglichkeit, die hier vor sich gehenden Beweisaufnahmen zu überwachen und zu beeinflussen'.

The emphasis of the nineteenth century writers was not just on the right to participation per se, but rather on a particular type of participation. The participation of the accused had also been a hugely important aspect of the inquisitorial laws preceding the nineteenth century reforms. Indeed the strict laws of evidence which were applied during this period meant that convictions were largely based on confessions, which in turn were dependent on the participation of the accused. Vargha confirms this when he refers to the hearing of the accused 'as the most important and essential means of discovering the material truth during this period'.[38] Whereas in the inquisitorial period the accused had been compelled (often through the use of torture) to confess, the essence of the reformed system was voluntary participation. But it was more than that. The nineteenth century marked a dramatic move away from conceptions of proof as based on strict statutory qualitative and quantitative presumptions and towards an adversarial idea of truth. Only through allowing the defence freedom to present its case and challenge that of the prosecution could there be certainty that the verdict had been correctly ascertained.[39]

The essential transformation was that the accused was no longer seen just as an individual, but rather as, in the context of 'the defence', a party to the proceedings.[40] It is interesting in this regard that the primary failings of the English procedural system were deemed to be the difficulties which would inevitably be faced by the accused in responding to the charges: '*[d]ie mangelhafte Vorsorge für die materielle Vertheidigung ist daher auch die Schattenseite des englischen Prozesses*'.[41] An inherent demand of the new accusatorial procedure model was that both parties were to have the same rights and opportunitites to convince the judge of their position. For this reason it was necessary to provide the accused with assistance, including the assistance of counsel, to allow him or her to function within this system.[42]

---

[38] *Ibid*, at 188: '*[d]ie Vernehmung des Beschuldigten galt dem inquisitorischen Processe für das wichtigste und wesentlichste Mittel der Erforschung materieller Wahrheit*'.

[39] F Hélie, *Traité de L'instruction Criminelle*, 2nd edn (Paris, Henri Plon, 1866–7), vii, at 383–4: '*[l]a défense, dans son système, revêt un double caractère: vis-à-vis de l'accusé, elle est un droit qu'il exerce librement pendant tout le cours du débat et jusqu'au jugement; vis-à-vis de la justice, elle est un moyen d'instruction, une des sources de la vérité, une forme essentielle de la procédure. Elle est à la fois instituée dans l'intérêt des accusés et dans l'intérêt de la société: dans l'intérêt des accusés, pour qu'il puissent faire valoir toutes les exceptions, toutes les justifications, tous les moyens de fait ou de droit qui leur appartiennent; dans l'intérêt de la société, car le premier besoin de la société est la justice, et il n'y a point de justice là où la défense n'est pas entière, car il n'y a pas certitude de la vérité*'.

[40] *Ibid*, vii, at 384: '*[l]a défense est le droit de l'accusé, mais elle est en même temps la garantie de la justice et le moyen le plus puissant d'arriver à la connaissance de la vérité. C'est parce qu'elle est non-seulement un droit un droit, mais une forme essentielle de l'instruction criminelle, que les accusés ne peuvent renoncer aux mesures établies pour l'assurer.*'

[41] J Glaser, *Handbuch des Strafprozesses* (Leipzig, Duncker & Humblot, 1883 & 1885), i, at 215, n 2: '[t]he inadequate provision for the rights of the defence represents the negative side of English criminal justice'.

[42] See also CJA Mittermaier, *Die Gesetzgebung und Rechtsübung über Strafverfahren nach ihrer neusten Fortbildung* (Erlangen, Ferdinand Enke, 1856) at 286.

The role of the defence was seen to be contingent on the institutional setting and on the relationship between the prosecution and the judiciary. The participatory role of the accused was therefore to be seen principally in the context of 'the defence' and was intended to counter the deficits of the inquisitorial period during which the accused completely lacked any sort of institutional status:

> *Ohne Stütze, ohne Vertheidiger, einsam, verlassen steht der Angeklagte vor dem Inquisitor, der ihm vielleicht schon vor der Untersuchung in seinem Herzen das Verdammungsurtheil gesprochen hat.*[43]

In direct contrast the reformed system was constructed around the notion of parties and the conception of the accused as part of a 'defence team' comprising lawyers and, where necessary, translators.[44] Counsel for the defence was to be seen as the 'procedural alter ego' and the 'legal ears and mouth' of the accused and any separation of the accused and his or her lawyers as contrary to the principles of the reformed accusatorial procedural system.[45] The determination of the charge was therefore seen not just as involving the unearthing of certain facts but also the explanation or interpretation of these in the course of the proceedings. Only through the assistance of counsel would those accused of criminal offences be able to engage with these vitally important legal formalities and make proper use of the guarantees afforded them in presenting their defence. Glaser highlights the importance placed on this idea by suggesting that 'the history of criminal procedure law' was in fact 'the history of the defence'.[46]

The participatory opportunities of the defence were seen therefore not just as individual rights but also as an integral part of the institutional and procedural form of the accusatorial legal system.[47] In the words of Glaser, '*die mündliche*

---

[43] J Vargha, *Die Verteidigung in Strafsachen* (Vienna, Manz'sche k k Hof-Verlag und Univ Buchhandlung, 1879) at 191: 'the accused stands without assistance, without defence counsel, isolated, abandoned before the inquisitor, who has possibly in his heart already convicted the accused before the investigation has even begun'.

[44] *Ibid*, at 286: '[d]er Anspruch auf "rechtliches Gehör" steht dem Beschuldigten nicht bloss für seine Person, sondern in seiner Eigenschaft als Processpartei zu. Zur Processpartei aber wird der Beschuldigte vom correcten accusatorischen Standpunkte aus erst in Gemeinschaft mit seinem Vertheidiger'.

[45] *Ibid*: '[d]er Beschuldigte hört also als Processpartei nicht, wo nicht auch sein Vertheidiger mithört und er wird auch nicht gehört, wo nicht auch letzterer mitgehört wird. Der Vertheidiger ist als ein processualer Alterego, gleichsam als das rechtliche Ohr und der rechtliche Mund des Beschuldigten aufzufassen. Jede gewaltsame Trennung der beiden Repräsentanten der Vertheidigungspartei ist principwidrig'. For a modern statement to this effect see the decision of the Swiss Federal Court in BGE 106 IA.

[46] J Glaser, *Handbuch des Strafprozesses* (Leipzig, Duncker & Humblot, 1883 & 1885), ii, at 223: '[m]ann kann sagen, dass die Geschichte des Strafprozesses die Geschichte der Vertheidigung ist'. See also HF Pfenninger, *Probleme des schweizerischen Strafprozessrechts: Ausgewählte Aufsätze von Prof. Dr. Hans Felix Pfenninger* (Zurich, Schulthess, 1966) at 140.

[47] F Hélie, *Traité de L'instruction Criminelle*, 2nd edn (Paris, Henri Plon, 1866–7), vii, at 382: '[l]a défense des accusés ne droit être considérée ni comme un privilége que la loi aurait établi, ni comme une mesure que l'humanité aurait conseillée'.

Hauptverhandlung ist nicht ohne lebendige und wirksame Vertreter der Vertheidigung wie der Anklage denkbar'.[48] A fundamental aspect of this was the importance of the procedural opportunities of the defence in relation to those of the prosecution. The nineteenth century writers were united in their belief that it was essential that both parties were to have the chance to convince the judge of their arguments. Compliance with the equality of arms principle required ensuring that the defence had the opportunity to respond to each of the prosecution's allegations.[49]

The participatory role of the accused must be seen therefore as being closely connected to the accusatorial conception of criminal proceedings and the corresponding development of an adversarial conception of the establishment of the truth, which had spread across the continent in the nineteenth century. The participation of the accused was not conceived of as a way of promoting communication with the court or permitting a dialogue between the accused and the judge; rather it was seen to be a natural and essential consequence of the procedural reforms which dictated that there be a levelling of the roles of the defence and prosecution. In this sense the participation of the accused was not only firmly tied to the role of the defence but also confined by the procedural structure that had been developed. This is not to say that these developments did not benefit the accused, but only to note that the 'rights' of the accused were developed in order to fit in with the procedural reforms and were secondary to the broader aim of developing an effective and legitimate system of criminal prosecutions. In order to examine this claim a little further, it is useful to look at the English reforms of the late nineteenth century which provided the accused with the 'right' to testify in court.

(b)   Understanding the Nature of the Accused's Participatory Rights: The English Reforms of the Late Nineteenth Century

The opportunity of the accused to participate in the proceedings was subject, in a number of European jurisdictions, to various restrictions. Undoubtedly one of the most significant of these was the rule as to the incompetence of the accused to testify, which applied in Scotland and England until it was abolished at the end of

---

[48]   J Glaser, *Handbuch des Strafprozesses* (Leipzig, Duncker & Humblot, 1883 & 1885), ii, at 224: 'The oral trial is unthinkable without the live and effective representatives of the defence and the prosecution'.

[49]   Eg CJA Mittermaier, *Die Gesetzgebung und Rechtsübung über Strafverfahren nach ihrer neusten Fortbildung* (Erlangen, Ferdinand Enke, 1856) at 286: *'[d]ie Gleichheit der Stellung des Anklägers und Angeklagten, daher keiner grössere Befugnisse als der Andere haben darf und gegen jeden Angriff des Anklägers dem Angeklagten die vollste Vertheidigung zustehen muss. Die Staatsregierung selbst muss erkennen, dass Strafurtheile nicht die nöthige Wirksamkeit haben, wenn nicht das Vertrauen begründet ist, dass das Strafverfahren auf voller Gleichheit der Waffen des Anklägers und des Angeklagten beruhte*; J Glaser, *Handbuch des Strafprozesses* (Leipzig, Duncker & Humblot, 1883 & 1885), i, at 239: '[d]ie contradictorische Verhandlung fördert ihrer Natur nach, dass den gegen einander verhandelnden Parteien gleiches Recht, gleiche Möglichkeit geboten sein müsse, auf den Richter einzuwirken'.

the nineteenth century. Until this point although those accused of criminal offences were permitted, or indeed required, to be present at trial there was a general prohibition on them testifying under oath. The abolition of this restriction is therefore often seen as a symbol of the developing 'respect for the accused as a rational and responsible agent' in the course of the nineteenth century. According to such claims, criminal proceedings are to be seen as moving towards a system, which has as its 'central purpose a process of argument and communication with the defendant': 'an accused will have a right to be heard, because the absence of that right would entail a refusal by the court to recognise the accused's status as a participant in the trial'.[50]

Initially, this argument seems somewhat uncontroversial. In a system based on the accusatorial trinity the role of the accused takes on considerable importance. On closer inspection however there is little evidence to demonstrate that the procedural developments of the nineteenth century were orientated towards upholding any sort of notion of the autonomy of the accused. On the contrary, the defence rights were adapted to fit the developing procedural model which depended on the participation of the accused as part of the defence, and not as an individual. Allen suggests that 'if the accused are to be treated as rational and responsible agents they cannot deny that status by refusing to participate in their trial'. He writes that 'the accused's status carries duties as well as rights, and these include the duty to give evidence and to submit to questioning by counsel for the prosecution'.[51] Statements like this however seem to misconstrue the nature of accusatorial criminal proceedings which were to be seen as affording the defence equal status to the prosecutor. The mandate of the defence was not to answer to a higher authority but rather to act in such a way as to further its interest in disputing the allegations of the prosecutor. From a procedural perspective, the accused was not to be seen as an individual but as an important institutional ingredient. The role of the defence, and thus that of the accused, was to a crucial extent predetermined by the structure of the criminal proceedings which had developed.

In order to gain a better understanding of the reasons for the abolition of the principle and the developing conception of the trial in nineteenth century England, it is useful to have regard to the claims and counter-claims made in the debates on whether or not to abolish the rule as to the accused's incompetence. The rationale underpinning the rule was apparently the belief that the evidence of the accused would be likely to be biased. The English writer Gilbert explained it in the following terms:

---

[50]   CJW Allen, *The Law of Evidence in Victorian England* (Cambridge, Cambridge University Press, 1997) at 174–5.
[51]   *Ibid*, at 175.

where a man who is interested in the matter in question, would also prove it, 'tis rather a cause for distrust than any just cause for belief... and the law removes from the testimony to stop them sliding into perjury.[52]

Importantly, the rule did not altogether prevent the accused from addressing the court, as he or she was still permitted to make 'unsworn' statements. Indeed there is evidence that the opportunity to allow an accused to make such a statement was taken seriously by the courts. In *Dyer*, for instance, the trial judge held:

> I would never prevent a prisoner from making a statement, though he has counsel. He may make any statement he pleases before his counsel addresses the jury, and then his counsel may comment upon that statement as part of the case. If it were otherwise, the most monstrous injustice might result to prisoners. If the statement of the prisoner fits in with the evidence, it would be very material, and we should have no right to shut it out.[53]

Furthermore the various possibilities for challenging the prosecution case meant that the accused was not left entirely without options in conducting his or her defence.[54]

The rule as to the accused's incompetence to testify was nevertheless regarded by many as a serious interference with the opportunity of the accused to defend him- or herself.[55] It was eventually abolished following the enactment of the Criminal Evidence Act in 1898.[56] Advocates of the new law pointed to the fact that it enabled those accused of criminal offences to speak in their defence, thereby increasing their autonomy:

> As we have already said, in a primitive state of society a party to a dispute tells his own tale – his opening statement as it may be called, is his evidence. Thus, to some extent,

---

[52]   G Gilbert, *The Law of Evidence* (London, 1754; reprinted London, Garland Publishers, 1979) at 122. See further AW Alschuler, 'A Peculiar Privilege in Historical Perspective' in RH Helmholz, CM Gray, JH Langbein, E Moglen, HE Smith and A Alschuler (eds), *The Privilege Against Self-Incrimination: Its Origins and Development* (Chicago, Ill, University of Chicago Press, 1997) at 198.

[53]   (1844) 1 Cox 113 at 114.

[54]   The inability of those accused of criminal offences to present their own arguments (although they were permitted to call witnesses for the defence) made the opportunity to challenge the prosecution case of paramount importance, and this perhaps goes some way to explaining the emphasis on the significance of the right to cross-examine prosecution witnesses. See eg JF Stephen, *A History of the Criminal Law of England* (London, Macmillan, 1883) at 431: '[s]o long as prisoners were really undefended by counsel in serious cases, their cross-examination of the witnesses against them was trifling and of little or no importance, though they did cross-examine to a greater or lesser extent. When they were allowed to have counsel to cross-examine, but not to speak for them, the cross-examination tended to become a speech thrown into the form of questions, and it has ever since retained this character to a greater or less extent.'

[55]   HE Smith, 'The Modern Privilege: Its Nineteenth-Century Origins' in RH Helmholz, CM Gray, JH Langbein, E Moglen, HE Smith and A Alschuler (eds), *The Privilege Against Self-Incrimination: Its Origins and Development* (Chicago, Ill, University of Chicago Press, 1997) at 146: '[f]ar from being a right to silence the disqualification was a burden on parties'.

[56]   62 Vict c 33. For an informative overview of the reform process see D Bentley, *English Criminal Justice in the Nineteenth Century* (London, Hambledon Press, 1998) at 147–204.

this enactment [Criminal Evidence Act 1898] restored to Englishmen a right of which they had been deprived by misplaced judicial ingenuity.[57]

The rule against the accused's competence was also criticised for interfering with the determination of the charge by virtue of the fact that it 'had the effect of excluding the evidence of the person who knew the most about the transaction'.[58] Bentham was a vociferous critic of the restrictions on the accused's competence to testify[59] and his arguments were instrumental in the prolonged campaign to have the rule abolished. He was of the opinion that only the guilty shrank from the opportunity to testify. According to him the only way to find out what had happened was to inquire:

> a proposition that from the beginning of the world to the present day has never been a secret to any human being, unless it be to English lawyers. And of whom to inquire? Of whom, but of the one person in the world who, if the fact be in existence, cannot fail to know of it?—the one person in the world, in comparison with whose evidence, every other imaginable species of evidence, direct or circumstantial (except in so far as this naturally best evidence happens, by the force of sinister motives, to be driven into mendacity), is a miserable makeshift.[60]

Similarly Stephen acknowledges that there were good grounds for allowing the accused to testify in his or her defence:

> I am convinced by much experience that questioning, or the power of giving evidence, is a positive assistance, and a highly important one, to innocent men, and I do not see why in the case of the guilty there need be any hardship about it. It must be remembered that most persons accused of crime are poor, stupid, and helpless. They are often defended by solicitors who confine their exertions to getting a copy of the depositions and endorsing it with the name of some counsel to whom they pay a very small fee, so that even when prisoners are defended by counsel the defence is often extremely imperfect and consists rather of what occurs at that moment to the solicitor and to counsel than of what the man himself has to say if he knew how to say it. When a prisoner is undefended his position is often pitiable, even if he has a good case. An ignorant uneducated man has the greatest difficulty in collecting his ideas, and seeing the bearing of facts alleged. He is utterly unaccustomed to sustained attention or systematic thought, and it often appears to me as if the proceedings on a trial, which to an experienced person appear plain and simple, must pass before the eyes and mind of the prisoner like a dream which he cannot grasp.[61]

This passage contains a number of reflections on the condition of nineteenth century criminal justice in England. The reference to the 'power of giving

---

[57] Anon, 'The Criminal Evidence Act, 1898: An Act to Amend the Law of Evidence' [1899] *Edinburgh Review* 194 at 202.

[58] Sir Charles Russell, Parl Debs, 1888, CCCXXIV, 70, cited in D Bentley, *English Criminal Justice in the Nineteenth Century* (London, Hambledon Press, 1998) at 171.

[59] J Bentham, *Rationale of Judicial Evidence* (Edinburgh, Bowring, 1843), vii.

[60] *Ibid*, at 14.

[61] JF Stephen, *A History of the Criminal Law of England* (London, Macmillan, 1883) at 442.

evidence' seems to indicate recognition of the importance of the accused being able to testify. Although it would perhaps be stretching the point somewhat to interpret this as acknowledging the importance of the accused's autonomy, it certainly seems to suggest recognition of the fact that the input of the accused could be of value to them in the determination of the charge. However this initial statement seems to be qualified by suggestions that the possibility of those accused of criminal offences presenting their cases was seriously, and perhaps fatally, hindered by their lack of education and/or experience in the criminal process and by the inadequacies of legal representation. It is thus difficult to see how, under these conditions, the accused would be able to exercise the rights afforded to him or her by the 1898 Act. The suggestion that the accused's autonomy and participatory rights were the main concern during the nineteenth century, when legal representation was the exception rather than the rule and when the majority of those accused of criminal offences were seen as 'poor, stupid, and helpless', seems rather suspect.

There can be no doubt, moreover, that the abolition of the rule as to the incompetence of the accused can also be seen as having had a detrimental impact on the position of the accused. The Act's detractors contended that it was 'hard upon a man to be obliged to criminate himself',[62] arguing instead that the law preventing the accused from testifying not only was 'highly advantageous to the guilty' but also contributed greatly 'to the dignity and humanity of the criminal trial' and stimulated 'the search for independent evidence'.[63] Several commentators opposed the abolition of the rule on the basis that it would promote the conviction of innocent prisoners. One of those was Herbert Stephen, the son of James Stephen. He argued that making the accused competent would mean that:

> innocent prisoners [would be] convicted because of the way that they gave their evidence. If they gave it badly or dishonestly it went against them, and yet there were many prisoners who could not answer a series of questions, concerning a matter in which they had a strong interest, without looking as though they were lying. Not a few people were absolutely incapable of answering questions straightforwardly and to the point.[64]

Others contended that the abolition of the rule would interfere with the privilege against self-incrimination as the failure to testify would inevitably be interpreted as evidence of the accused's guilt.[65]

---

[62] J Bentham, *Rationale of Judicial Evidence* (Edinburgh, Bowring, 1843), vii, at 452; this view was of course criticised by Bentham who believed that 'evidence is the basis of justice; to exclude evidence is to exclude justice'.

[63] JF Stephen, *A History of the Criminal Law of England* (London, Macmillan, 1883) at 441.

[64] H Stephen, 'A Bill to Promote the Conviction of Innocent Prisoners' [1896] *Nineteenth Century* 566, at 566, quoted in D Bentley, *English Criminal Justice in the Nineteenth Century* (London, Hambledon Press, 1998) at 193.

[65] See AW Alschuler, 'A Peculiar Privilege in Historical Perspective' in RH Helmholz, CM Gray, JH Langbein, E Moglen, HE Smith and A Alschuler (eds), *The Privilege Against Self-Incrimination: Its*

Although the debate was framed mainly in terms of a play-off between the rights of the accused and the interests of society in an accurate determination of the charge, it is perhaps more accurate to see these developments in the context of the broader procedural reforms of the nineteenth century. The growing disquiet with the judicial role in relation to the examination of the evidence and the increasing involvement of prosecuting counsel at trial meant that the proceedings were quite obviously unbalanced. Indeed in his argument against the reforms Herbert Stephen draws attention to the fact that 'where prisoners gave evidence, prosecuting counsel examined them and addressed the jury, not as ministers of justice but as if striving for a verdict at Nisi Prius'.[66] He seems therefore not just to attack the reform of the rule as to the accused's incompetence but also to criticise the new conception of criminal proceedings which was emerging towards the end of the century. The reference to aggressive prosecutors striving for conviction is presumably intended as a contrast with proceedings in which the judge was primarily responsible for the examination of the evidence and for the protection of the interests of the accused. But the procedural reforms dictated that the role of the defence had to change. The defence role mutated as the procedural environment changed, and the role of the defence was tailored in response to the demands of this new procedural setting.

The solution to the debate on finding the correct balance between the rights of the defence and the facilitating of the prosecution was an evidential rather than a procedural one. The 1898 Act stripped the accused of his or her old immunity from cross-examination and exposed an accused 'who attacked the character of Crown witnesses to a new peril: retaliation in kind should he venture into the witness box'.[67] The decision to testify laid the accused open to cross-examination by the prosecutor. On the other hand, the importance of the right of the accused not to testify was also protected by a provision included in the 1898 Act which prohibited the prosecutor from commenting on the accused's failure to give evidence.[68] The Act also contained a general prohibition on the cross-examination of the accused as to his or her character.[69]

These concerns and the guarantees built into the 1898 Act can also be seen as being of relevance to a broader point about the scope of the rights of the defence and the context within which they should operate. The defence 'right' to present evidence is seen as something of a double-edged sword with the potential to count against the accused. In some cases it undoubtedly enabled the accused to set the record straight and lead evidence proving his or her innocence. In others,

---

Origins and Development (Chicago, Ill, University of Chicago Press, 1997) at 198; JN Bodansky, 'The Abolition of the Party–Witness Disqualification: An Historical Survey' (1981–2) 70 *Kentucky Law Journal* 91 at 115.

[66]   *Ibid.*

[67]   D Bentley, *English Criminal Justice in the Nineteenth Century* (London, Hambledon Press, 1998) at 204.

[68]   It should be noted that this protection, set out in s 1(c), was abolished in England in 1994.

[69]   S 1(f) of the 1898 Act.

however, where the accused was unable successfully to challenge the prosecution's case, the impression made by the accused may have actually contributed to the finding of guilt. This possibility was clearly acknowledged by commentators at the time of the reforms, and the evidential provisions built into the Act seem to have been expressly intended to protect the accused from him- or herself.[70] Thus, although the right to present evidence was of importance to the accused, it was equally important that the manner in which it was exercised was also regulated. The rules of evidence can be seen as dictating what type of evidence was not to be used to ground the conviction, thereby reducing the negative potential of the accused's testimony (or the manner in which it was delivered). Various other rules which set out exactly when and in which context the right to present evidence in the defence should be allowed were viewed as equally important.[71]

Bentley writes that the 1898 Act 'decisively and drastically' altered the criminal trial,[72] but alternatively it might be argued that the decisive alterations to the criminal trial in the course of the latter half of the nineteenth century actually resulted in the Act's introduction by removing the procedural basis for the existence of the old rule as to the accused's incompetence. The conception of judicial impartiality paved the way for the introduction of prosecuting counsel, which in turn necessitated a corresponding alteration in the role of the defence in order to address the apparent imbalance in the proceedings. Importantly there is little evidence to suggest that these reforms were based on notions of individual responsibility; indeed it is difficult to assess whether the individual accused was better or less well off following these reforms. It was the institutional form of the criminal proceedings that determined the extent of the role and autonomy of the defence, rather than the rights of the defence influencing the form of the proceedings. The evidential provisions on the other hand seem to have played an important role in safeguarding the interests of the defence, protecting the decision of the accused not to contribute to the proceedings.

(iii)   The Assistance of Counsel

The significance of the assistance of counsel can be seen to be directly connected to the corresponding importance of the defence's institutional role in procedural systems based on two opposing sides and an impartial judge. In many European jurisdictions the institutional reforms of the nineteenth century led to an

---

[70] Bentley, above n66.

[71] Stephen for instance favoured leaving the examination of the accused to counsel for the defence and the prosecution: '[b]y leaving him to be examined in chief by his own counsel and cross-examined by the counsel for the crown the danger of placing the judge in a position hostile to the prisoner would be avoided': JF Stephen, *A History of the Criminal Law of England* (London, Macmillan, 1883) 445.

[72] D Bentley, *English Criminal Justice in the Nineteenth Century* (London, Hambledon Press, 1998) at 204.

understanding of the trial not only as oral, public and adversarial[73] but also as the most desirable forum for the examination of the evidence.[74] The increasing role of the defence was thus connected to the reformation of the nature of proceedings. Whereas under the old procedural system the accused had had a relatively passive role, with the judiciary assuming primary responsibility for the examination of the evidence, the system that developed in the nineteenth century required the defence to be more active.[75] This meant that in order for the accused to be able to mount an effective defence it was essential that he or she had the opportunity to appoint counsel.[76] Legal assistance was held to be so important that the German federal Code of Criminal Procedure of 1877 made provision for the presence at trial of the defence lawyer, even in cases where the accused had been excluded.[77]

The right to counsel was seen by most commentators to be the most important aspect of the rights of the defence.[78] According to President Lamoignon, commenting on the relevant provision in Ordinances of 1670, the assistance of a lawyer had to be considered as a freedom grounded in the principles of natural justice.[79] Vargha goes as far as to suggest that the accused could be properly considered to be a 'party' to the process only if he or she was assisted by counsel,[80]

---

[73] J Glaser, *Handbuch des Strafprozesses* (Leipzig, Duncker & Humblot, 1883 & 1885), ii, at 490–2: '[d]ie Hauptverhandlung ist derjenige Abschnitt des Strafprozesses, in welchem die erhobene Anklage durch mündliche Verhandlung vor dem erkennenden Gerichte zu unmittelbarem Austrag durch das Endurtheil gebracht wird. Sie bildet den Hauptbestandtheil jedes Strafprozesses in welchem die für die Reform des Strafverfahrens vorangestellten Grundsätze (mündlich-öffentlich-contradictorische Verhandlung) zu voller Gestaltung gelangen; sie repräsentirt die neuen, wie die Voruntersuchung die aus dem alten Recht herübergenommenen Elemente des modernen Strafprozesses'.

[74] *Ibid*, i, at 374: '[d]ie Gestaltung des Beweisverfahrens, als des Hauptbestandtheils des gesammten Strafverfahrens . . .'.

[75] *Ibid*: '[a]uf der anderen Seite beruht der moderne Strafprozess, im Gegensatz zu dem gemeinen deutschen Inquisitionsprozess, dessen Theorie aus jenem Grundgedanken die Folgerung nahezu vollständiger Passivität der Parteien (oder vielmehr, da die Anklage kein selbständiges Organ hatte, des Beschuldigten) abgeleitet hatte, auf der Anerkennung der selbständigen Berechtigung der Betheiligten zur Mitwirkung im Beweisverfahren'.

[76] *Ibid*, ii, at 224: 'die mündliche Hauptverhandlung ist nicht ohne lebendige und wirksame Vertreter der Vertheidigung wie der Anklage denkbar'.

[77] Para 246 of the German StPO of 1877.

[78] F Hélie, *Traité de L'instruction Criminelle*, 2nd edn (Paris, Henri Plon, 1866–7) at 384: '[l]e premier corollaire du droit de défense est que l'accusé soit assisté d'un conseil'; J Vargha, *Die Vertheidigung in Strafsachen* (Vienna, Manz'sche k k Hof-Verlag und Univ Buchhandlung, 1879) at 286: '[d]er Beschuldigte muss nämlich nicht nur hören und gehört werden, er muss das Gehörte auch sachlich und sprachlich verstehen und sich auch in correcter Weise hören lassen und verständlich machen können, was ihm im Allgemeinen ohne die Unterstützung durch einen Vertheidigungstechniker, der dem Anklagetechniker die Waage zu halten vermag, nicht möglich sein wird'.

[79] *Ibid*, at 286: '[d]er Rechtsbeistand welchen man Angeklagten zu geben pflegt, stellt nicht etwa ein von Ordonnanzen oder Gesetzen gewährtes Privilegium dar, sondern vielmehr eine Freiheit, die im natürlichen Rechte gründet, welches älter ist, als alle menschlichen Gesetze. Die Natur selbst lehrt dem Menschen, die Kenntnisse Anderer anzurufen, wenn er selbst nicht über die zu seinen Zwecken nöthigen Mittel verfügt, und die Hülfe Anderer zu erborgen, wenn er sich selbst zu seiner Vertheidigung nicht hinlänglich stark fühlt'.

[80] *Ibid*: '[z]ur Processpartei aber wird der Beschuldigte vom correcten accusatorischen Standpunkte aus erst in Gemeinschaft mit seinem Vertheidiger'.

while Glaser writes that it was a 'fundamental principle' of procedural law that the trial could not proceed 'in the absence of the representatives of the defence and the prosecution'.[81] In France the right to counsel was even seen as instrumental to the functioning of the criminal justice system,[82] and in some cases the accused was not permitted to refuse to be assisted by counsel,[83] a fact which emphasises the institutional conception of the role of the defence. Vargha appeals to the notion of equality of arms, and states that in order to respect this principle it was essential for an expert for the defence to appear to act as a counterbalance to the legal expertise of the prosecutor.[84] Holtzendorff takes a similar approach, noting that while the old procedure had been sceptical of the involvement of defence counsel, the new procedural code was intended to guarantee equality of arms between the prosecution and defence, at least during the trial hearing.[85]

In England too the right to counsel underwent important developments in the course of the nineteenth century, although it is more common to find reference to their eighteenth century origins. Langbein refers to the emergence of solicitors for the prosecution in the eighteenth century as the primary factor in prompting the introduction of counsel in English trials: '[b]y allowing defence counsel to cross-examine prosecution witnesses, the judges of the 1730s undertook to correct for the imbalance that had opened between the unaided accused and a criminal prosecution that increasingly reflected the hand of lawyers and quasi-professional thieftakers'.[86] He writes that it was not 'until the 1780s, when there was a spurt in the reported use of defense counsel' that the adversary combat came to 'typify the seriously contested criminal trial'. But this 'spurt' does not change the fact that the right to counsel during the nineteenth century was, in England as in the vast majority of European countries, a patchy affair dependant on a number of variables including the nature of the charge.[87] Even in those cases

---

[81] J Glaser, *Handbuch des Strafprozesses* (Leipzig, Duncker & Humblot, 1883 & 1885) at 500: '*[d]ass eine Hauptverhandlung ohne die Anwesenheit von Repräsentanten der Anklage und Vertheidigung nicht zulässig sei, ist feststehender Grundsatz*'.

[82] '*[Q]ue les accusées ne peuvent valablement renoncer à l'exécution des formes que la loi a prescrites d'une manière absolue dans l'intérêt de leur défense*': Cass, 19 June 1823 (JP, tome XVII, 1496); 10 July 1823 (tome XVIII, 23); 19 Mar 1825 (tome XIX, 319); **52** 7 Jan 1836 (Bull no 6).

[83] Eg Cass, **53** 27 vend. an VIII (JP, tome I, 509); see F Hélie, *Traité de L'instruction Criminelle*, 2nd edn (Paris, Henri Plon, 1866–7), vii, at 384.

[84] J Vargha, *Die Verteidigung in Strafsachen* (Vienna, Manz'sche k k Hof-Verlag und Univ Buchhandlung, 1879) at 293: '*[d]em fachmännischen "Anklagekünstler" muss ein fachmännischer "Vertheidigungskünstler" gegenüber stehen, sonst kann von einer principiellen Waffengleichheit der Parteien nie und nimmer die Rede sein*'.

[85] F von Holtzendorff (ed), *Handbuch des Deutschen Strafprozessrechts* (Berlin, Carl Habel, 1879), i, at 409: '*[w]aren die älteren Prozeßgesetze vielfach darauf bedacht, die formale Vertheidigung in mißtrauischer Weise einzuschränken, so hat die Deutsche Str. Pr. O. wenigstens für die Hauptverhandlung den Grundsatz der sg. Waffengleichheit zwischen der Vertheidigung und der Anklagebehörde durchzuführen gesucht*'.

[86] JH Langbein, *The Origins of the Adversary Criminal Trial* (Oxford, Oxford University Press, 2002) at 168.

[87] Accused persons charged with impeachment (Geo II, c 30) or treason (7 & 8 Will III, c 3) were allowed to engage counsel. In felony cases counsel were sometimes allowed, and this became more

in which counsel were permitted to act for the accused, a large proportion of cases were tried without the participation of counsel. Beattie writes that by the end of the eighteenth century 'between a quarter and a third of defendants at the Old Bailey had the benefit of counsel'.[88] The proportion of accused assisted by counsel does not appear to have changed much by the 1830s,[89] in spite of the passing of the Prisoner's Counsel Act 1836. Bentley writes that for 'the majority of prisoners the Act was cruelly irrelevant. Whatever their legal right, in practice they were denied counsel by their poverty'.[90]

In fact, it was not until the second half of the nineteenth century, when there was growing awareness of the need to reform the prosecution and to ensure that prosecutors appeared regularly at trial, that there was corresponding consideration of the need for defence counsel. Reformers argued that the lack of an effective prosecutorial structure meant that criminals were escaping justice because victims were unwilling to prosecute. Although there had been resistance in England to the creation of a public prosecutor's office, which by this time existed in the majority of other European countries, by 1850 prosecutions 'were increasingly overseen by either the police, clerks to magistrates or borough solicitors, and were financed out of public funds'.[91] Further, in 1879 a Director of Public Prosecutions was appointed in order to oversee prosecutions. It is instructive that a right to legal aid (which precipitated the biggest 'spurt' of all in terms of the percentage of those accused of criminal offences represented by counsel) was introduced only after the reform of the system of prosecutions at the end of the nineteenth century.[92] The growing conception of prosecutions as a public, rather than merely a private, matter meant that the lack of representation for the accused gave rise to an appearance of imbalance which threatened to undermine the legitimacy of the system, now that judges were no longer charged with looking after the interests of the accused.

In Scotland too there is a clear historical link between the introduction of prosecutors at trial and the right to defence counsel. According to Hume, the

---

common during the 18th century, although counsel were not permitted to address the jury. See JH Langbein, 'The Prosecutorial Origins of Defence Counsel in the Eighteenth Century: The Appearance of Solicitors' (1999) 58 *Cambridge Law Journal* 314; JH Langbein, 'The Criminal Trial Before The Lawyers' (1978) 45 *University of Chicago Law Review* 263. See more generally JH Langbein, *The Origins of the Adversary Criminal Trial* (Oxford, Oxford University Press, 2002).

[88] JM Beattie, 'Scales of Justice: Defense Counsel and the English Criminal Trial in the Eighteenth and Nineteenth Centuries' (1991) 9 *Law and History Review* 221 at 228.

[89] Allyson May, using the Old Bailey Session Papers, calculates that counsel appeared in 27.7% of the cases; cited in DJA Cairns, *Advocacy and the Making of the Adversarial Criminal Trial 1800–1865* (Oxford, Clarendon Press, 1998).

[90] D Bentley, *English Criminal Justice in the Nineteenth Century* (London, Hambledon Press, 1998) at 108. This is still a concern in modern times: S Trechsel, *Human Rights in Criminal Proceedings* (Oxford, Oxford University Press, 2005) at 270: '[i]t is a sad joke that the law, like the Ritz Hotel, is open to all'.

[91] D Bentley, *English Criminal Justice in the Nineteenth Century* (London, Hambledon Press, 1998) at 7.

[92] Poor Prisoner's Defence Act 1903; see Bentley, above n90, at 108–10.

Scottish accused, unlike his English counterpart, was not left to 'take charge of these difficult and interesting matters [pleading in court], alone and unassisted'; instead the law entitled the accused to enjoy 'in every instance the benefit of counsel, to guide him in his choice, and enable him to conduct his defence with skill and discretion'.[93] This right to counsel derived from an Act of 1587 which provided:

> That all and whatsumever lieges of this realme, accused of treason or quhatsumever crime, sall have their advocates and procuratoures, to use all the lauchful defences, quhom the Judge sall compel to procure for them, in case of their refusal; that the sute of the accuser be not tane pro confesso, and the party accused prejudged in ony sute, before he convicted be lauchful trial.[94]

It is of little surprise that the establishment of the Lord Advocate's office as a public prosecutor was also provided for in an earlier Act of the same year.[95]

The development of the right to defence counsel can be seen to be directly related to the understanding of criminal proceedings as based on the accusatorial trial. Whereas in earlier times the judge had had responsibility for protecting the interests of the accused, these interests were now to be the responsibility of counsel for the defence. As a result the equality of procedural opportunities between the defence and the prosecution became an absolutely essential element of the understanding of European criminal proceedings sustained by the jurists of the nineteenth century.

C The Role of the Defence in the Pre-trial Phase

(i) The Pre-trial Phase as 'Investigative'

Although criminal proceedings were seen to be firmly orientated towards the public and oral trial,[96] the investigative phase continued to play an important role. Pue writes that even in England (which is generally seen as the procedural system which was traditionally least reliant on the investigative phase) 'pre-trial procedures in 1843 were manifold'.[97] The purpose of the investigation was generally accepted as providing a forum for establishing whether there was

---

[93] D Hume, *Commentaries on the Law of Scotland, Respecting Crimes* (Edinburgh, Bell & Bradfute, 1844), ii, at 283.

[94] Statute of 1587 c 91.

[95] *Ibid*, c 77.

[96] J Vargha, *Die Verteidigung in Strafsachen* (Vienna, Manz'sche k k Hof-Verlag und Univ Buchhandlung, 1879) at 390: '[i]m reformierten Anklageprocesse hingegen liegt der Schwerpunkt des Verfahrens wirklich in der Hauptverhandlung . . .'.

[97] WW Pue, 'The Criminal Twilight Zone: Pre-Trial Procedures in the 1840s' (1983) 21 *Alberta Law Review* 335 at 337.

sufficient evidence to prosecute.[98] The 'double purpose' of the investigation consisted, according to Hume, of 'doing justice to the prisoner, if it shall appear that there are no sufficient grounds to detain him; and of accurately informing the prosecutor, in the opposite event, concerning the whole particulars of the fact, so as he may lay his charge with fullness and precision'.[99] A similar understanding of the investigation is advanced by Vargha, who writes that its aim was to ensure on the one hand that those accused of criminal offences could learn of the suspicions against them and to enable prosecutors on the other to convince themselves of the plausibility of these suspicions.[100] Hélie refers to the French investigation phase as the sole basis of the charge and draws attention to the fact that it also assisted accused persons in preparing their defence by providing them with a copy of all of the evidence against them.[101]

It is clear therefore that the investigation phase was intended to be a subordinate part of the criminal proceedings.[102] As a general rule the examination (in the sense of the testing and determination) of the evidence was not to take place during this phase. Indeed this factor was deemed to be the primary point distinguishing the reformed procedural laws from those of the inquisitorial period.[103] But this meant in turn that there was not the same need for the accusatorial structure during this phase. Although some writers, notably Vargha and Zachariä, argued strongly in favour of an accusatorial understanding of the investigation phase,[104] legislators and judges across the continent seemed to reject this on the basis that it would compromise the effectiveness of the investigation. A good example of this is evident in the judgment of Best J in *Cox v Coleridge*:

> Besides, if this right exists [to be assisted by counsel], there can never be any private examinations, which are very frequent, and often very necessary for the purposes of

---

[98]   F Hélie, *Traité de L'instruction Criminelle*, 2nd edn (Paris, Henri Plon, 1866–7), iv, at 39.

[99]   D Hume, *Commentaries on the Law of Scotland, Respecting Crimes* (Edinburgh, Bell & Bradfute, 1844), ii, at 81.

[100]   J Vargha, *Die Verteidigung in Strafsachen* (Vienna, Manz'sche k k Hof-Verlag und Univ Buchhandlung, 1879) at 390: '*und seine Voruntersuchung hat bloss den Zweck, Gelegenheiten zu bieten, dass einerseits der Beschuldigte die gegen ihn vorliegenden Verdachtsgründe behufs seiner Rechtfertigung erfahre, andererseits aber der Ankläger sich von der Haltbarkeit derselben überzeuge, wogegen Beweismittel für die Hauptverhandlung ausnahmsweise eben nur dann in der Voruntersuchung festgestellt werden dürfen, wenn zu besorgen stünde, dass sie für den Moment der Hauptverhandlung nicht mehr vorliegen könnten*'. See also J Glaser, *Handbuch des Strafprozesses* (Leipzig, Duncker & Humblot, 1883 & 1885), ii, at 381.

[101]   Hélie, above n97, iv, at 37.

[102]   J Glaser, *Handbuch des Strafprozesses* (Leipzig, Duncker & Humblot, 1883 & 1885), i, at 212: '*[d]iese inquisitorische, geheime und schrifliche Procedur soll aber nur ein untergeordneter Bestandtheil des Prozesses sein*'.

[103]   J Vargha, *Die Verteidigung in Strafsachen* (Vienna, Manz'sche k k Hof-Verlag und Univ Buchhandlung, 1879) at 390.

[104]   *Ibid*; HA Zachariä, *Die Gebrechen und die Reform des deutschen Strafverfahrens, dargestellt auf der Basis einer consequenten Entwicklung des inquisitorischen und des accusatorischen Prinzips* (Göttingen, Dieterichschen Buchhandlung, 1846) at 64, 73; see too CJA Mittermaier, *Die Gesetzgebung und Rechtsübung über Strafverfahren nach ihrer neusten Fortbildung* (Erlangen, Ferdinand Enke, 1856) at 272

justice. They are useful, not merely to take down in writing such evidence as is to be offered at trial, but to find where further evidence may be obtained, and to get at accomplices. These objects would be defeated if any one had a right to be present who could convey intelligence of what had passed... It may be extremely hard that an innocent person should be confined for an hour, when, if he were allowed professional assistance and witnesses, he could demonstrate his innocence and entitle himself to his discharge. But there is no rule, however wise, that does not produce some inconvenience or hardship, and the question always must be, does the good outweigh the evil. Considering how many desperate offenders might escape justice, and proceed uninterrupted in their guilty career, if this right were allowed, I have no hesitation in saying that it ought not to be admitted, and that we ought to give judgements for the defendants.[105]

A similar statement can be found in the work of the German writer Planck, who notes that the accused was neither entitled, nor compelled, to participate in the investigation hearings. The former meant that he had no right to information about the nature of the suspicions against him, while the latter provided that he could not be compelled to make a confession.[106] Despite assurances however as to the preparatory and subsidiary nature of the investigative phase, it was nevertheless the forum for a number of important activities, and this gave rise to something of a conundrum: if the accusatorial form was to be so important at trial, then what reasons could justify the decision not to respect its ethos in the investigation phase?

(a) The Questioning of the Accused

The questioning of the accused during the investigation phase was an essential aspect of nineteenth century criminal proceedings in Europe. These hearings were generally carried out by an investigating judge, or sometimes by a prosecutor, and the accused was seldom allowed the assistance of counsel. Even though these hearings were intended to be merely investigative and not determinative, there seems to be evidence nevertheless of the importance of ensuring that they could be presented as fair. The reluctance to enforce the familiar accusatorial regulatory structure in the investigation phase meant that this had to be achieved by other means. It is no coincidence in this regard that around this time many jurisdictions played up the importance of the 'voluntary' nature of the

---

[105] (1822) 1 Barn & Cress 37 at 54–5.

[106] JW Planck, *Systematische Darstellung des deutschen Strafverfahren auf Grundlage der neuen Strafprozessordnung seit 1848* (Göttingen, Dieterichschen Buchhandlung, 1857) at 241: '[d]er künftige Angeklagte ist an und für sich zu einer Theilnahme und Mitwirkung dabei weder berechtigt, noch verpflichtet. Nicht berechtigt: Daher kann er weder Einsicht des gesammelten Stoffes, noch vorgängiges Gehör, ehe die Anklage, gegen ihn erhoben wird, verlangen. Nicht verpflichtet: Daher kann von ihm ein Aufschluss, ein Geständnis oder sonstige Unterstützung zur Sammlung der Beweise gegen ihn nicht verlangt werden'.

co-operation and participation of the accused.[107] Much was made of the warning that was to be given to the fact that 'his declaration may, and probably will be used against him, on his trial'.[108] This was said to guarantee that the statements of the accused were made voluntarily and to support the notions of a developing nineteenth century respect for the individual and the importance of the 'free will' of the accused. In England an Act of 1848 provided that the magistrate, prior to taking a statement from the accused, 'shall state to him, and give him clearly to understand, that he has nothing to hope from any promise of favour, and nothing to fear from any threat which may have been holden out to him to make any admission or confession of his guilt, but that whatever he shall then say may be given against him upon his trial'.[109]

Archbold was highly complimentary about the caution, writing that 'this address to the accused is in that true spirit of fairness towards him which distinguishes the administration of criminal justice in this country, from its administration in any other country in Europe'.[110] But variations on this warning were also to be found in the various European legal systems. The importance of being able to characterise the statements of the accused as 'voluntary', rather than having been made under compulsion, was indeed of significant important in countries which were struggling to emerge from the shadow of the inquisition.[111] The emphasis on guaranteeing that the statements of the accused were made voluntarily is sometimes seen in the context of developing nineteenth century respect for the accused as an individual; it is however perhaps better understood as a response to the precarious legitimacy and obvious deficiencies of the institutional structure of the investigation phase.

Concerns about the legitimate regulation of the investigation phase were evident in nineteenth century Scotland, where the accused was questioned in a pre-trial judicial examination and his or her statements used to support the case against him or her at trial.[112] In theory judicial examinations were to be conducted by a magistrate, but in practice it was more common for the procurator fiscal to do so.[113] This was criticised in *Brims and Brims*, where Lord

---

[107] For a good overview of the situation in England see D Bentley, *English Criminal Justice in the Nineteenth Century* (London, Hambledon Press, 1998) at 161 ff.

[108] D Hume, *Commentaries on the Law of Scotland, Respecting Crimes* (Edinburgh, Bell & Bradfute, 1844), ii, at 81; see eg JF Stephen, *A History of the Criminal Law of England* (London, Macmillan, 1883) at 441, who writes that the accused was 'absolutely protected against all judicial questioning before trial'.

[109] S 18 of 11 & 12 Vict, c 42 (1848).

[110] JF Archbold, *Pleading and Evidence in Criminal Cases* (London, Sweet, 1862) at 48.

[111] JW Planck, *Systematische Darstellung des deutschen Strafverfahren auf Grundlage der neuen Strafprozessordnung seit 1848* (Göttingen, Dieterichschen Buchhandlung, 1857) at 241.

[112] For an overview of the procedure see AV Sheehan and DJ Dickson, *Scottish Criminal Procedure*, 2nd edn (Edinburgh, Butterworths, 2003) at 32, para 48.

[113] JHA MacDonald, *A Practical Treatise on the Criminal Law of Scotland* (Edinburgh, William Green & Son, 1894) at 265: '[t]he magistrate is the proper person to put the questions, although in practice the Procurator fiscal generally does so', referring to *HM Advocate v James Brims and John M Brims*, Inverness, 27 Sept 1887, 1 White 462.

Young referred to it as 'bad practice' and stated that 'no questions should be put by the Procurator-Fiscal at any time before the Magistrate, and when the prisoner intimates that he declines to answer further questions, none should be put by anyone'.[114] His explanation for this was based on the procedural inequalities at this stage in the proceedings:

> [t]o take a prisoner alone with no professional assistance, and subject him to an examination by a professional man who is his prosecutor, in which examination questions are apparently put in order to involve him in contradictions, or elicit statements from him which may be contradicted, is, in my judgment, departing from the purpose of the examination before a Magistrate.[115]

He continues, 'I think our law, although our practice is not so prescribed or limited, is governed by the same spirit as that of England. The Magistrate with us may suggest to the prisoner matters which he considers require explanation; and I think it ought to be distinctly stated to the prisoner what it is the Magistrate requires explanation from him about.'[116]

Macdonald seems to endorse a less demanding test where he suggests that the procurator fiscal can conduct the examination providing that a magistrate was present during the examination 'to act as a safeguard against unfair or oppressive questioning'.[117] Consequently 'a declaration emitted in his absence, although acknowledged afterwards in his hearing as correctly taken down before being signed' was to be considered invalid.[118] Similarly, in the case of *John Erskine*, the court held that 'the declaration having been taken by a Clerk and not in presence of any Magistrate, ought not to have been founded on as part of the process against him'.[119] The emphasis on the fact that the accused had voluntarily made the incriminatory statements seems to have been orientated less towards upholding the accused's autonomy and more towards ensuring, in the absence of an 'accusatorial regulatory structure', that the investigation hearings could be characterised as being 'fair' and thereby reducing the accused's opportunity to complain that the investigation authorities were biased. Similarly there is evidence of the importance of demonstrating the efficacy of the proceedings in Hume's reference to the requirement that the whole investigation hearing take place 'in the presence of creditable witnesses, who have heard and seen the examination, from first to last (not the subscription only of the magistrate and

---

[114] *Ibid*, at 465.

[115] *Ibid*, at 464.

[116] *Ibid*.

[117] JHA MacDonald, *A Practical Treatise on the Criminal Law of Scotland* (Edinburgh, William Green & Son, 1894) at 265.

[118] Dietrich Mahler and Marcus Berrenhard, HC, 15 June 1857, 2 Irv 634, 29 SJ 562. See too D Hume, *Commentaries on the Law of Scotland, Respecting Crimes* (Edinburgh, Bell & Bradfute, 1844), ii, at 327, referring to *James Davidson*, Aberdeen, 18 Apr 1827: it is obviously indispensable that the examination take place in the presence of the magistrate, and be conducted by him.

[119] Judgment of 14 Dec 1818; see D Hume, *Commentaries on the Law of Scotland, Respecting Crimes* (Edinburgh, Bell & Bradfute, 1844), ii, at 328, note a.

the prisoner); and who in testimony thereof put their names to the writing, that, if necessary on the trial, they may be able to authenticate it, and swear to all that passed on the occasion'.[120] These comments are indicative of a realisation of the importance of the investigation phase for the subsequent determination of the charge.

In reality there can be little doubt that throughout the nineteenth century the position of the accused in the investigation phase was precarious, not least because he or she was seldom allowed the assistance of counsel. In England the right to counsel generally differed depending on the classification of the crime. The accused was not, for example, 'entitled as of right to the assistance of an attorney or counsel on a charge of felony; the permitting such assistance is discretionary with the magistrate or the court'.[121] According to the majority of the court in *Cox v Coleridge*, for instance, the preliminary investigation conducted by the English magistrate was just an investigation into the circumstances of the case, and it would not therefore have been appropriate to grant the accused legal assistance.[122] Although there are some cases where the English courts seem to have upheld the right of an accused to counsel in the pre-trial phase, these represent the exception rather than the rule, not least because there was no entitlement during the nineteenth century to legal aid and the majority of those accused of criminal offences were unable to afford to employ counsel themselves.[123] This was also the case in the majority of European countries. Even after the reforms in the second half of the nineteenth century counsel were not permitted to be present during the pre-trial questioning of the accused in France, Germany or Austria..[124]

Unlike Archbold, several nineteenth century writers were sceptical of the advantages of warnings in the absence of any right to legal advice. Mittermaier argued that, precisely because the aim of the state was to question the accused, it was essential that right from the beginning of the investigation he or she be in a position to destroy the basis for all suspicion,[125] but this could be achieved only with the assistance of counsel.[126] Similarly Vargha argues that without legal

---

[120] D Hume, *Commentaries on the Law of Scotland, Respecting Crimes* (Edinburgh, Bell & Bradfute, 1844), ii, at 81.

[121] See WW Pue, 'The Criminal Twilight Zone: Pre-trial Procedures in the 1840s' (1983) 21 *Alberta Law Review* 335 at 339.

[122] *Cox v Coleridge*, 1 Barn & Cress, 54–5.

[123] See SA Farrar, 'Myths and Legends: An Examination of the Historical Role of the Accused in Traditional Legal Scholarship: A Look at the 19th Century' (2001) 21 *Oxford Journal of Legal Studies* 331 at n 61.

[124] Austria: Code of Criminal Procedure (StPO) para 198; Germany: Code of Criminal Procedure of 1877 (StPO) para 190.

[125] 'Gleich beim ersten Schritte schon, den der Staat gegen einen Beschuldigten vornehmen will, muss dieser in den Stand gesetzt werden, die vorhandenen Vedachtsgründe zu zerstören', quoted by J Vargha, *Die Verteidigung in Strafsachen* (Vienna, Manz'sche k k Hof-Verlag und Univ Buchhandlung, 1879) at 407.

[126] *Ibid*: '[d]as wirksamste Mittel hierzu ist die formelle Vetheidigung, und diese muss ihm also auch schon hier gewährt werden'.

assistance the accused reverted to the position of an object of the proceedings rather than a procedural party.[127] It is instructive, however, that these arguments were ignored.

(b) The Examination of Evidence

A number of exceptions to the principle that the examination and determination of evidence was not to occur in the investigation phase were to be found in the procedural laws of many countries. One of the most common concerned evidence which was likely to be lost before the trial took place.[128] In many jurisdictions witnesses were questioned before the trial by the investigating judge. Procedural codes providing for the presence of defence counsel during such hearings were very much the exception rather than the rule. A notable exception was the German federal Code of Criminal Procedure of 1877 which made provision for the attendance of the accused and counsel at the hearing of witnesses if it was deemed likely that the witnesses would be unable to attend the trial.[129] But the investigating judge could refuse to allow the accused to be present if the judge had reason to fear that his or her presence would prevent the witness from speaking the truth.[130]

The importance of counsel at such hearings was deemed by many German commentators to be essential to upholding the spirit of the reformed procedural system. Vargha noted, for instance, that in view of the fact that the final determination of evidence occurred not just at trial but also sometimes during the pre-trial phase, it was essential that the accused and his or her lawyer be present.[131] He was especially critical of procedural provisions which prevented the accused and counsel from attending hearings with witnesses in the pre-trial phase, writing that this meant that the investigating judge was freed from the control or restraint of the parties.[132] In general, as we have seen, the nineteenth

---

[127] *Ibid*, at 396.

[128] J Glaser, *Handbuch des Strafprozesses* (Leipzig, Duncker & Humblot, 1883 & 1885), i, at 212.

[129] Para 191 of the German StPO: '*wenn eine Zeuge oder Sachverständiger vernommen werden soll, welcher voraussichtlich am Erscheinen in der Hauptverhandlung verhindert oder dessen Erscheinen wegen grosser Entfernung besonders erschwert wird*'.

[130] *Ibid*, para 192: '*wenn zu befürchten ist, dass ein Zeuge in seiner Gegenwart die Wahrheit nicht sagen werde*'.

[131] J Vargha, *Die Verteidigung in Strafsachen* (Vienna, Manz'sche k k Hof-Verlag und Univ Buchhandlung, 1879) at 393: '*[n]icht nur in der Hauptverhandlung jedoch, sonder möglicher Weise auch schon während des Vorverfahrens ist die endgültige Fixierung von Beweisen möglich und unter Umständen geboten. Auch hinsichtlich dieser muss es vom Standpunkt des accusatorischen Processes dem Beschuldigten mit seinem Anwalte gestattet sein, behufs unmittelbarer Wahrnehmung der Vertheidigungsrechts anwesend zu sein*'. It is worth noting that some of the old regional procedural codes had allowed this, eg para 7 of the Brunswick Criminal Procedure Code (StPO), which allowed both the accused and counsel to be present during all hearings. See also HA Zachariä, *Handbuch des deutschen Strafprozesses* (Göttingen, Verlag der Dieterichschen Buchhandlung, 1861 & 1868) at 293–7.

[132] J Vargha, *Die Verteidigung in Strafsachen* (Vienna, Manz'sche k k Hof-Verlag und Univ Buchhandlung, 1879) at 396.

century European criminal procedural laws were united in not allowing counsel to become involved in the investigation hearings.

It is interesting, though perhaps not altogether surprising, that those systems which afforded the defence the most significant pre-trial rights were also those which had proven slow to adapt to the general nineteenth century institutional developments and which continued to use the 'investigation' as the correct forum for the determination of the evidence. According to Ruth,[133] for instance, Zurich was one of the few Swiss cantons to permit defence counsel to take part in all of the 'formal hearings' (*förmliche Verhandlungen*) of the investigation phase, and in particular to be present during confrontation hearings and to have the right to put questions to the witnesses.[134]

(ii)   The 'Determinative' Reality of the Investigation

Although in theory the investigation phase was billed as very much secondary to the oral and public trial, the reality was somewhat different. Every European legal system allowed, albeit to varying extents, evidence collected and examined during the investigation phase to be submitted in written form at trial. And this meant in reality that the testing and evaluation of the evidence was taking place in the investigative phase, despite the fact that it was not subject to the same institutional guarantees that were deemed to be so important in the regulation of the trial. This tendency was particularly pronounced in France, where the written protocols of the pre-trial testimony of witnesses were routinely submitted to the court in place of oral testimony.[135] But France was by no means alone in this regard. Cleric, for instance, criticises the procedural model of the Canton of Zurich on the basis that the examination of witnesses at trial was very unusual.[136] Moreover and perhaps even more controversially, the majority of procedural systems allowed for the submission of statements made by the accused to be read out at trial.[137]

Dissatisfaction with the nature of the investigation phase can therefore be seen as being based, not on the belief that it should have been public and oral, but rather on the knowledge that the activities of the investigation phase were of

---

[133]   M Ruth, *Der Verteidiger im schweizerisches Strafprozessrecht* (Bern, Stämpfli, 1904) at 86.

[134]   G z R (Gesetz betreffend die zürcherische Rechtspflege, 2 Dec. 1874), para 784 ᴵ ᵘ· ᴵᴵ (similar rules were part of the cantonal procedural codes of the Tessin, Geneva, Aargau, Neuchâtel, Solothurn and Vaud). See also the draft of 1900, para 15.

[135]   See the section on oral and immediate proceedings in Ch 2.

[136]   GF von Cleric, 'Die Prinzipien der Unmittelbarkeit und der Mündlichkeit im Strafprozess' (1915) XII *Schweizerische Juristen Zeitung* 41 at 44: '*höchst selten*' .

[137]   Eg Germany: para 234 of the Criminal Procedure Code (StPO) 1877; Austria: para 245 of the Criminal Procedure Code (StPO); for Scotland see D Hume, *Commentaries on the Law of Scotland, Respecting Crimes* (Edinburgh, Bell & Bradfute, 1844), ii.

considerable importance and were providing the authorities with the opportunity to bypass the strict institutional guarantees afforded by the trial.[138] Thus, in the words of Vargha:

> *Die richterliche Thätigkeit im accusatorischen Processe kann ohne Mitwirkung und Controle der Parteien gar nicht gedacht werden und es heisst wohl den letzteren ihre Rechtsausübung sehr verkümmern, wenn man ihre Gegenwart von so einem wichtigen Theile des Untersuchungsverfahrens ausschliesst, wie es die Vernehmung sind.*[139]

The importance of the investigation phase and the failure to regulate it in a manner that corresponded to the regulation of the trial allowed the re-emergence of 'inquisitorial tendencies'. According to Schwarze this meant that there was room for considerable suspicion that the investigation phase was primarily orientated towards enabling the preparation of the evidence supporting the charge, while the interests of the accused were of very much secondary importance.[140] The nature of the secret investigation phase which excluded the parties and which derived its sole legitimacy from the already discredited neutrality of the investigating authorities was seen as being irreconcilable with the reformed accusatorial procedural system:

> *Die Voruntersuchung als Vorbereitung der Hauptverhandlung muss, so wenig sie auch ihren vorbereitenden Charakter verläugnen darf, auf den Anschuldigungs- wie auf den Entschuldigungsbeweis Rücksicht nehmen. Diese Rücksicht wird bisweilen nicht gleichmässig in Obacht genommen, zumal die Ansicht nicht selten vertreten wird, dass die Voruntersuchung und das Anklageerkenntniss vorzugsweise den Belastungsbeweis berücksichtigen müsse, während in der Hauptverhandlung selbst genügende Gelegenheit zur Vorführung des Entlastungsbeweises geboten sei. Es wird hierdurch in die Voruntersuchung eine Einseitigkeit hineingetragen, welche weder mit dem Charakter einer gehörigen Vorbereitung der Handlung, noch auch mit dem Charakter der letzteren vereinbar sei.*[141]

---

[138] A Esmein, *A History of Continental Criminal Procedure with Special Reference to France* (trans J Simpson, Boston, Mass, Little Brown & Co, 1913; reprinted Union, NJ, The Lawbook Exchange, 2000) at 512–17; F Hélie, *Traité de l'Instruction Criminelle*, 2nd edn (Paris, Henri Plon, 1866–7), vii, at 487–94; J-E Boitard, *Leçons sur les Code Pénal et d'Instruction Criminelle*, 3rd edn (Paris, Gustave Thorel, 1844) at 562–3, 595–6; J Vargha, *Die Vertedigung in Strafsachen* (Vienna, Manz'sche k k Hof-Verlag und Univ Buchhandlung, 1879) at 391.

[139] *Ibid*, at 395: '[t]he judicial role in the accusatorial procedure system cannot even be envisaged without the participation and control of the parties and it would seriously interfere with the parties' exercise of their rights if one were to exclude them from being present during such an important a part of the investigation proceedings as the questioning of the accused and of witnesses'.

[140] FO Schwarze, 'Die Vertheidigung im mündlichen Verfahren' (1878) 15 *Zeitschrift für Rechtspflege und Verwaltung in Sachsen* 8.

[141] J Vargha, *Die Vertedigung in Strafsachen* (Vienna, Manz'sche k k Hof-Verlag und Univ Buchhandlung, 1879) at 395, n 2: '[t]he investigation as the means for preparing the trial must, to the degree made possible by virtue of its preparatory nature, allow for consideration of both the incriminatory and exculpatory evidence. This issue is not always sufficiently addressed, not least because it is not uncommon for the view to be expressed that the investigation and the formulation of the charge should principally be influenced by the incriminatory evidence, as there will be sufficient opportunity offered at trial for the presentation of exculpatory evidence. Because of this, an imbalance is introduced into the investigation phase, which is compatible neither with the proper preparation of the trial nor with the nature of the trial itself'.

The disparity between the institutional form of the investigation phase and that of the trial was simply too big. This is clearly evidenced in the French *Code d'instruction criminelle* of 1808, which provided that the investigative aspects of the pre-trial proceedings such as the hearing of the witnesses and the investigation of written proof were to be the responsibility of the investigating judge. The investigation was to retain its secret, written form with regard to the hearings both of the witnesses and of the accused. The accused was not permitted to have the assistance of counsel during the interrogation.[142] At the trial stage, things looked quite different. According to Esmein, 'We pass from obscurity into the full light of day'. Whereas the procedure during the investigation was secret, written and always favourable to the prosecution, the trial hearing was public, oral, and allowed both discussion and the opportunity for the defence to state its case freely.[143] After the conclusion of the investigation hearings, the accused was to receive all the files of the investigation,[144] to be moved within 24 hours to the court and within 24 hours of his arrival to be interrogated by the president of the court and informed of his or her right to be assisted by counsel.[145] Here the Code of 1808 contained impressive rules which expressly protected various aspects of the exercise of the rights of the defence, such as the right of the lawyer to communicate with the accused.[146] The defence was to be provided with copies of all of the witness statements taken in the investigation phase,[147] was to be free to conduct its defence and to question witnesses[148] and was to be guaranteed the 'last word' in order to allow it to respond to all the allegations raised in the course of the proceedings.[149]

But, as Hélie observes, this was the first chance that the lawyer had to intervene in the proceedings, as until this point the proceeding had been entirely secret and the accused had had no right to the assistance of counsel.[150] The emphasis on the fairness of the trial, the rights of the accused and the institutional guarantees to

---

[142] Eg A Esmein, A *History of Continental Criminal Procedure with Special Reference to France* (trans J Simpson, Boston, Mass, Little Brown & Co, 1913; reprinted Union, NJ, The Lawbook Exchange, 2000) at 504.

[143] *Ibid*, at 510.

[144] Art 242 of the Code of 1808.

[145] *Ibid*, Art 294.

[146] *Ibid*, Art 302: '*le conseil pourra communiquer avec l'accusé après son interrogatoire*'.

[147] *Ibid*, Art 305.

[148] See *ibid*, Arts 315, 318, 319, 322, 330 and F Hélie, *Traité de L'instruction Criminelle*, 2nd edn (Paris, Henri Plon, 1866–7), vii, at 409–11.

[149] Art 335 of the Code of 1808. According to Cass, 5 May 1826 (JP tome XX, 452): '*qu'aux termes de l'article 335, l'accusé ou son conseil doivent toujours avoir la parole les derniers; que cette règle fondamentale domine tous les débats et ne s'applique point exclusivement à cette dernière période de l'examen pendant laquelle l'accusé, la partie civile ou son conseil et le ministère public sont entendus et développent les moyens de l'accusation; qu'elle s'applique à tous les incidents qui peuvent s'élever dans le cours des débats et qui peuvent intéresser la défense ou la justification de l'accusé, soit que ces incidents doivent être terminés par une ordonnance du président ou par un arrêt*'.

[150] F Hélie, *Traité de L'instruction Criminelle*, 2nd edn (Paris, Henri Plon, 1866–7), vii, at 399: '[c]*'est là le premier acte de la défense: jusqu'à cet interrogatoire la procédure est restée secrète et l'accusé n'a été assisté d'aucun conseil*'.

uphold the legitimacy of the criminal process was therefore significantly under-mined by the lack of regulation of the investigation phase. It seems therefore that Vargha had good reason to characterise the failure correctly to regulate the investigation as a 'sad sign' of how little notice was taken in practice of the theoretical understanding of criminal proceedings as based on the accusatorial trinity:

> *Nach unsern reformierten Processgesetzen findet jedoch ein solcher Ausschluss der Verthei-digungspartei dennoch statt und der Vorwand, den man zur Rechtfertigung hierfür vorschützt, ist merkwürdiger Weise die hierdurch angeblich bewirkte Vereinfachung des Verfahrens. Es ist in der That höchst eigenthümlich, dass man alle von den Praktikern für nothwendig erkannte Entlastung der Gerichte und Vereinfachung des Verfahrens stets nur auf Kosten der formellen Vertheidigung anstreben will. Diese Tendenz ist ein trauriges Zeichen, wie wenig noch immer das in der Theorie zur Herrschaft berufene accusatorische Princip in der Praxis recht erfasst und in's Fleisch und Blut unserer Gerichtsfunctionäre übergegangen ist.*[151]

D Conclusions

Vargha's complaint is of particular relevance in modern times when there is a widespread tendency to view criminal procedural developments as involving a trade off between 'defence rights' (read: due process) and efficiency in prosecut-ing crime (read: crime control). Such arguments significantly misconstrue, and thereby undermine, the theoretical underpinnings of European criminal pro-ceedings. The defence plays an important institutional role which, like all institutional legal principles, promotes the effectiveness and legitimacy of the proceedings. Defence 'rights' cannot therefore be balanced against crime control issues, because the role of the defence is integral to the institutional conception of the criminal procedural system. Any debate about procedural values must take place on the institutional level and must not be used as an excuse for restricting procedural 'rights' as this will seriously unbalance the proceedings. That this flawed efficiency–due process argument is also frequently made in the context of the immediacy principle is particularly unfortunate. There can be little doubt that the immediacy principle is absolutely essential to the theoretical conception

---

[151] J Vargha, *Die Verteidigung in Strafsachen* (Vienna, Manz'sche k k Hof-Verlag und Univ Buchhandlung, 1879) at 289: '[a]ccording to our reformed procedural system, defence parties can be excluded (ie from the investigation hearings) and the pretext used to justify this is, strangely enough, the resulting simplification of the proceedings. It is in fact very odd that all those measures advocated by the practitioners as essential to relieving the strain on the courts and simplifying the proceedings are always at the expense of the formal rights of the defence. This tendency is a sad sign of how little understanding there is in practice of the notion developed in the theory of the accusatorial principle as the ruling characteristic of the proceedings and is evidence of the fact that this understanding of the proceedings has not yet become second nature to our judicial authorities'.

of accusatorial proceedings developed across the continent in the works of the nineteenth century jurists. Only by accepting the trial as the only acceptable forum for the determination of the evidence is it possible to accept the extreme differences in the regulation of the trial and investigation phases and to accept the trial's claim to legitimacy. The continuation of the determinative role of the under-regulated investigation phase means, however, that it casts a long shadow over the claims of procedural equality underpinning the adversarial conception of the trial. Far from combating the dangers of the investigation, the adversarial trial both masks and benefits from the 'abuses' carried out during this phase. It must be doubted whether it is possible to take seriously claims that the procedural developments of the nineteenth century were orientated principally towards the rights of the accused; even those concerns such as the importance of the voluntary nature of the accused's statements which could have been construed as beneficial to the accused, seem instead to have been principally aimed at preventing more 'invasive' defence activities during the investigative phase.

The role of the defence is dependent on the nature of the procedural or institutional setting. Only by ensuring correlation between the rights of the defence and the procedural context is it possible to conceive of the common application of procedural values. If fair proceedings are taken to be those in which those accused of criminal offences have the opportunity to know of and challenge the evidence against them, as well as to present their own evidence, then fairness depends not just on their ability to exercise these rights, but also on the context in which they can exercise them. The failure to recognise this necessarily impedes the application of common values, while simultaneously suppressing the problem and endorsing the flawed status quo. The nineteenth century debate on the rights of the defence suggests moreover that the strengthening of the participatory rights of the defence was targeted neither at guaranteeing the accused's autonomy in criminal proceedings nor at improving the efficiency of criminal prosecutions, but was rather a consequence of the institutional reforms of the nineteenth century which advocated a very particular understanding of criminal proceedings as based on the accusatorial trinity.

The acknowledgement of the existence of the procedural tradition as developed by the nineteenth century jurists provides an alternative starting point for examining the nature and extent of the fair trial provisions in Article 6 ECHR. As will be shown in the next chapters, there has been a tendency in the case law of the Court, caused, or at least exacerbated, by the persistent reliance of the criminal law scholarship on the comparative adversarial/inquisitorial approach, to neglect not only this procedural tradition but also the importance of the relationship between defence rights and institutional forms. In the next Part, it will be argued that the focus in Article 6 on the 'rights of the accused' has been at the expense of the procedural understanding of fair trials advocated by the nineteenth century reformers, and has led to a neglect of the institutional aspects of fairness in the case law of the Strasbourg authorities. Consideration will be given not only to whether an awareness of the European criminal procedure tradition might help to improve the coherence and consistency of the guarantees set out in Article 6, but also to the inherent tension between the rights focus of the ECHR and the argument for an institutional understanding of fairness.

Part Two

4

Defining Fairness in Article 6(1) ECHR

A Introduction

T HE RIGHT TO a fair trial is a recognisable feature of every significant international normative instrument charged with protecting human rights.[1] Deriving legitimacy from the various preambles to these Conventions and Treaties which proclaim an allegiance to both democracy and the rule of law, the guarantee of fair procedure becomes a standard by which a state's commitment to these ideals is measured. As a theoretical principle, the right to a fair trial is unilaterally endorsed by every European country and the conviction that their trials are indeed fair explains why states are content to sign treaties proclaiming a common heritage based on the rule of law.[2] That the rule of law may have a variety of meanings throughout the continent is conspicuously ignored.[3]

In spite of this it is widely acknowledged that within Europe there are different systems of criminal procedure. As we have seen, these are often separated into two caricature procedural models—inquisitorial (or non-adversarial) and accusatorial (or adversarial)—and each is subject to the suspicion and distrust of

---

[1] See, *inter alia*, Art 8 of the American Convention on Human Rights (ACHR); Art 6 of the European Convention for the Protection of Human Rights and Fundamental Freedoms (ECHR); Art 14 of the International Covenant on Civil and Political Rights (ICCPR); Art 10 of the Universal Declaration of Human Rights (UDHR); common Art 3 of the four Geneva Conventions of 12 Aug 1949 and Art 6 of Additional Protocol II to the Geneva Conventions which contain indispensable judicial guarantees for the protection of the right to a fair trial during non-international armed conflicts; Arts 96 and 99–108 of the Geneva Convention relative to the Treatment of Prisoners of War prescribe the rights of prisoners of war in judicial proceedings; Arts 54, 64–74 and 117–126 of the Geneva Convention relative to the Protection of Civilian Persons in Time of War provide for the right to a fair trial and a remedy in occupied territories and extend fair trial guarantees in international armed conflicts to all persons, including those arrested for actions relating to the conflict.

[2] For an examination of the relationship between the trial and the rule of law see R Burns, *A Theory of the Trial* (Princeton, NJ, Princeton University Press, 1999) at 11.

[3] On the differing interpretations of the rule of law in Europe see D Mineshima, 'The Rule of Law and EU Expansion' (2002) 24 *Liverpool Law Review* 73 at 73.

those schooled in the tradition of the other.[4] That states are willing to ratify provisions such as Article 6 of the European Convention on Human Rights (ECHR) is testimony, however, to the tacit belief that the theoretical principle of a fair trial is not dependant on a particular criminal procedural model, and it is on this basis that Article 6 attempts to regulate multiple criminal procedure systems, an attempt which, though comprising a significant practical challenge, does not attract much theoretical evaluation.[5] Just as it is assumed that there are two traditions in European criminal procedure law, it is somewhat taken for granted that it is possible to regulate different models of criminal procedure based on a vague theoretical principle, while at the same time remaining neutral among competing visions of how a criminal procedural system should look or indeed function. The underlying incompatibility of these essentially competing assumptions is ignored.

At the heart of much of the Article 6 case law on criminal proceedings lies the implicit belief that systems need not be procedurally identical to be fair. In this sense the Court seems to subscribe to Harlow's view that:

> There is… no absolute advantage of adversarial over inquisitorial procedure; one is not inevitably more independent or inherently less arbitrary than the other; each can operate fairly.[6]

There is little analysis, however, of the viability of the assertion that it is possible to create a definition of fairness which does not, by its very nature, require a defined procedural structure. Instead, the evaluation of the successes and difficulties of the Court have tended to be framed in terms of the difficulties of reconciling accusatorial and inquisitorial procedural systems. The overview of the historical developments in the field of criminal procedure during the nineteenth century suggests, however, that there is a close relationship between

---

[4] See generally Ch 1.

[5] This is also evidenced in the case law of the Court: *Pretto and Others v Italy* judgment of 8 Dec 1983 Series A no 71, (1984) 6 EHRR 182, para 22; *Axen v Germany* judgment of 8 Dec 1983, Series A no 72, (1984) 6 EHRR 195, para 26; *B v United Kingdom* and *P v United Kingdom* nos 36337/97 & 35974/97 judgment of 24 Apr 2001, (2002) 34 EHRR 19, para 45: '[t]he formal aspect of the matter is, however, of secondary importance as compared with the purpose underlying the publicity required by Article 6 para 1'.

[6] C Harlow, 'Voice of Difference in a Plural Community' in P Beaumont, C Lyons and N Walker (eds), *Convergence and Divergence in European Public Law* (Oxford, Oxford University Press, 2002) at 219, citing MR Damaška, *The Faces of Justice and State Authority: A Comparative Approach to the Legal Process* (New Haven, Conn, Yale University Press, 1986) and PH Lindblom, 'Harmony of the Legal Spheres' (1997) 5 *European Review of Private Law* 11 at 20. See also M Pieth, *Der Beweisantrag des Beschuldigten im Schweizer Strafprozessrecht* (Basel, Helbing & Lichtenhahn, 1984) at 212: '[w]enn im kontinentaleuropäischen Bereich die Verantwortung für die Beweisaufnahme beim Gericht liegt, gehört dies zu den systemkonstituierenden Elementen, die von der EMRK respektiert werden müssen. Somit kann die Verteidigung nicht, gestützt auf die EMRK, das Recht beanspruchen, beliebige Zeugeneinvernahme zu verlangen': '[t]he responsibility for the examination of the evidence lies, in continental European systems, with the courts and thus belongs to the constituent elements of the system which must be respected by the ECHR. Consequently, the defence cannot rely on the ECHR to demand the right to a witness confrontation hearing with whichever witnesses it pleases'.

institutional forms and procedural rights and provides a basis on which to challenge these claims. The Court's case law on fairness will be examined in order to ascertain whether its success can be explained, not by a procedurally neutral account of fairness, but rather by way of the application of principles which gained European-wide recognition in the course of the nineteenth century. An examination of what the Court believes to be the essence of the right to 'a fair trial' will provide the basis, first, for determining the influence of the principles developed during the nineteenth century; secondly, for assessing how closely the problems which the court has encountered in the application of Article 6 are related to its failure to articulate a clear version of fairness based on a particular procedural context and, thirdly, for suggesting a legitimate theoretical basis for the regulation of trials which can accommodate the dual demands of coherency and European-wide application.

B Identifying Vargha's 'Accusatorial Trinity'

Article 6(1) ECHR is entitled 'The right to a fair trial'[7] and provides that 'in the determination of his civil rights and obligations or of any criminal charge against him, everyone is entitled to a fair and public hearing within a reasonable time by an independent and impartial tribunal established by law'.[8] As such it does not provide much guidance on the foundation of the notion of a fair trial in criminal proceedings in the sense of determining the form that the proceedings should take. This can be partly explained, of course, by the decision of the drafters to combine civil and criminal regulatory structures in one paragraph. It is of little surprise therefore that there is no specific reference to 'public prosecutions' or to the relationship between the defence and the prosecution. The notion of fair criminal proceedings in Article 6(1) is supplemented by two further paragraphs guaranteeing the presumption of innocence and the rights of the defence. But there is no reference in either of these to the relationship between the prosecution and the defence.

Some guidance in this matter can be obtained from the case law on judicial impartiality. Judicial impartiality has been held to require 'the absence of prejudice or bias' and has been interpreted as comprising both 'subjective' and 'objective' elements.[9] The subjective element relates to the personal conviction of

---

[7] This title was introduced by Protocol No 11 to the ECHR.

[8] The 'civil rights and obligations' case law will be considered here only in so far as it is relevant to the definition of fairness in the context of the criminal trial.

[9] *Piersack v Belgium,* judgment of 1 Oct 1982, Series A no 53, (1983) 5 EHRR 169, para 30: '[w]hilst impartiality normally denotes absence of prejudice or bias, its existence or otherwise can, notably under Article 6 § 1 of the Convention, be tested in various ways. A distinction can be drawn in this context between a subjective approach, that is endeavouring to ascertain the personal

the judge, while the objective part refers to whether the judge offered guarantees sufficient to exclude legitimate doubt about his or her partiality. There have been very few cases in which the Court has found a violation on the basis of subjective personal bias, such as, for instance, racism.[10] There have, however, been a number of cases involving 'objective' institutional-type bias, in which the judge failed to maintain sufficient distance from the prosecutorial role. In many of these cases the primarily cause for concern was the fact that the judge had had responsibility for a succession of functions by virtue of his or her involvement in the prosecution. In *Piersack v Belgium*, for instance, the Court held that a judge who had earlier been involved in the case as the prosecutorial supervisor of the deputies responsible for prosecuting the applicant could not be considered impartial:

> If an individual, after holding in the public prosecutor's department an office whose nature is such that he may have to deal with a given matter in the course of his duties, subsequently sits in the same case as a judge, the public are entitled to fear that he does not offer sufficient guarantees of impartiality.[11]

Similar problems of institutional bias have arisen in a number of cases involving the British system of court martial.[12] In *Findlay v United Kingdom*, the convening officer 'decided which charges should be brought and which type of court martial was most appropriate. He convened the court martial and appointed its members and the prosecuting and defending officers.' Furthermore, all those involved in the court martial were subordinate to him. In determining the application the Court noted that the convening officer was 'central to Mr Findlay's prosecution and closely linked to the prosecuting authorities'.[13] In view of his central role in the determination and confirmation of the charge, the court martial could not be considered to be compatible with the impartiality requirement of Article 6(1).[14]

---

conviction of a given judge in a given case, and an objective approach, that is determining whether he offered guarantees sufficient to exclude any legitimate doubt in this respect.'

[10] There was held to be no violation in either *Remli v France*, judgment of 23 Apr 1996, Reports 1996-II, 559, (1996) 22 EHRR 253 or *Gregory v United Kingdom*, judgment of 25 Feb 1997, Reports 1997-I, 296, (1998) 25 EHRR 577 which both involved allegations of racism on the jury. There was a violation in *Kyprianou v Cyprus*, no 73797/01, judgment of 27 Jan 2004 where a defence lawyer who argued with judges after being interrupted during his cross-examination was convicted by the same judges on the spot and sentenced to 5 days' imprisonment.

[11] *Piersack v Belgium*, judgment of 1 Oct 1982, Series A no 53, (1983) 5 EHRR 169, para 30.

[12] See eg *Findlay v United Kingdom*, judgment of 25 Feb 1997, Reports 1997-I, 263, (1997) 24 EHRR 211; *Morris v United Kingdom*, no 38784/97, judgment of 26 Feb 2002, (2002) 34 EHRR 52; *Cooper v United Kingdom* (Grand Chamber), no 44843/99, judgment of 16 Dec 2003, (2004) 39 EHRR 8.

[13] *Findlay v United Kingdom*, judgment of 25 Feb 1997, Reports 1997-I, 263, (1997) 24 EHRR 211, para 74.

[14] *Ibid*, at para 80.

The involvement of police officers in the investigation was also held in *Kristinsson* to be incompatible with a subsequent judicial role in the proceedings.[15]

Of particular interest is the Court's approach to the relationship between the investigating judge and the trial judge. In *De Cubber v Belgium*, the Court had to consider a case where an investigating judge was subsequently involved in the determination of the charge.[16] The government argued that in Belgium investigating judges were independent in the performance of their duties, that they did not have 'the status of a party to criminal proceedings' and that they were not 'an instrument of the prosecution'. Moreover, it stressed that the object of their activity was not 'to establish the guilt of the person' whom they believed to be guilty but to 'assemble in an impartial manner evidence in favour of as well as against the accused, whilst maintaining a just balance between prosecution and defence'. The investigating judge was merely responsible for presenting to the judges at trial 'objective reports describing the progress and state of the preliminary investigations, without expressing any opinion of his own, even assuming he has formed one'.[17]

In spite of these arguments, the Court was not convinced that the investigating judge could be seen as an 'impartial' authority in the sense of Article 6(1). Essentially this scepticism was based on the fact that the relationship between investigating judges and the prosecution was far from clear. In this regard the Court drew attention to the fact that the investigating judge, like the 'procureurs du Roi and their deputies', had 'the status of officer of the criminal investigation police' and, as such, was 'placed under the supervision of the procureur général'. Moreover not only did investigating judges have 'very wide-ranging powers', they also presided over a preparatory investigation 'which is inquisitorial in nature, is secret and is not conducted in the presence of both parties'. In view of this the Court concluded:

> One can accordingly understand that an accused might feel some unease should he see on the bench of the court called upon to determine the charge against him the judge who had ordered him to be placed in detention on remand and who had interrogated him on numerous occasions during the preparatory investigation, albeit with questions dictated by a concern to ascertain the truth. Furthermore, through the various means of inquiry which he will have utilised at the investigation stage, the judge in question, unlike his colleagues, will already have acquired well before the hearing a particularly detailed knowledge of the—sometimes voluminous—file or files which he has assembled. Consequently, it is quite conceivable that he might, in the eyes of the accused, appear, firstly, to be in a position enabling him to play a crucial role in the trial court and, secondly, even to have a pre-formed opinion which is liable to weigh heavily in the balance at the moment of the decision. In addition, the criminal court (*tribunal*

---

[15] *Kristinsson v Iceland*, Report of 8 Mar 1989, attached to the judgment of 22 Feb 1990, Series A no 171-B. See further S Trechsel, *Human Rights in Criminal Proceedings* (Oxford, Oxford University Press, 2005) at 507 ff.

[16] Judgment of 26 Oct 1984 Series A no 86, (1985) 7 EHRR 236, para 29.

[17] *Ibid*, at para 28.

correctionnel) may, like the court of appeal (see paragraph 19 in fine above), have to review the lawfulness of measures taken or ordered by the investigating judge. The accused may view with some alarm the prospect of the investigating judge being actively involved in this process of review.[18]

The Court's judgment in this case demonstrates very clearly not just the importance of the separation of the functions of investigating and judging as set out in the accusatorial trinity, but also the conception of criminal proceedings as involving two quite separate phases calling for separate regulatory structures.

Although these cases go some way to suggesting the importance in Article 6 of the separation of the functions of prosecuting and judging, they are of limited assistance in achieving an understanding of the nature of the relationship between the defence and the prosecution in a 'fair hearing'. Pinpointing the Court's definition of 'fair hearing' is complicated, moreover, by the use of the term 'fair' in different contexts. It is not uncommon in some commentaries on the ECHR for the time and publicity elements to be included within one large notion of fairness, assuming that in order to be fair a trial must be public, independently supervised and conducted within a reasonable time.[19] Indeed, the idea that fairness is an overarching concept achieved by respecting a number of different guarantees is frequently proclaimed by the Strasbourg authorities.[20] If, however, one accepts that publicity and reasonable time are part of the term 'fair hearing', it becomes necessary to question why the word 'fair' as used in the text of Article 6 was repeated in the title.[21] The use of the word 'fair' in the text suggests that it has a different role from the notion of fairness as a whole, defined by the title. A literal reading of the text suggests that these are in fact separate guarantees, ie the trial must be fair *and* it must be public, independently adjudicated and conducted within a reasonable time. A better understanding of this 'hidden' notion of fairness may provide some guidance on the Court's acceptance or rejection of the accusatorial trinity.

It could be argued, in relation to the determination of the parameters of this notion of fairness, that 'fairness' is wholly represented by the minimum guarantees set out in Article 6(3). This seems, however, to have been rejected by the Commission in *Nielsen v Denmark*, where it held:

> Article 6 of the Convention does not define the notion of 'fair trial' in a criminal case. Paragraph 3 of the Article enumerates certain specific rights which constitute essential

---

[18] *Ibid*, at para 29.
[19] Eg R Reed and J Murdoch, *A Guide to Human Rights Law in Scotland* (Edinburgh, Butterworths, 2001).
[20] Eg *Can v Austria*, App no 9300/81 report of 12 July 1984, Series B no 79, para 48, where the Commission held that 'the guarantees enshrined in Article 6(3) are not an aim in themselves . . . Their intrinsic aim is always to ensure, or to contribute to ensuring the fairness of the criminal proceedings as a whole . . . They must accordingly be interpreted in the light of the function they have in the overall context of the proceedings.' See also *Barberà, Messegué and Jabardo v Spain*, judgment of 6 Dec 1988, Series A no 146, (1989) 11 EHRR 360 where the Court found a breach on the basis that a number of failures in the process rendered unfair the 'trial as a whole'.
[21] Added by Protocol No 11 to the ECHR.

elements of that general notion, and paragraph 2 may be considered to add another element. The word 'minimum rights', however clearly indicate that the six rights specifically enumerated in paragraph 3 are not exhaustive, and that a trial may not conform to the general standard of a 'fair trial', even if the minimum rights guaranteed by paragraph 3—and also the right set forth in paragraph 2—have been respected'.[22]

It could still be argued, if one takes the fairness mentioned in *Nielsen* to be a reference to the institutional or general notion, that the term 'fair' contained within Article 6(1) is in fact represented by the criteria in Article 6(3). This, however, seems rather unlikely. Not only is there no such cross-reference in the Convention itself, but as Article 6(3) applies only to cases involving the determination of a criminal charge, such an interpretation would call into question the notion of fair procedure in cases concerning civil rights or obligations. It is indisputable that the right to a fair hearing also applies to civil proceedings. The fair procedure element in Article 6(1) must therefore be seen as having an existence independent of both the general notion of fairness in Article 6 and the specific examples of fairness set out in Article 6(3). In order to determine how this specific notion of fairness is defined it is essential to examine the Court's case law.

Determining the approach of the Court to this concept is complicated by the lack of differentiation in the case law between these notions of fairness. It is difficult to find concrete examples of the use of specific fairness; the Court rarely refers to this notion, which is clearly overshadowed by the dominance of the importance of 'fairness as a whole'.[23] An examination of the case law reveals some principles which, while not expressly set out in the text of the Convention, have nonetheless been attributed by the Court to Article 6(1), and which have the potential to be of assistance in the quest better to understand the relationship between the defence and the prosecution.

C The Role of the 'Equality of Arms' Doctrine

A number of factors point to the possibility that equality of arms is at least related to the more specific notion of fairness in Article 6(1). First, it has been held to apply to both civil and criminal cases and has been attributed to Article 6(1). A brief glance at Article 6(1) shows that it does not fit within the other guarantees: 'reasonable time'; 'public trial'; 'independent and impartial tribunal'. More convincing evidence however comes from four Commission decisions from

---

[22] *Nielsen v Denmark*, App no 343/57, report of 15 Mar 1961, (1961) 4 YB 494, para 52.
[23] See S Trechsel, *Human Rights in Criminal Proceedings* (Oxford, Oxford University Press, 2005) at 86; see also R Reed and J Murdoch, *A Guide to Human Rights Law in Scotland* (Edinburgh, Butterworths, 2001) at 303, para 5.54.

the early 1960s, which introduced the principle into the Strasbourg case law.[24] Although the cases concerned different procedures, the unifying point was that they all revolved around the determination of an appeal in a non-public setting, in which the accused had not had an opportunity to be heard, even though the opposing side had been given this chance. The Commission determined that the issues ought not to be addressed under the specific guarantees of Article 6(3), but rather that they all concerned the 'procedural equality of the accused with the public prosecutor'. This was later referred to by the Court as the principle of equality of arms, and was determined to be an 'inherent element of a "fair trial"'.[25] Equality of arms therefore seems to be the ideal starting point for any examination of the specific procedural fairness under Article 6(1).

Although the term 'equality of arms' is perhaps more commonly associated with certain legal systems, it is clear that the Court does not believe this principle to be culturally specific. It has applied it in criminal and civil cases concerning, *inter alia*, the United Kingdom, France, Austria, Belgium, the Netherlands, Switzerland and Finland. Equality of arms is often defined in a broad and relatively neutral sense as being the requirement that a balance of fairness is maintained between the parties. It was contrary to the principle, for instance, for a prosecutor to be heard during a court hearing while the accused or his representative had been prohibited from attending.[26] This idea of balance is a vital part of understanding the scope of the principle.

Equality of arms does not guarantee specific rights, such as the right to be heard, but instead it seeks to ensure that these rights are fairly applied;[27] thus if one party has the right to be heard, the other side must also be permitted this

---

[24] *Ofner and Hopfinger v Austria*, App nos 524/59 and 617/59, report of 23 Nov 1962, (1963) 6 YB 680; *Pataki and Dunshirn v Austria*, App nos 596/59 and 789/60, report of 28 Mar 1963, (1963) 6 YB 718. Although the term 'equality of arms' was first mentioned in the above cases, the concept behind the term was introduced in an earlier case concerning civil proceedings: *X v Sweden*, App no 434/58, (1959) 2 YB 354, 370.

[25] See eg *Neumeister v Austria*, judgment of 27 June 1968, Series A no 8, (1979–80) 1 EHRR 91. See further S Trechsel, *Human Rights in Criminal Proceedings* (Oxford, Oxford University Press, 2005) at 94–102; M Wasek-Wiaderek, *The Principle of Equality of Arms in Criminal Procedure Under Article 6 of the European Convention on Human Rights and its Function in Criminal Justice of Selected European Countries: A Comparative View* (Leuven, Leuven University Press, 2000); S Trechsel, 'Die Verteidigungsrechte in der Praxis zur Europäischen Menschenrechtskonvention' (1979) 96 *Schweizerische Zeitschrift für Strafrecht* 337.

[26] *Neumeister v Austria*, judgment of 27 June 1968, Series A no 8, (1979–80) 1 EHRR 91, para 22; here the Court noted that this procedure would have violated Art 6(1). However there was no violation as the point at issue, an examination of a provisional request for release, was not covered by Art 6(1). See also *Matznetter v Austria*, judgment of 10 Nov 1969, Series A no 10, (1979–80) 1 EHRR 198, para 13. It is doubtful however whether this would be upheld today; cf eg *Sanchez-Reisse v Switzerland*, judgment of 21 Oct 1986, Series A no 107, (1987) 9 EHRR 71.

[27] S Stavros, *The Guarantees for Accused Persons Under Article 6 of the European Convention on Human Rights* (Dordrecht, Kluwer Law, 1993) at 53 is thus wrong to criticise the Court for holding, eg in *Monnell and Morris v United Kingdom*, judgment of 2 Mar 1987, Series A no 115, (1988) 10 EHRR 205, para 62, that there had been no violation of the equality of arms because, while the defence could not attend the hearing, the prosecution was similarly absent. This situation could well however have constituted a violation of the adversarial proceedings requirement.

opportunity. Other imbalances have arisen in relation to unequal access to the file,[28] inequalities in submitting arguments and observations,[29] failure to disclose relevant evidence[30] and in the unequal status of expert witnesses.[31] More generally and according to the most commonly used phrase in this area of the Court's case law, equality of arms dictates that 'everyone who is a party to the proceedings shall have an opportunity to present his case under conditions which do not place him at a disadvantage vis-à-vis his opponent'.[32] It is notable that the Court frequently stresses that equality of arms is just one element of the 'wider concept of a fair trial'.[33] This is not incidental, but has a methodological significance. Establishing a lack of balance is just the first part of the Court's approach; once this has been determined the Court will examine the effect that this has had on the fairness of the proceedings as a whole.[34]

In determining the scope of the equality of arms it is instructive to look to its development in the Convention's case law. The principle that one party should not be placed in an advantageous position during the trial hearing was first mentioned in the context of civil proceedings in the case of *X v Sweden*.[35] Civil

---

[28] *Foucher v France*, judgment of 18 Mar 1997, Reports 1997-II, 452, (1998) 25 EHRR 234, paras 26–38; *Bendenoun v France*, judgment of 24 Feb 1994, Series A no 284, (1994) 18 EHRR 54, paras 49–53; *Mialhe v France (no 2)*, judgment of 26 Sept 1996, Reports 1996-IV, 1319, (1997) 23 EHRR 491, paras 38 and 44; *McMicheal v United Kingdom*, judgment of 24 Feb 1995, Series A no 307-B, (1995) 20 EHRR 205; *Vermeulen v Belgium*, judgment of 20 Feb 1996, Reports 1996-I, 224, (2001) 32 EHRR 15, para 33.

[29] *Borgers v Belgium*, judgment of 30 Oct 1991, Series A no 214-B, (1993) 15 EHRR 92, paras 27–29; *Ruiz-Mateos v Spain*, judgment of 23 June 1993, Series A no 262, (1993) 16 EHRR 505, paras 61–63; *Nideröst-Huber v Switzerland*, judgment of 18 Feb 1997, Reports 1997-I, 101, (1998) 25 EHRR 709, paras 19–32; *Van de Hurk v Netherlands*, judgment of 19 Apr 1994, Series A no 288, (1994) 18 EHRR 481, paras 56–57; *FR v Switzerland*, no 37292/97, judgment of 28 June 2001, paras 35 and 40–41; *Bulut v Austria*, judgment of 22 Feb 1996, Reports 1996-II, 346, (1997) 24 EHRR 84, paras 44–50; *Apeh Üldözötteinek Szövetsége and Others v Hungary*, no 32367/96, ECHR 2000-X, 361, (2002) 34 EHRR 34, paras 42–43; *Werner v Austria*, judgment of 24 Nov 1997, Reports 1997-VII, 2496, (1998) 26 EHRR 310, para 67.

[30] *Jasper v United Kingdom*, judgment of 16 Feb 2000, (2000) 30 EHRR 441, paras 55–57; *Rowe and Davis v United Kingdom*, no 28901/95 ECHR 2000-II, (2000) 30 EHRR 1; *Fitt v United Kingdom*, no 29777/96 ECHR 2000-II, (2000) 30 EHRR 480, paras 46–50; *Kress v France*, no 39594/98 ECHR 2001-VI, 41, para 73; *Kuopila v Finland*, no 27752/95, judgment of 27 Apr 2000, (2001) 33 EHRR 25, para 38.

[31] *Boenisch v Austria*, judgment of 6 May 1985, Series A no 92, (1987) 9 EHRR 191, paras 31–35; *Brandstetter v Austria*, judgment of 28 Aug 1991, Series A no 211, (1993) 15 EHRR 378, para 45; *Dombo Beeher BV v Netherlands*, judgment of 27 Oct 1993, Series A no 274, (1994) 18 EHRR 213, paras 30–35.

[32] *Struppat v Federal Republic of Germany*, App no 2804/66, (1968) 27 CD 61; *Kaufman v Belgium*, App no 10938/84, (1986) 50 DR 98 at 115; *Foucher v France*, judgment of 18 Mar 1997, Reports 1997-II, 452, (1998) 25 EHRR 234.

[33] *Delcourt v Belgium*, judgment of 17 Jan 1970, Series A no 11, (1979–80) 1 EHRR 355, para 28; *Monnell and Morris v United Kingdom*, Series A no 115, (1988) 10 EHRR 205, para 62.

[34] For criticism see S Trechsel, *Human Rights in Criminal Proceedings* (Oxford, Oxford University Press 2005) at 86.

[35] *X v Sweden*, App no 434/58, decision of 30 June 1959, (1959) 2 YB 354, 370–2: the applicant was refused an entry permit to Sweden and was thus unable to make a personal appearance in proceedings involving his right of access to his son. The Commission noted in finding, *inter alia*, a violation of Art 6 that 'Article 6, paragraph 1, of the Convention appears to contemplate that everyone who is a party

proceedings, which throughout Europe generally follow the pattern of opposing sides and a judge who decides on the outcome of the case, provided a relatively uncontroversial basis for the introduction of this principle into the Court's case law. In relation to civil proceedings it is clear that the principle will not be able to rectify disadvantages inherent in the strengths of the opponents. It is inevitable that one side will have bigger resources or greater leverage than the other. The principle simply exists to ensure that one side is not given procedural possibilities greater than the other. Each side must have an equal opportunity to present its case *at trial* and to challenge the case of the other side. Suggestions that this principle cannot exist in practice because of initial inequalities between opponents, an argument which frequently invokes the difference in strength between an accused and the prosecuting authorities, misconstrue the scope of the provision.

The label 'equality of arms' seems to have been first applied in the criminal context in the early joined cases of *Pataki* and *Dunshirn v Austria* and *Opfer* and *Hopfinger v Austria*. In *Pataki* the public prosecutor, in the course of appealing against the applicants' sentences, had had the opportunity to appear and to make submissions to the Court of Appeal suggesting that their sentences be increased. Neither the applicants themselves nor their legal representatives were permitted either to be present or make counter submissions. Their sentences were duly raised. The Commission held that there was no need to show actual prejudice, and that in order for a violation to be found it was sufficient if one party was afforded an opportunity to influence the court that was not awarded to the other party:

> Even on the assumption . . . that the Public Prosecutor did not play an active role at this stage of the proceedings, the very fact that he was present and thereby had the opportunity of influencing the members of the Court, without the accused or his counsel having any similar opportunities or any possibility of contesting any statements made by the Prosecutor, constitutes an inequality which . . . is incompatible with the notion of a fair trial.[36]

The Commission's perception of the parties involved in the case is particularly important. The Commission viewed the Public Prosecutor as an 'opposing party' who was seeking to impose more severe sanctions on the applicants. In this capacity he could not be viewed as a neutral observer, but was rather seen as creating a bias in favour of the state and thus creating a deficit of fairness for the applicants. The fairness of the hearing can be seen to be prejudiced by the apparent one-sidedness of the process whereby the applicants, unlike the prosecutor, have no opportunity to influence the decision-making process. Although

---

to civil proceedings shall have a reasonable opportunity of presenting his case to the Court under conditions which do not place him under a substantial disadvantage vis-à-vis his opponent'.

[36] *Pataki and Dunshirn v Austria*, App nos 596/59 and 789/60, report of 28 Mar 1963, (1963) 6 YB 718, 732.

this seems to accord with the nineteenth century understanding of the accusatorial trinity, there is some evidence of initial uncertainty about the application of the principle.

Following this interpretation there would be no interference with the equality of arms principle in the event of the involvement of someone in the proceedings who could be viewed as neutral and objective. This was the case in *Opfer and Hopfinger v Austria*.[37] Here the Commission held that the involvement of the Attorney General in the proceedings did not serve to create a bias against the applicant. The Commission explicitly distinguished the Attorney General's role from that of the Public Prosecutor, noting that he had simply 'rubber stamped' the opinion of the Juge Rapporteur and had not influenced the decision-making process in any way. These cases demonstrate that although the content of the equality of arms is relatively neutral, in the sense that it merely requires that each party have the opportunity to present his or her case without being at a disadvantage with regard to his or her opponent, the context within which it is applied is anything but neutral. Even in the early cases it is clear that the equality of arms exists as a guarantee within the framework of Article 6(1), and perhaps most importantly alongside the guarantee of the right to an impartial judge, and envisages a relatively specific type of proceedings. Although these judgments indicate a movement towards acceptance of the accusatorial trinity, at this stage there had not yet been acknowledgement of the importance of the application of a strict conception of the institutional setting for the determination of the charge.

That the case law in this area has evolved considerably since these early cases is demonstrated by a comparison of the Court's reasoning in two cases against Belgium in which the applicants complained about the same procedure. In *Delcourt v Belgium*, decided in 1970, the Court examined the issues and broadly followed the approach of the Commission, determining whether there could be said to be a violation on the basis of whether the person involved could really be seen to be an opposing party. When, however, the Commission and the Court came to consider the same procedure 20 years later they came to a radically different conclusion. A comparison of the Court's reasoning in these cases illustrates the substantial transformation that occurred.

In *Delcourt* the Court held that there was no violation of the principle of equality of arms despite the applicant's complaint concerning the involvement of the Avocat Général, a member of the Public Prosecutor's office, in the course of his appeal hearing. Although the Public Prosecutor's department did not file a counter memorial, the appeal court heard submissions from the Juge Rapporteur and the Avocat Général that the appeal be dismissed, and the latter was permitted to be present during the court's deliberations, though he had no right to cast a vote. The Court found that the Avocat Général could not be seen to be an

---

[37] *Ofner and Hopfinger v Austria*, App nos 524/59 and 617/59, report of 23 Nov 1962, (1963) 6 YB 680.

'adversary' of the applicant. His task was simply to ensure the observance by the judges of the law, and had nothing to do with the establishment of the guilt or innocence of the accused. Instead he was an objective authority in the proceedings, he was deemed to be independent and impartial and his involvement was not such as unfairly to disadvantage the accused. The Court thus found unanimously that there had been no violation of the equality of arms.[38]

The Court emphasises understanding of the difficulties involved in reconciling century old legal traditions with the principles of Article 6. In keeping with its attempt to regulate fairness on a case-to-case basis and its tendency to link 'fairness' to the effect of the alleged defects on the outcome of the proceedings, it held, *inter alia*:

> the system now challenged dates back for more than a century and a half. Whilst it is true that the long standing of a national legal rule cannot justify a failure to comply with the present requirements of international law, it may under certain conditions provide supporting evidence that there has been no such failure. The Court is of the opinion that this is the case here. In this connection, the Court notes that on two occasions a parliament chosen in free elections has deliberately decided to maintain the system, the first time unchanged (preparatory work to the Act of 19th April 1949), the second time in substance and after studying the question in the context of the Convention (preparation of the new Judicial Code). Furthermore, the propriety and fairness of the rule laid down in Article 39 of the Decree of 15th March 1815 and then in Article 1109 of the 1967 Judicial Code—as it operates in practice—appears never to have been put in question by the legal profession or public opinion in Belgium. This wide measure of agreement would be impossible to explain if the independence and impartiality of the men on whose shoulders fell the administration of this institution at the Court of Cassation were doubted in Belgium, if the worth of their contribution to the body of decisions of the highest court were disputed or if their participation at the deliberations of the judges had been thought in any single case to open their door to unfairness or abuse.[39]

Twenty years later, in the case of *Borgers v Belgium*,[40] in which an applicant challenged the same procedure, things looked rather different. In this case the Court, noting that the rights of the defence and the principle of the equality of arms had 'undergone a considerable evolution in the Court's case-law', held that this procedure could no longer be deemed to be compatible with the principles inherent in Article 6. Although it stated that no one could question the objectivity with which the Avocat Général discharged his or her functions, the opinion of the Public Prosecutor's department could nevertheless not be regarded as being neutral. The inability of the applicant to reply to the Avocat Général's submissions thus created an inequality that was incompatible with the rights of the

---

[38] *Delcourt v Belgium*, judgment of 17 Jan 1970, Series A no 11, (1979–80) 1 EHRR 355, paras 33 and 34.
[39] *Ibid*, at para 36
[40] *Borgers v Belgium*, judgment of 30 Oct 1991, Series A no 214, (1993) 15 EHRR 92.

defence. The reasons for the Court's decision are not entirely apparent. Although the Court hints that this change in direction relates to the 'increased sensitivities of the public to the fair administration of justice',[41] it must be noted that this was a factor that was also considered in the earlier *Delcourt* decision.

Borgers was by no means unanimously decided, and there were a number of strong dissenting opinions from several judges, including Judge Martens and the ad hoc Belgian judge, Judge Storme, who in his dissenting opinion noted:

> The principal reason for my dissenting opinion lies in the fact that the detailed and comprehensive analysis which I have conducted of the case has not enabled me to understand why the *Borgers* case should be decided differently from the *Delcourt* case: the complaints are identical, the legislation and judicial practice in Belgium are the same, the facts of the case are the same.

Martens was similarly disturbed, noting that, in his opinion, the Court had failed to state its reasons 'clearly and convincingly'. In suggesting that there was a need for a careful approach to 'filling in' the vague concept of the right to a fair trial, he noted that the Court's case-by-case approach exacerbated the danger that the 'rules which emerge from such a case-law develop a momentum of their own and a tendency to engender specific new rules'. These new rules might 'overstrain a concept which, after all, refers to very basic principles of procedure'. He noted that particular caution was required since the Court was 'confronted in a double sense with various procedural systems: its members have been schooled in different procedural traditions and those of the respondent State permeate the issues under Article 6(1)'. Moreover he pointed out that it was possible that 'those who are completely unfamiliar with a particular procedural institution will be more readily inclined to find it incompatible with the requirements of "fair trial" than those who form part of the same tradition'. This meant that there was a 'risk that the former will be more inclined to view as a question of fair trial—i.e. as a question concerning *basic principles*—issues which in the latter's view concern merely questions of *procedural expediency* (about which procedural law specialists may differ) yet which fall outside the province of "fair trial"'.

The judgment in *Borgers* reflects a movement away from a conception of unfairness as based on evidence of a negative impact on the accused, inevitably linked to the outcome of the trial and reflected in the dissenting judges' desire to accommodate existing national practices and the fact that procedural fairness was dependent on a particular procedural setting. In this sense they represent a tightening of focus and an endorsement of the perception of fairness in Article 6 as reliant on procedural systems involving two opposing parties and an impartial judge. In view of this, those affiliated with the prosecution cannot logically be seen, particularly on the institutional level, as impartial, and thus cannot be

---

[41] *Ibid*, at para 24; see also JD Jackson, 'The Effect of Human Rights on Criminal Evidentiary Processes: Towards Convergence, Divergence or Realignment' (2005) 68 *MLR* 737 at 751.

permitted to communicate privately with the judiciary. The views of the dissenting judges in *Borgers* and the majority in *Delcourt* must be viewed as inconsistent with the European procedural tradition and as incompatible with the principle of fairness in European criminal proceedings. Indeed, the seeds of the *Borgers* decision were already sown in the reforms of the nineteenth century. While it is understandable that at the time the judgment appeared to be an extraordinary break with the Court's own case law, with the benefit of hindsight it fits neatly within a series of judgments from the early 1990s which start openly to equate equality of arms with a seemingly more controversial factor, that of adversarial procedure.

D The Relationship Between the Adversarial Procedure Requirement and the Equality of Arms

In the late 1980s references to 'adversarial procedure' began to appear in the Court's case law: 'all evidence must be produced in the presence of the accused… with a view to adversarial argument'.[42] The first Article 6 case[43] which includes any reference to adversarial procedure seems to be *Barberà, Messegué and Jabardo v Spain*,[44] where the applicants alleged a violation of the 'equality of arms and adversarial procedure'. The Court noted that among the guarantees of Article 6 were the rights of those accused of criminal offence to examine or have examined witnesses against them and to obtain the attendance and examination of witnesses on their behalf under the same conditions as witnesses against them. It held that this right 'not only entails equal treatment of the prosecution and the defence in this matter but also means that the hearing of witnesses must in general be adversarial'. Although the finding of a violation was achieved by only a small majority (by 10 votes to eight), none of the dissenting opinions commented on the use of the phrase 'adversarial procedure'.

With the development of the case law it becomes increasingly common to find the concepts cited together: '[t]he principle of equality of arms is only one feature of the wider concept of a fair trial, which also includes the fundamental right that criminal proceedings should be adversarial';[45] and 'it is a fundamental aspect of

---

[42] *Barberà, Messegué and Jabardo v Spain*, judgment of 6 Dec 1988, Series A no 146, (1989) 11 EHRR 360, para 78.

[43] There is evidence of the requirement of adversarial procedure in earlier cases, but these relate to Art 5(4), not to Art 6: see eg *Sanchez-Reisse v Switzerland*, judgment of 21 Oct 1986, Series A no 107, (1987) 9 EHRR 71, paras 50–51.

[44] *Ibid.*

[45] *Belziuk v Poland*, judgment of 25 Mar 1998, Reports 1998-II, 338, (2000) 30 EHRR 614, para 37; *Ruiz-Mateos v Spain*, judgment of 23 June 1993, Series A no 262, (1993) 16 EHRR 505, para 63; *Brandstetter v Austria*, judgment of 28 Aug 1991, Series A no 211, (1993) 15 EHRR 378, para 66.

the right to a fair trial that criminal proceedings, including elements of such proceedings which relate to procedure, should be adversarial and that there should be equality of arms between the prosecution and the defence'.[46]

The right to an adversarial trial means 'in a criminal case, that both prosecution and defence must be given the opportunity to have knowledge of and comment on the observations filed and the evidence adduced by the other party'[47] as well as those made by an independent member of the national legal service, with a view to influencing the court's decision.[48] This is extremely close to the definition applied in some cases to the equality of arms. Indeed in *Borgers v Belgium* the Court invoked the principle of equality of arms and found a violation where the accused had had no opportunity to reply to submissions put before the Court of Cassation.[49] Similarly in *Pataki v Austria*[50] a breach of the equality of arms occurred where the defence could not challenge the prosecution's submissions. It is consequently easy to become confused about the exact relationship between these principles in the case law. In fact they do have distinct roles, but these will often come together, especially in the context of criminal proceedings.

Equality of arms is a consequence of the acceptance of the accusatorial trinity and means that there must always be a balance achieved between the parties to the proceedings. Where, for instance, one party is given the chance to make submissions to the Court or to challenge the submissions of the other side, the other party must also be offered this chance. The adversarial procedure requirement involves a specific concern, namely that both parties to the proceedings have the chance to challenge the other side's submissions. In civil proceedings it would thus be possible for there to be no violation of the equality of arms, for instance in a case where neither side was able to challenge a piece of evidence, but a violation of adversarial procedure, on the basis that one party was unable to

---

[46] *Rowe and Davis v United Kingdom,* no 28901/95, ECHR 2000-II, (2000) 30 EHRR 1, para 60.

[47] *Belziuk v Poland,* above n45, at para 37; see, *inter alia, Brandstetter v Austria,* above n45, paras 66–67; *Lobo Machado v Portugal,* judgment of 20 Feb 1996, Reports 1996-I, 195, (1997) 23 EHRR 79, para 31; *Rowe and Davis v United Kingdom,* above n46,; *IJL, GMR and AKP v United Kingdom,* nos 29522/95, 30056/96 and 30574/96, ECHR 2000-IX, (2001) 33 EHRR 11, para 112; *Fitt v United Kingdom,* no 29777/96, ECHR 2000-II, (2000) 30 EHRR 480, para 44; *Ruiz-Mateos v Spain,* above n45, para 63; *Brandstetter v Austria,* above n45, para 67.

[48] See also *JJ v Netherlands,* judgment of 27 Mar 1998, Reports 1998-II, 603, (1999) 28 EHRR 168, para 43; *Vermeulen v Belgium,* judgment of 20 Feb 1996, Reports 1996-I, (2001) 32 EHRR 15, para 33; *Van Orshoven v Belgium,* judgment of 25 June 1997, Reports 1997-III, 1039, (1998) 26 EHRR 55, para 41; *KDB v Netherlands,* judgment of 27 Mar 1998, Reports 1998-II, 620, para 44; *Morel v France,* no 34130/96, ECHR 2000-VI, (2001) 33 EHRR 47, para 27; *Goc v Turkey,* no 36590/97, judgment of 9 Nov 2000, (2002) 35 EHRR 6, para 34. Being able to influence the Court's decision was also a factor deemed significant in a number of other cases including: *Krcmar and others v Czech Republic,* no 35376/97, judgment of 3 Mar 2000, (2001) 31 EHRR 41; *Mantovanelli v France,* judgment of 18 Mar 1997, Reports 1997-II, 436, para 33, and *Nideröst-Huber v Switzerland,* judgment of 18 Feb 1997, Reports 1997-I, 108, (1998) 25 EHRR 709, para 24.

[49] *Borgers v Belgium,* judgment of 30 Oct 1991, Series A no 214, (1993) 15 EHRR 92, paras 24–27.

[50] *Pataki and Dunshirn v Austria,* App nos 596/59 and 789/60, report of 28 Mar 1963, (1963) 6 YB 718, para 70.

challenge evidence before the court.[51] In *Krcmar and Others v Czech Republic*, for instance, documentary evidence that had been collected by the court was not communicated to either side, thus neither side was at a disadvantage and there could be no violation of the equality of arms. The court nevertheless found a violation of Article 6 based on a failure to respect the adversarial procedure principle. It held that this required that parties have 'the opportunity not only to make known any evidence needed for their claims to succeed, but also to have knowledge of, and comment on, all evidence adduced or observations filed, with a view to influencing the court's decision'.[52] Despite the fact that this evidence was manifestly aimed at influencing the court's decision, the applicant had had no possibility 'to familiarise itself with the evidence before the court' or 'to comment on its existence, contents and authenticity in an appropriate form and within an appropriate time, if need be, in a written form and in advance';[53] given the character and importance of the evidence, this was incompatible with Article 6.[54]

The distinction between these principles is less clear in the context of criminal proceedings. The equality of arms means that there must be a balance of procedural opportunities between defence and prosecution, while adversarial procedure guarantees the right of the defence to be informed of and be able to challenge the prosecution's submissions. In a criminal case, it is unlikely that the evidence which the defence wants to challenge will come from any source other than the prosecution, thus it is likely that if evidence is led which the defence is unable to challenge, then there will be a violation of both the equality of arms and the adversarial procedure requirement. It is notable that the temporal development of these principles in the Court's case law mirrors their development in the works of the nineteenth century writers. The recognition of criminal proceedings as party-orientated necessarily requires that attention be paid to the sufficiency of the procedural opportunities of the defence.

E The Court's Interpretation of the Adversarial Procedure Requirement in Criminal Proceedings

Given the terminology of the comparative criminal procedure law scholarship, the use of the term 'adversarial procedure' might have been expected to prove

---

[51] See *Krcmar and others v Czech Republic*, no 35376/97, judgment of 3 Mar 2000, (2001) 31 EHRR 41.

[52] Citing *Nideröst-Huber v Switzerland*, judgment of 18 Feb 1997, Reports 1997-I, 108, (1998) 25 EHRR 709, para 24, and *Mantovanelli v France*, judgment of 18 Mar 1997, Reports 1997-II, 436, (1997) 24 EHRR 370, para 33.

[53] *Krcmar and others v Czech Republic*, no 35376/97, judgment of 3 Mar 2000, (2001) 31 EHRR 41, para 42.

[54] *Ibid*, at para 42.

controversial. It has however received little attention from commentators.[55] Reed and Murdoch note that 'an adversarial hearing is a vital characteristic in both criminal and civil proceedings',[56] while Harris, O'Boyle and Warbrick state that 'a principle that underlies Art 6 as a whole is that judicial proceedings must be adversarial'.[57] Similarly the Dutch writers van Dijk and van Hoof quote without comment the Court's requirement that the proceedings be adversarial.[58] In order to understand this lack of controversy it is essential to have an understanding of the scope of the principle. An examination of the cases where a lack of adversarial procedure has been challenged and of the Court's response to these challenges will serve to illuminate the scope of this requirement. The right to adversarial procedure encompasses two main facets: first the requirement that the accused be present and, secondly, the requirement that the defence be able to challenge the submissions and observations of the prosecution and to lead its own evidence.

(i) The Right to be Present at Trial

As a general rule, the right to participate effectively in a criminal trial requires both the presence of the accused and the guarantee that he or she be able to understand and follow the proceedings.[59] The importance of this guarantee in the context of criminal proceedings is emphasised by the Court's indication that it is to be treated more strictly in criminal proceedings than in civil cases.[60]

In spite of the emphasis on the presence of the accused, proceedings held in an accused's absence are not in principle incompatible with the Convention, particularly if the accused person can subsequently obtain from a court which has heard him or her a fresh determination of the merits of the charge, in respect of both law and fact.[61] Even in those cases however where there is no possibility of a re-trial, trial *in absentia* may be compatible with Article 6.[62] Unfortunately much of the case law in this area is expressed in terms of fault. Distinctions are drawn

---

[55]   Cf S Trechsel, *Human Rights in Criminal Proceedings* (Oxford, Oxford University Press, 2005) at 89 ff.

[56]   R Reed and J Murdoch, *A Guide to Human Rights Law in Scotland* (Edinburgh, Butterworths, 2001) at 304, para 5.55.

[57]   D Harris, M O'Boyle and C Warbrick, *Law of the European Convention on Human Rights* (London, Butterworths, 1995).

[58]   P Van Dijk and GJH van Hoof, *Theory and Practice of the European Convention on Human Rights* (The Hague, Kluwer Law, 1998) at 435 and 474.

[59]   *Stanford v United Kingdom,* judgment of 23 Feb 1994, Series A no 282-A, para 26; See also *Colozza v Italy,* judgment of 12 Feb 1985, Series A no 89, (1985) 7 EHRR 516, para 27; *Belziuk v Poland,* judgment of 25 Mar 1998, Reports 1998-II, 558, (2000) 30 EHRR 614, para 37.

[60]   *Dombo Beheer BV v Netherlands,* judgment of 27 Oct 1993, Series A no 274, (1994) 18 EHRR 213, para 32: 'the contracting States have a greater latitude when dealing with civil cases concerning civil rights and obligations than they have when dealing with criminal cases'.

[61]   *Colozza v Italy,* above n59, paras 27–29; *Poitrimol v France,* judgment of 23 Nov 1993, Series A no 277-A, (1994) 18 EHRR 130, para 31; for an overview of the Convention case law in this area see S Trechsel, *Human Rights in Criminal Proceedings* (Oxford, Oxford University Press, 2005) at 252 ff.

[62]   *FCB v Italy,* judgment of 28 Aug 1991, Series A no 208-B, (1992) 14 EHRR 909, para 35.

between those cases where the accused knew of the summons and failed to appear at trial and those cases where the accused was not aware of the summons. Not only does the case law suggest some uncertainty about what ought to be protected but the Court also seems to express support for the importance of respecting the institutions of justice at the expense of the 'rights of the accused'. Especially problematic is its attempt to dress this up in the language of individual autonomy by connecting it to the notion of waiver. Consequently, where the accused deliberately wants to waive the right to appear, member states are permitted to impose sanctions:

> It is of capital importance that a defendant should appear, both because of his right to a hearing and because of the need to verify the accuracy of his statements and compare them with those of the victim—whose interests need to be protected—and of the witnesses.
>
> The legislature must accordingly be able to discourage unjustified absences.[63]

Conversely, it is legitimate for member states to characterise the failure of the accused to appear as implicit waiver, and thus to carry out a trial *in absentia.*

In relation to appeal hearings, the Court has taken a more restrictive approach, ruling that the presence of the accused is not always required at second or third instance providing that there has been a public hearing at first instance. This means that leave to appeal and appeal hearings will not necessarily require the presence of the appellant,[64] although this will depend, in part, on the role of the appeal court in the member state. In *Ekbatani*, the Court of Appeal was called upon to examine the case as to the facts and the law and to make a full assessment of guilt or innocence. The Court decided that in the circumstances of the case 'that question could not, as a matter of fair trial, have been properly determined without a direct assessment of the evidence given in person by the applicant— who claimed that he had not committed the act alleged to constitute the criminal offence'. Accordingly, the Court of Appeal's re-examination of the applicant's conviction at first instance 'ought to have comprised a full rehearing of the applicant and the complainant'.[65] Similarly the Court found a violation in *Kremzow v Austria*, where the applicant had been denied the opportunity to be present at the appeal against sentence, holding that 'given the gravity of what was at stake for the applicant, he ought to have been able "to defend himself in person" as required by Article 6 para. 3 (c) and that the State was under a positive duty, notwithstanding his failure to make a request, to ensure his presence in

---

[63] *Poitrimol v France,* judgment of 23 Nov 1993, Series A no 277-A, (1994) 18 EHRR 130, para 35.

[64] See *Monnell and Morris v United Kingdom,* judgment of 2 Mar 1987, Series A no 115, (1988) 10 EHRR 205 (leave to appeal hearings); *Sutter v Switzerland,* judgment of 22 Feb 1984, Series A no 74, (1984) 6 EHRR 272, para 30 (appeal hearings).

[65] *Ekbatani v Sweden,* judgment of 26 May 1988, Series A no 134, (1991) 13 EHRR 504, para 32; see also *Helmers v Sweden,* judgment of 29 Oct 1991, Series A no 212-A, (1993) 15 EHRR 285, paras 38 and 39.

court in such circumstances'.[66] As a general rule, where the appeal court is able to address questions of fact as well as law and to make a full assessment of the guilt or innocence of the appellant, the appellant has the right to be present.[67] The reference to the ability of the court to address questions of fact seems to connect the defence right to be present to the examination of the evidence. Where the evidence can be examined, there is a right to be present, but where there is no room for such an examination, there is no corresponding defence right.

One consequence of the lack of express reference to this principle in the text of the Convention is that there is no consistency in the case law as to the foundation of the principle that the accused be present. Some of the early case law confuses the issue of self-representation and the right to be present—often only considering the representation issue.[68] As the principle has evolved it has been linked with several different aspects of Article 6. In the case of *Ensslin, Baader and Raspe v Germany* the Commission noted that the right to be heard could be considered independently of the right to represent oneself. It stressed that the applicants' complaint that they were not able to be present had to be considered in the light of 'the general principle of a fair trial, not all aspects of which are set forth in Article 6 (3)'.[69] It noted:

> In criminal cases, for the accused to appear personally and be heard by the judge should normally contribute to a fair examination of the case.[70] In order to determine, in the case in point, whether the continuation of the trial when the accused were absent (though not excluded) may have infringed the right secured by Article 6(1), account must however be taken of the particular circumstances of the case and of the requirement that justice be done, and be done within a reasonable time.

This approach was followed by the Court in *Colozza v Italy* where it stated that, although not expressly mentioned in Article 6(1), 'the object and purpose of Art. 6 taken as a whole show that a person "charged with a criminal offence" is entitled to take part in the hearing'.[71] As the applicant's case was never heard in his presence by a 'tribunal' which was competent to determine all the aspects of the matter, there had been a violation of Article 6(1).[72] In *Goddi v Italy*, however,

---

[66] Judgment of 21 Sept 1993, Series A no 268-B, (1994) 17 EHRR 322, para 68, although the Court found that there was no need for him to be present at the proceedings concerning a declaration of nullity. The Court reached the same conclusion in *Botten v Norway,* judgment of 19 Feb 1996, ECHR 1996-I, 126, (2001) 32 EHRR 3, para 53.

[67] *Tierce and others v San Marino,* nos 24954/94, 24971/94 and 24972/94, ECHR 2001-IX, (2002) 34 EHRR 25, para 95. Although there are some exceptions including *Fejde v Sweden,* judgment of 29 Oct 1991, Series A no 212-C, (1994) 17 EHRR 14, where the Court ruled that on the specific facts of the case the accused did not need to be present at the appeal hearing.

[68] *X v Norway,* App no 5923/72, decision of 30 May 1975, (1975) 3 DR 43 at 44; *X v Austria,* App no 2676/65, decision of 3 Apr 1967, (1967) 23 CD 31; *X v Austria,* App no 2645/65, (1969) 28 CD 43.

[69] *Ensslin, Baader and Raspe v Germany,* App nos 7572/76, 7586/76 and 7587/76, (1978) 14 DR 91 at 115; see also *Nielsen v Denmark,* App no 343/57, report of 15 Mar 1961, (1961) 4 YB 494, para 52.

[70] Cf *X v Germany,* App no 1169/61, (1964) 13 CD 1.

[71] *Colozza v Italy,* judgment of 12 Feb 1985, Series A no 89, (1985) 7 EHRR 516, para 27.

[72] *Ibid,* at para 32.

the Court reverted to considering the issue of the applicant's presence at trial (as well as the absence of his lawyer) under Article 6(3)(c), finding a violation on the basis that the authorities failed to ensure that the applicant was informed about the hearing resulting not only in his absence but also in an inadequate opportunity to prepare his defence.[73]

The right to be present has been linked to various other aspects of the right to a fair trial. Its relationship to the opportunity of the accused to examine important witnesses was evident in *Barberà, Messengué and Jabardo v Spain*.[74] Here the Court noted that it could be inferred from the right of the accused to be present that 'all the evidence must in principle be produced in the presence of the accused at a public hearing with a view to adversarial argument'. Similarly in *Austria v Italy*[75] the applicants complained that they were not allowed to accompany the judge and lawyers to the scene of the crime where the judge had carried out an interrogation of one of the witnesses. Although the Commission noted that it would have been better 'if the witness had not been heard in the absence of the seven prisoners', it found no violation on the basis that counsel for the defence had requested the hearing.[76] The right to be heard has also been affiliated to the right to a public hearing guaranteed in Article 6(1).[77] In *Stefanelli v San Marino*, the accused had the chance to question witnesses before the investigating judge, but not before the trial judge—there was no public hearing as the determination of the charge was carried out by way of a written procedure. As there was no opportunity for the accused to be heard on appeal the Court concluded that the right to a public hearing had been violated.[78]

Therefore the Court's case law, the right to be present has been considered under Article 6(1)[79] as part of the right to a public hearing,[80] as part of the equality of arms,[81] as part of the right guaranteed by Article 6(3)(c),[82] and even in some cases as being a constitute element of several of these together.[83] This is

---

[73] Judgment of 9 Apr 1984, Series A no 76, (1984) 6 EHRR 457, paras 27–32.

[74] Judgment of 6 Dec 1988, Series A no 146, (1989) 11 EHRR 360, para 78.

[75] *Austria v Italy (Pfunders case)*, App no 788/60, report of 30 Mar 1963, (1963) 6 YB 740.

[76] It is likely that this judgment would now be decided differently and that the judge, as the 'ultimate guardian of fairness' (*Cuscani v United Kingdom*, no 32771/96, judgment of 24 Sept 2002, (2003) 36 EHRR 2, paras 38–40) would have the responsibility for ensuring that the accused be present: see *Botten v Norway*, judgment of 19 Feb 1996, Reports 1996-I, 126, (2001) 32 EHRR 3, para 53, where the Court held that '[t]he Supreme Court was under a duty to take positive measures to this effect, notwithstanding the fact that the applicant neither attended the hearing, nor asked for leave to address the court nor objected through his counsel to a new judgment under Article 362 para 2 being given by the Supreme Court'.

[77] This is also the view of some academic commentators: see eg D Harris, M O'Boyle and C Warbrick, *Law of the European Convention on Human Rights* (London, Butterworths, 1995) at 203.

[78] *Stefanelli v San Marino*, no 35396/97, ECHR 2000-II, (2001) 33 EHRR 16.

[79] Eg *Colozza v Italy*, judgment of 12 Feb 1985, Series A no 89, (1985) 7 EHRR 516.

[80] Eg *Stefanelli v San Marino*, above n78.

[81] *Belziuk v Poland*, judgment of 25 Mar 1998, Reports 1998-II, (2000) 30 EHRR 614, para 39.

[82] Eg *Goddi v Italy*, judgment of 9 Apr 1984, Series A no 76, (1984) 6 EHRR 457, para 29.

[83] In *Belziuk* the Court found a violation of Art 6 (3)(c) and (1)—apparently with regard to equality of arms: *Belziuk v Poland*, above n81,.

an unfortunate approach, which inevitably and needlessly prevents a clear elucidation of principle. There is in fact a clear theoretical distinction between these guarantees. The right to a public hearing in a criminal trial has significance beyond, and is quite separate from, the presence of the accused; it is broader and serves primarily to maintain public confidence in the administration of justice.[84] It is clearly possible for the hearing not to take place in public, despite the presence of the parties. Indeed the accused cannot really be considered to be 'the public'; this is emphasised by the fact that the exceptions specified in Article 6(1) never permit the exclusion of the accused.[85] Similarly the suggestion that the right to be heard constitutes part of the equality of arms is problematic in that, as we have seen, the principle serves only to ensure that the accused receive the same procedural opportunities as the prosecution. Thus, the absence of the accused would not violate the equality of arms if the prosecutor were similarly absent.[86]

Neither does the right to be heard sit especially well within the right guaranteed by Article 6(3)(c). The right to defend oneself in person is by its nature closely linked to the right to be defended by counsel. Indeed both the Court and Commission have made it clear that the guarantee in Article 6(3)(c) is deliberately phrased as an alternative: the accused has a right to be represented by counsel or to represent him- or herself, and the decision as to which to apply will depend on the law of the member state.[87] If the accused elects to be represented by counsel, the right to defend oneself loses any application, but this cannot mean that the accused then has no right to be present at the hearing. Indeed, restrictions on the right to defend oneself should not necessarily interfere with the right to be present in court. Where, for instance, legislation prohibits an accused from directly questioning the victim in a rape case, this does not necessarily prohibit the accused from being present during the hearing. These are separate guarantees serving different purposes.

The right of the accused to be present at trial is perhaps more accurately expressed as the right to be present during the examination of the evidence. While the Strasbourg authorities seem reluctant to admit this, the importance of the accused person's presence during the examination of the evidence is apparent in the emphasis that is placed on determining whether the court at issue has the opportunity to examine the facts or the evidence rather than merely the law.

---

[84] As the Court itself has often noted: see eg *Axen v Germany,* judgment of 8 Dec 1983, Series A no 72, (1984) 6 EHRR 195, para 25.

[85] See cases such as *B v UK,* judgment of 8 July 1987, Series A no 121, (1988) 10 EHRR 87 (exclusion of press and public in child custody hearings).

[86] This was the reasoning of the Court in *Monnell and Morris v United Kingdom,* judgment of 2 Mar 1987, Series A no 115, (1988) 10 EHRR 205.

[87] Eg *X v Norway,* App no 5923/72, decision of 30 May 1975, (1975) 3 DR 43 at 44. It should be noted however that this alternative really works only one way; a state may not refuse an accused legal assistance (assuming, of course, that he or she would be entitled to legal assistance by virtue of Art 6(3)(c)) on the basis that he or she could represent him- or herself—*Pakelli v Germany,* judgment of 25 Apr 1983, Series A no 64, (1984) 6 EHRR 1, para 31.

(ii)   Knowledge of the Other Side's Submissions

The second main aspect of the adversarial procedure requirement is the requirement that the accused be aware of and have the opportunity to challenge the prosecution's submissions. The first requirement involves the communication of submissions to the defence. The ramifications of the Court's insistence that the adversarial procedure requirement includes the right to have advance knowledge of the other side's submissions have been particularly felt in the country that is widely held to have the greatest affiliation to the adversarial tradition. The Court has had to consider a number of cases against the United Kingdom, where evidence was withheld from the defence on the basis of public interest considerations, ie so as to preserve the fundamental rights of another individual or to safeguard an important public interest.

Generally, while the withholding of evidence cannot be said to be compatible with the notion of 'adversarial procedure', the Court has held that it may be acceptable providing that the defence was given the opportunity to challenge the decision to exclude the evidence and providing that the trial judge has the role of deciding whether or not the evidence should be withheld. This latter point was at issue in *Rowe and Davis v United Kingdom,* where the prosecution's unilateral decision to withhold certain relevant evidence on the grounds of public interest without notifying the trial judge was held to be incompatible with the demands of adversarial procedure. Although there could be instances where evidence could be excluded from the requirement of disclosure, it was incompatible with the principle of adversarial procedure for the prosecution unilaterally to decide to withhold evidence. The failure of the prosecution to lay the evidence in question before the trial judge and to permit him to rule on the question of disclosure thus deprived the applicants of a fair trial.[88]

This case demonstrates that the approach of the Court is not to determine whether the withholding of the evidence was 'strictly necessary', as this is deemed to be a task for the national authorities. Instead, the Court's role is to ensure that the decision-making procedure complied with the principles necessary to ensure adversarial procedure. That the Court is not interested in acting as a Court of fourth instance is further evidenced by its decision in *Jasper and Fitt v United Kingdom.*[89] Here the trial judge had examined the material himself and decided that the evidence should not be disclosed; the defence in turn had been notified of the existence of the material and had had the chance to make submissions and to participate in the decision-making process. Thus the Court held that the principles of adversarial procedure and equality of arms had been complied with and there was no violation of Article 6.

---

[88] *Rowe and Davis v United Kingdom,* no 28901/95, ECHR 2000-II, (2000) 30 EHRR 1, paras 66–67.

[89] *Jasper v United Kingdom,* no 27052/95, judgment of 16 Feb 2000, (2000) 30 EHRR 441; *Fitt v United Kingdom,* no 29777/96, ECHR 2000-II, (2000) 30 EHRR 480; see too S Trechsel, *Human Rights in Criminal Proceedings* (Oxford, Oxford University, 2005) at 92 ff.

The question whether an appeal court could rectify an erroneous decision to withhold evidence at the trial itself was considered in *Edwards v United Kingdom*. Here, evidence that a principal witness had failed to pick out the applicant from volumes of photographs in which he had appeared was withheld. This evidence was examined by the Court of Appeal, which decided on the basis of all the evidence, including a confession by the applicant, that the conviction was safe. Although the court had not re-examined witnesses, this would have been possible had the defence requested it. The Court decided by seven votes to two that there had been no violation of Article 6, holding that 'the defects of the original trial were remedied by the subsequent procedure before the court of appeal'.[90] Judge Pettiti, dissenting, was not convinced. He noted that proceedings *in camera* might be required in relation to state secrets. In this case, however, there were no secrets involved; the prosecution had simply concealed 'exonerating evidence'. The failure of the defence to raise this matter at the Court of Appeal was for him irrelevant. He noted:

> Such concealment is comparable to a ground of nullity for reasons of public policy in the continental system. Grounds of nullity can and must be raised by the Court *ex officio*, even if the defence itself does not rely on them. In fact, one cannot leave to a possibly inexperienced defence alone the burden of ensuring respect for the fundamental procedural rule which prohibits the concealment of documents or evidence. . . . Cases where evidence has been hidden from the trial court have left bitter memories in the history of justice.

Judge Pettiti thought that the Court of Appeal ought to have remitted the case to a jury to reconsider the evidence. It could be argued that in finding no violation of Article 6 the Court was influenced by evidence of the applicant's confession. Bearing in mind, however, the Court's repeated refusals to examine the value of evidence—a matter which it says must be left to the domestic courts—and to concentrate solely on the procedure involved, this would seem incompatible with the Court's own approach. It seems more likely that the Court puts substantial emphasis on the failure of the defence to complain about the disclosure before the Court of Appeal.

The possibility of curing trial process defects on appeal was again at issue in *Atlan v United Kingdom*.[91] Here the prosecution had repeatedly denied the existence of evidence relating to an informer. The applicants' defence was that they had been falsely implicated in the importation of cocaine by an undercover customs and excise officer. No evidence relating to the informer was served on the defence or put before the judge, and under cross-examination the officers involved refused to confirm or deny that they had used an informer. After their conviction and prior to their appeal hearing the applicants were informed by the

---

[90] *Edwards v United Kingdom*, judgment of 16 Feb 1992, Series A no 247-B, (1993) 15 EHRR 417, para 39.
[91] *Atlan v United Kingdom*, no 36533/97, judgment of 19 June 2001, (2002) 34 EHRR 33, paras 44–46.

prosecution that unserved, unused material did in fact exist. The Court noted that it was clear that the 'repeated denials by the prosecution at first instance of the existence of further undisclosed relevant material, and their failure to inform the trial judge of the true position, were not consistent with the requirements of Article 6(1)'. The Court had then to decide whether this had been corrected by the *ex parte* procedure before the Court of Appeal which had also decided not to disclose the evidence to the applicants. The Court held unanimously that the failure of the prosecution to lay the evidence in question before the trial judge and to permit him to rule on the question of disclosure deprived the applicants of a fair trial. It noted that the trial judge was best placed to decide whether or not the non-disclosure of public interest immunity evidence would be unfairly prejudicial to the defence.[92] Moreover, in this case, had the trial judge seen the evidence he might have chosen a very different form of words for his summing up to the jury. Thus the failure to lay the evidence before him and to allow him to rule on the question of disclosure deprived the applicants of a fair trial. This case seems to make it clear that, if the prosecution wants to withhold evidence contrary to the requirements of adversarial procedure, it has an obligation to put this evidence before the trial judge. Failure to do so will be incompatible with the procedural requirements of a fair trial. Having said that and following the ruling in *Edwards*, the possibility of a Court of Appeal being held to have 'remedied' such a violation cannot be ruled out.

(iii) Opportunity to Comment on the Other Side's Submissions

The requirement of adversarial proceedings also requires that the defence have a genuine opportunity to challenge all the evidence before the court. In *Reinhardt and Slimane-Kaïd v France*,[93] the applicants' complaint related to the appeal procedure before the Court of Cassation. The reporting judge's file, including his report and one or more draft judgments, had been communicated to the Avocat Général but not to the applicant, who had been informed only of the recommendations set out in the report. The Commission held not only that this imbalance was incompatible with the equality of arms, but also that the violation of the right to a fair trial was accentuated by the fact that the Avocat Général's submissions had not been communicated to the applicants, who had thus had no 'genuine opportunity' to comment on the submissions, contrary to the principle of adversarial procedure.[94] The Court relied on the latter ground as the principal basis for its finding of a violation. The role of the Avocat Général was again of particular importance. The Government argued that the Avocat Général did not

---

[92] Citing *Rowe Davis v United Kingdom*, no 28901/95, ECHR 2000-II, (2000) 30 EHRR 1, para 65.
[93] Judgment of 31 Mar 1998, Reports 1998-II, 640, (1999) 28 EHRR 59. See the Commission's opinion, para 103.
[94] *Ibid*, at para 107.

act as a prosecutor; rather that he expressed his views in complete independence on the way in which the law should be construed and applied, and thus could not be seen to be a 'party' to the proceedings. In this case, the Court's opinion on this point is not entirely clear. The Court notes that the Avocat Général's role is to ensure that the law is correctly applied and he has the ability to influence the decision in favour of or against the applicant. Judge Pettiti in his concurring opinion suggests that the Court recognised that the Avocat Général was not a party to the proceedings *per se* but 'a "party" joined to the criminal proceedings'. In fact, whether the Avocat Général is explicitly referred to as a party to the proceedings or not is of little relevance, because it is implicitly clear from the Court's approach that he could not be characterised as a neutral observer, and was thus construed as an opposing party. Judge Vilhjálmsson, dissenting, seems to suggest that the Court misunderstood the role of the Avocat Général, noting:

> The rules on the procedure before the Court of Cassation have been developed over a long period of time. I find them balanced, finely tuned and unbiased, even if they are somewhat foreign to lawyers from other European countries with other traditions and systems.

The dissenting opinion of Judge DeMeyer is also of interest. He too was unimpressed by the Court's judgment that the right to a fair trial had been violated. He noted that the Court had always accepted that 'in Court systems such as those in France and Belgium, members of the Principal State Counsel's Office at the Court of Cassation perform their duties entirely independently, impartially and objectively and save, in exceptional circumstances, cannot in any way be considered as parties to appeals to the Court of Cassation'. Despite this the Court had 'on more than one occasion condemned their presence at deliberations and the fact that they address the Court last without communicating their submissions to the parties beforehand'. Judge De Meyer's opinion is worth quoting at length, because of the strength of feeling it conveys towards what he perceives to be an irrational and unnecessary

> In the instant case the Court also disapproves of the practice whereby, with a view to the hearing, the advocate-general is given the reporting judge's reports and draft judgements, but the parties are not. What harm lies in these practices? In what way do they adversely affect the fairness of the proceedings? Surely representatives of State Counsel's Office at the Court of Cassation are, like the judge of that court and in particular the reporting judges, independent, impartial and objective, both in law and in practice? Should they not be so presumed until proved otherwise? . . . The fact is that neither the reporting judge nor the advocate-general can be dissociated from the court itself. The reporting judge's report and draft judgment and the advocate-general's submissions remain independent of the debate between the parties, as they form part of the process of preparation of the decision, in readiness for the actual deliberations. The fact that the reporting judge and the advocate-general communicate these documents to each other before the hearing without informing the parties of their content does not in any way adversely affect the fairness of the proceedings. The position here is very difficult from cases concerning the observations of a 'prosecuting authority', such as, in the present

case, the Chartres public prosecutor or the public prosecutor attached to the Versailles Court of Appeal, or in the *Bulut* case, the Attorney-general attached to the Austrian Supreme Court, as it is obvious that the prosecution cannot be allowed to bring anything to the court's attention without the defence being informed.

Judge De Meyer's impassioned plea for the Court actually to examine both the procedure and the effect on the applicant's trial is rightly ignored. It would be impossible to reconcile this with the case law on adversarial procedure and equality of arms. The Court has firmly acknowledged a procedural model of fairness during the trial which does not have any room for parties other than the prosecution, defence and the judiciary. Any party which is involved in the proceedings and which could theoretically negatively affect the defence's case is thus perceived to be allied to the prosecution and to be on the other side.

The decision in *Reinhardt and Slimane-Kaïd* reflects an approach which has been applied by the Court in a number of judgments. In *Borgers v Belgium*, as mentioned above,[95] the Court found a violation of the equality of arms when a member of the Public Prosecutor's office, though independent of the prosecution, made submissions suggesting that the accused's appeal be dismissed to which the accused was unable to reply. Similarly, in *Kress v France* the Court found a violation where a Commissioner who made submissions unfavourable to the applicant's case was able to attend the deliberations with the judges.[96] In *Bulut v Austria*, the applicant complained that after he had lodged his appeal with the Court, the Attorney General submitted observations (*croquis*) which were not served on the defence.[97] Citing *Borgers* and *Lobo Machado v Portugal*, the Court noted that while the objectivity of the Attorney General was unquestionable, his opinion could not be regarded as neutral. This was particularly so in this case as the Attorney General's office was responsible for bringing the prosecution. Thus Article 6(1) required that the rights of the defence and the principle of equality of arms be respected. The Government argued that the submissions were of a purely procedural nature and stated that it was appropriate to deal with the appeal under a section of the criminal code. It contained no arguments as to the merits and thus there were no new elements for the defence to comment on. This argument was however rejected by the Court, which found Article 6(1) to have been violated. It held:

> In the present criminal appeal, the submission of the observations allowed the Attorney-General to take up a clear position as to the applicant's appeal, a position which was not communicated to the defence and to which the defence could not reply. In any event, as the Commission rightly pointed out, the principle of equality of arms

---

[95] *Borgers v Belgium*, judgment of 30 Oct 1991, Series A no 214-B, (1993) 15 EHRR 92, paras 28–29. See also *Apeh Üldözötteinek Szövetsége and others v Hungary*, no 32367/96, ECHR 2000-X, 361, (2002) 34 EHRR 34.

[96] *Kress v France*, no 39594/98, ECHR 2001-VI, 41.

[97] *Bulut v Austria*, judgment of 22 Feb 1996, Reports 1996-II, 346, (1997) 24 EHRR 84.

does not depend on further quantifiable unfairness flowing from a procedural inequality. It is a matter for the defence to assess whether a submissions deserves a reaction. It is therefore unfair for the prosecution to make submissions to a court without the knowledge of the defence.[98]

These cases demonstrate clearly that the Strasbourg authorities apply a strict test both in relation to the opportunity to comment on the submissions of the other side, and to the constitution of the term 'other side'. The Court will not conduct a substantial examination of whether or not someone else involved in the proceedings was neutral. It appears now, in criminal proceedings at least, that any parties to the process who are not either affiliated to the defence or independent members of the judiciary will be deemed to be members of the other side, and their involvement in the proceedings will precipitate the application of the principle of adversariality. Moreover the Court does not make any attempt to weigh up the nature of the submissions made and their effect on the defence's case, simply stating that adversarial procedure means that it is for the defence to decide whether the submissions are relevant for it or not.

In *Kuopila v Finland*, for instance, the applicant received a copy of a statement, which she referred to as 'vital evidence', only after the proceedings on the merits had come to an end.[99] Although this statement was given to the court by the prosecutor the court did not rely on it in its reasoning. Nevertheless the Court felt that this was not decisive from the point of view of the applicant's right to adversarial proceedings. The Court noted that the prosecutor had expressed his opinion to the court on the relevance of the report, thereby intending to influence the court's judgment. The Court thus considered that fairness required that the applicant, too, should have had the chance to assess the evidence and to comment on it. Thus the Court held that 'the procedure did not enable the applicant to participate properly and in conformity with the principle of equality of arms in the proceedings before the court'. Conversely, the need for adversarial procedure will arise only in the event that the applicant's adversary uses documents or submissions against him. Similarly, where the applicant has the opportunity to challenge the submissions or to examine the files and fails to do so, there will be no breach of either the adversarial principle or the equality of arms.[100]

The adversarial proceedings requirement seems therefore to be not only the basis of the 'rights of the defence' but also the product of a specific understanding of criminal proceedings, with its roots in the nineteenth century developments as governed by the accusatorial trinity and as comprising two distinct phases: the public trial and the investigative pre-trial phase. These defence rights must therefore be seen not only as guaranteeing the autonomy of the accused, but also as an important aspect upholding the institutional basis of criminal proceedings.

---

[98]   *Ibid*, at para 49.
[99]   *Kuopila v Finland*, no 27752/95, judgment of 27 Apr 2000, (2001) 33 EHRR 25, para 38.
[100]   *Bendenoun v France*, judgment of 24 Feb 1994, Series A no 284, (1994) 18 EHRR 54, para 52. See also *Schuler-Zgraggen v Switzerland*, judgment of 24 June 1993, Series A no 263, (1993) 16 EHRR 405, para 52.

F The Relationship Between the Defence and the Prosecution

The Court has interpreted the fairness requirement in Article 6(1) as requiring not only that there is a balance of procedural opportunities between those involved in the criminal process but also that the principle of adversarial procedure is recognised. It is clear, too, that the adversarial procedure requirement has an autonomous meaning in the Convention's case law and thus differs substantially from notions expounded by commentators on comparative criminal procedure. It is clear, for instance, that there is no correlation between the doctrine applied by the Court and that applied by those engaged in the comparative criminal procedure debate. Both structurally and with regard to the content, the Court's approach is considerably narrower. Indeed in so far as it requires the presence of the accused and the guarantee that he or she be permitted to challenge the evidence of the prosecution and lead his or her own evidence, it embodies the principle of the right to be heard.

The problems that have been encountered in the case law are very similar to those issues that were addressed in the nineteenth century, and primarily relate to the relationship between the defence and the prosecution. In those countries where there is a resolutely partial prosecution, there is a danger that prosecutorial over-zealousness could lead to the suppression of evidence, thus endangering the safety of the conviction. Meanwhile, in those systems where the investigation and prosecution authorities are supposedly neutral, the primary concerns involve their institutional partiality and the potential for this to interfere with the verdict. In spite of this the Court's case law on the need for adversarial procedure—a principle seemingly bound up in notions of culturally defined legal principles—has produced surprisingly few significant challenges. Indeed, the majority of the cases have concerned a specific type of appeals procedure followed by Austria, Belgium, France, Poland and Portugal, or by the prosecution's failure in England to disclose important information to the defence. With the exception of these areas, however, the Court's 'adversarial procedure' and 'equality of arms' principles seem to have been, with an almost disappointing lack of controversy, accepted as applicable throughout Europe.

The explanation for the uncontroversial adoption of the adversarial procedure and equality of arms requirements is quite simple. By the end of the nineteenth century the majority of European countries, including England, France and Germany, had accepted an understanding of criminal proceedings as based on two opposing parties and an independent judge. Insofar as Stavros' criticism that such a notion is 'far removed from the inquisitorial organization of the criminal trial in most continental systems' where the prosecution, 'being part of the judiciary, is traditionally seen as the accessory of the court striving with it for the discovery of the truth and not for victory over the accused', implies that the prosecution is not a party to the proceedings it must be rejected.[101]

Broadly speaking, most European systems of criminal procedure can accommodate such a distinction at the trial stage (in the sense of the main hearing before the judge charged with determining the guilt or innocence of the accused) itself. Whether or not the prosecution is perceived to be acting with the Court in the quest for the truth or not is actually of very little relevance. Any notion of co-operation between prosecution and judge at trial has been firmly rejected by the Court, as it was by the nineteenth century European jurists, in favour of a distinct separation of the roles of investigating and judging.[102] In fact, at the trial stage itself, every system of criminal procedure in western Europe makes provision for those charged with criminal offences to reply to the accusations levelled against them; and every European legal system claims to have a judiciary impartial of the parties which controls the proceedings and either decides on the guilt or innocence of the accused, or regulates the decision-making body.

There are some problems, however, even at the trial stage, with such a distinction, especially with regard to the role of experts in the proceedings. If there is deemed to be such a strong dividing line between the sides, where does the expert fit in? He or she is certainly not a 'judge' and could conceivably be seen as someone giving evidence against the defence. In a system such as those to be found in Scotland or England and Wales, where both sides have the opportunity to call experts, it is clear that the experts for the prosecution shall be treated as witnesses for the prosecution. Where, however, experts are appointed by the Court, as is the case in a number of jurisdictions, and where they are supposed to be 'neutral', their position becomes a little more complicated. In *Bönisch v Austria*,[103] the applicant complained of an inequality in treatment between the defence's expert, who was treated simply as a witness, and the court-appointed expert, who had significantly greater status. Here the Court invoked the equality of arms and unanimously found a violation, not on the basis of a lack of witness independence but on the basis that, as the court-appointed expert had prompted the bringing of a prosecution, he was more like a witness for the prosecution, and consequently treating him differently from the defence expert constituted a violation of the equality of arms.[104] The Commission had additionally found a violation of Article 6(1) on the basis that Austrian law provided that the expert would, in the event that the accused was convicted, receive a financial bonus![105] The Court however did not examine this issue.

In a later case,[106] also against Austria, the Austrian court had refused to hear any expert other than the one appointed by the court. The Commission found a

---

[101] S Stavros, *The Guarantees for Accused Persons Under Article 6 of the European Convention on Human Rights* (Dordrecht, Kluwer Law, 1993).

[102] See Ch 2.

[103] *Bönisch v Austria*, judgment of 6 May 1985, Series A no 92, (1987) 9 EHRR 191.

[104] *Ibid*, at paras 32–35.

[105] This provision has since been abolished.

[106] *Brandstetter v Austria*, judgment of 28 Aug 1991, Series A no 211, (1993) 15 EHRR 378.

violation on the basis that, as in *Boenisch*, the expert belonged to the same institute which had raised the initial suspicions against the defendant; as such he had to be considered as a witness for the prosecution.[107] The Court however disagreed. It applied the test set out in *Hauschildt*[108] for the independence of the judge: 'what is decisive is whether the doubts raised by appearances can be held objectively justified'.[109] The Court felt that such objective justifications were lacking and that the fact that the expert was based at the same institute as the person who had raised the suspicions does not justify fears that he will be unable to act with proper neutrality: '[t]o hold otherwise would in many cases place unacceptable limits on the possibility for courts to obtain expert evidence'.[110]

The Court also attached weight to the fact that the defence had not challenged the appointment of the expert at the first two hearings. Moreover it noted that '[t]he right to a fair trial does not require that a national court should appoint, at the request of the defence, further experts when the opinion of the court-appointed expert supports the prosecution case'.[111] Neither the approach of the court in *Boenisch* nor that in *Brandstetter* appears particularly satisfactory. In *Boenisch* the Court puts the emphasis on the equality of arms and the ability of the defence to call its own witness on equal terms to counter effectively the 'prosecution' witness. This does not sit at all well in a system where the court appoints one witness. On the other hand in *Brandstetter*, the Court applies a lesser test of independence than that used for ensuring the impartiality of the judge, ignores the clear appearance of a lack of impartiality on the part of the expert and rejects the defence's right to call a counter expert. In view of the fact that the role of the expert will differ substantially in different legal systems, ie depending on whether he or she is perceived to be partial or a neutral appointee of the court, the court should adopt an approach that takes this into account. Where the expert acts as a prosecution witness, the defence should be given the chance to call its own expert. Where, however, the court appoints a neutral expert, this expert should be required to fulfil the same guarantees of independence and impartiality that would be required of a judge. The failure of the Court openly to make this distinction between different legal systems leads to unfair proceedings and to an inevitably incoherent case law.

G Fairness and Implied Procedural Forms

It would seem that far from espousing a procedurally neutral version of fairness, the Court has developed an account of it which is closely related to a particular

---

[107] *Ibid*, at para 116.
[108] *Ibid*, at para 48.
[109] *Ibid*, at para 44.
[110] *Ibid*, at paras 44–45.
[111] *Ibid*, at para 46.

understanding of criminal proceedings. These proceedings involve partial prosecutors, independent and impartial adjudicators and accused persons assisted by
counsel and equipped with various procedural opportunities to counter the
prosecution's allegations. In view of the nineteenth century developments, and
despite apparent proclamations to the contrary from some quarters, this can only
be viewed as unsurprising. The Strasbourg authorities seem to have, at least to a
certain extent, come to accept Vargha's notion of the accusatorial trinity, and as
such the European procedural tradition. By rejecting all applications claiming a
violation of Article 6 based on the partiality of the investigating authorities, for
instance, they have ensured that any notion of impartial (in the sense of Article 6)
investigators or prosecutors has no place in the European criminal procedural
order.[112] This is rejected by Stavros,[113] but can be simply rationalised if one
accepts the Court's construction of a criminal trial in which the investigators are
automatically assumed to be partial to be an automatic and indeed consistent
extension of the principle of adversarial procedure and opposing sides applied
during the trial phase into the pre-trial phase.

Its acceptance of a distinct, and relatively inflexible, procedural model, comprising opposing sides as being the only mechanism for guaranteeing 'a fair trial',
has posed few problems during the trial phase. But it is to be doubted whether
this unanimity can be said to have been extended to include the transfer of such
notions into the pre-trial phase. Indeed the somewhat ambivalent approach to
the regulation of the investigative phase leaves the impression that acceptance of
the European procedural tradition is instinctive rather than deliberate.

Essentially the Court's concept of fairness, tied as it is to the 'rights' of the
accused, is not, and could never hope to be, 'procedurally neutral'. Inevitably the
extent of the rights of the accused will depend significantly on the manner in
which they are to be applied. In this sense the 'fairness' of the proceedings will
inevitably be tied to the form of criminal proceedings. Despite this there has been
no express acknowledgement of the relationship between the Court's notion of
fairness and the form of the proceedings. That this has not proven more
problematic is at least partly due to the pervasive reach of the nineteenth century
reforms. Many of the institutional aspects of fairness identified by the nineteenth
century jurists are expressly set out in Article 6, notably the requirements that
trials be oral, public and supervised by an impartial judge.

It is notable, however, that the issue which proved especially controversial in
the nineteenth century, namely the treatment of evidence during the investigation and at trial, continues, as we will see in the next chapter, to pose considerable
problems. While the case law suggests that the Court has reconciled itself to

---

[112] *Schertenleib v Switzerland*, App no 8339/79, (1980) 23 DR 137; *X v Germany*, App no 6541/74,
decision of 9 July 1975, (1975) 3 DR 86; *X v X*, App no 11669/85, (1987) 54 DR 95; *Crociani and others
v Italy*, App nos 8603/79, 8722/79, 8723/79 and 8729/79, (1980) 22 DR 147.

[113] S Stavros, *The Guarantees for Accused Persons Under Article 6 of the European Convention on
Human Rights* (Dordrecht, Kluwer Law, 1993) at 71.

applying a defined procedural structure in the context of the trial, it has continually shied away from setting out a comprehensive understanding of the role of the pre-trial phase. It has shown itself unwilling to insist on the public, oral trial as the only acceptable forum for determining the evidence and the charge. At the same time, it has proven slow to impose restrictions on the regulation of the investigation phase. The investigation continues to play a shadowy and ambiguous role in criminal proceedings, undermining both doctrinal certainty and the principle of fairness in Article 6.

As we will see in the next chapter, the Court has faced considerable difficulties in its attempt to propagate such a vision, which in turn has resulted in doctrinal uncertainty in relation to the principles underlying fairness in criminal proceedings.

5

The Structure of the 'Trial' in Article 6 ECHR

A Introduction

IN CONSIDERING THE definition of the fair trial there can be little doubt that the emphasis has been on determining the extent of the rights of the defence rather than on considering the form which the trial should take. Both the work of the nineteenth century jurists and the Court's definition of fairness in Article 6(1) demonstrate however that 'fairness', in the sense of the procedural rights of the defence, is closely connected to the institutional and procedural form of the proceedings. The determination of what constitutes a 'trial' is thus central to achieving an understanding of the Court's approach to fairness. In accordance with the European criminal procedural tradition, Article 6 sets out an understanding of the public and impartially adjudicated trial as the essence of criminal proceedings. This has been reinforced by the case law of the Court, which has interpreted the specific fairness requirement in Article 6(1) as requiring equality of procedural opportunities between the parties to the proceedings, namely the defence and the prosecution. The definition of fairness, far from being generally applicable in different procedural systems, is in fact based on a particular understanding of criminal proceedings.

This is not entirely uncontroversial. It is fair to say that there are many modern commentators in Europe who oppose the idea that European criminal proceedings could have a common institutional basis.[1] It is not uncommon to find reference to the fact that the term 'trial' in Article 6 is often translated in a broader way than its English usage might suggest. The German term *Verfahren*, for instance, is understood as referring to the 'proceedings' and not just to the trial, which would be translated rather as the *Hauptverhandlung*. The Swiss criminal procedure lawyer Schmid argues that, despite this inexact translation, Article 6 is orientated towards the criminal trial and not to the pre-trial and

---

[1] See Ch 1.

investigation stages.[2] His vision of trial is confined to the examination and determination of a cause by a judicial tribunal. Although this argument is quite at odds with the case law of the Court, in which the difficulties of separating the trial from the proceedings as a whole are often emphasised,[3] there may in fact be grounds for suggesting that the broad approach adopted by the Court has led to inconsistency and doctrinal uncertainty.

A typical example of the way in which the Court frames its recognition of the importance of the earlier stages of the proceedings can be found in the *Pisano* case:

> Certainly the primary purpose of Article 6 as far as criminal matters are concerned is to ensure a fair trial by a 'tribunal' competent to determine 'any criminal charge', but it does not follow that Article 6 has no application to pre-trial proceedings... Other requirements of Article 6—especially of paragraph 3—may also be relevant before a case is sent for trial if and in so far as the fairness of the trial is likely to be seriously prejudiced by an initial failure to comply with them.[4]

The approach of the Court is to try to fit the procedural guarantees developed in the context of the trial into the investigation proceedings, rather than setting out principles for the regulation of the investigation phase and determining which opportunities the defence should have in the earlier phases of the proceedings. Despite developing defence participatory rights on the basis of the public, oral and immediate trial, the Court has proven reluctant to insist on the trial as the correct forum for the examination and determination of the evidence in criminal proceedings. It is true that some express reference to the importance of immediacy can be found in the case law,[5] but such allusions to the principle represent the exception rather than the rule.

It is nevertheless clear that as Article 6 stands it envisages that the principal examination of the evidence will occur at 'the trial' itself, fairness dictates that this is possible. If, however, such examinations are moved outwith the trial itself and take place instead, for instance, during the pre-trial phase, then this has an

---

[2] '*Wie der Name schon besagt, ist das Prinzip von fair Trial an sich auf das gerichtliche Verfahren, also nicht das Ermittlungs- und Untersuchungsstadium, zugeschnitten, und diese Beschränkung gilt nach der Praxis der Europäischen Menschenrechtskommission auch für die Anwendbarkeit von EMRK Ziff 1*': N Schmid, *Strafprozessrecht*, 4th edn (Zurich, Schulthess, 2004) at 78, para 235. See also the decision of the Swiss Federal Court: BGE 106 IV 86.

[3] Fairness at the trial will be insufficient if important aspects of the process have already occurred unfairly at an earlier stage in the proceedings. See eg *John Murray v United Kingdom*, judgment of 8 Feb 1996, Reports 1996-I, 30, (1996) 22 EHRR 29. Conversely, where unfairness has occurred, the Court may find no violation providing that there has been rectification of defects at a later instance: see eg *Edwards v United Kingdom*, judgment of 16 Dec 1992, Series A no 247-B, (1993) 15 EHRR 417.

[4] *Pisano v Italy*, App no 36732/97, judgment of 27 July 2000, (2002) 34 EHRR 27, para 27.

[5] Eg *PK v Finland*, App no 37442/97, decision of 9 July 2002: '[t]he Court considers that an important element of fair criminal proceedings is also the possibility of the accused to be confronted with the witness in the presence of the judge who ultimately decides the case. Such a principle of immediacy is an important guarantee in criminal proceedings in which the observations made by the court about the demeanour and credibility of a witness may have important consequences for the accused'.

effect not only on the structure of the process but also on the proper functioning of the principle of fairness. Instead of upholding the notion of fairness by insisting on a rigid approach to defining the trial, the Court has chosen to allow states a certain flexibility in organising their criminal processes, but in doing so it has struggled to find a method of applying its notion of fairness outwith the 'traditional' scope of application of the trial.

In this chapter it will be argued that the failure of the Court to outline its conception of the correct forum for the examination and determination of the evidence means that it is applying different standards of fairness in different jurisdictions.[6] Further, it will be argued that the solution which it has adopted in an attempt to rectify this situation has contributed to the incoherence rather than alleviating it. While there has been acceptance in principle of the nineteenth century conception of criminal proceedings as comprising determinative trials and partial investigations, insufficient attention has been paid to the type of regulation which is required in the investigation phase. The reluctance of the Strasbourg authorities to insist on the application of adversarial principles during the investigation stage gives rise to some serious tensions as to the theoretical ability of the provision to set out consistent principles for regulating fair trials. Just as in the nineteenth century, legislatures and courts proved unwilling to strengthen the participatory rights of the defence in the investigation for fear of compromising its effectiveness, so too have the Strasbourg authorities proven reluctant either to afford the defence significant rights during this phase or to reject the investigation as a forum for the challenging of the evidence. Instead, they have chosen to emphasise the power of the privilege against self-incrimination as a means of upholding the rights of the accused in the investigation. The under-regulation of the investigation phase however puts severe strain on the accusatorial conception of the trial. If evidence is heard and challenged solely in a non-public forum which is not supervised by an impartial judge, it must be questioned to what extent the 'trial rights' in Article 6(1) can still be said to have application and meaning. This necessarily raises questions of legitimacy in relation both to the trial and to the Court's notion of fairness. In order to demonstrate the tension in the Court's case law and the difficult relationship between the trial and the investigative phases of the proceedings, two distinct aspects of its case law will be examined. First, the right of those accused of criminal offences to challenge the evidence of witnesses testifying against them and, secondly, the development of the case law on the privilege against self-incrimination

---

[6] This uneven application of the Convention guarantees contradicts the intentions set out in the Preamble to the Convention, in which it is stated: '[c]onsidering that this Declaration aims at securing the universal and effective recognition and observance of the Rights therein declare…'.

B The Defence's Right to Challenge Witness Evidence

Inconsistencies in relation to the application of the defence's participatory rights are especially apparent in relation to the Court's case law on the right to challenge witnesses under Article 6(3)(d). This provision is unique in the sense that it is the only provision in the Convention which expressly refers to the challenging, determination or regulation of evidence.[7] Moreover the regulation of witness evidence is complicated by the fact that the point at which the examination takes place differs throughout Europe. The approach of the Court to witness evidence clearly shows the problems that it has encountered in regulating fairness when vitally important aspects of the process precede the hearing and the determination of the charge. The problems are partly a result of the text of the Convention, in that there is no express regulation of the 'investigation' phase, but they are also due to the longstanding failure of European courts and legislatures to acknowledge the significance of the investigative phase and to recognise the fundamental importance of the institutional form of the proceedings for the rights of the defence. The problem in this regard relates generally to the treatment of evidence and to the correct surroundings for its examination and determination. The case law relating to Article 6(3)(d) will be examined in order to demonstrate how the Court's notion of fairness has been affected by its failure to set out the institutional form of European criminal proceedings, and in particular the nature of the forum for the determination of the evidence. On the basis of this the Court's approach will be assessed in order to determine to what extent it has led to the arbitrary application of guarantees which were meant to be universally applied.

C Witness Evidence in Europe: An Overview

Until recently, any suggestion that there could be considered to be a common European law of evidence would have been met with extreme scepticism. While in England evidence law is an independent discipline defined as 'a series of disparate exceptions to a single principle of freedom of proof',[8] in the Netherlands the commentaries do not know concepts such as admissibility, relevance and materiality.[9] Whereas in France 'evidence is generally not excludable unless

---

[7] The regulation of witness evidence is an ideal subject for analysis precisely because it is expressly regulated in the Convention, whereas other subjects that would also be of interest, such as the questioning of accused persons during the investigation phase, are not expressly regulated and thus are less discussed in the case law.

[8] W Twining, *Rethinking Evidence: Exploratory Essays* (Oxford, Blackwell, 1990) at 178.

[9] See JF Nijboer, 'Common Law Tradition in Evidence Scholarship Observed from a Continental Perspective' (1993) 41 *American Journal of Comparative Law* 299.

the violation has caused "harm to the interests of the party it concerns" or affects public interests',[10] in Scotland there are numerous grounds for excluding evidence.[11] Each legal system, defined by its own tradition, has a different approach to tackling the regulation of proof, whether it be by regulating the presentation of evidence during the trial or by controlling the subsequent decision-making process.[12] These differences are so obvious and so irrefutable that any discussion of standardisation or harmonisation in Europe seems so unlikely as to be bordering on the absurd. Yet, although indisputable differences exist, particularly in relation to the admissibility of evidence, the Court has had to consider evidential matters, at least insofar as these relate to the procedural opportunities of the defence to challenge and present evidence. While commentators often focus on questions of admissibility[13]—this terminology has been rejected by the Court, which has instead focussed on the way in which the evidence is 'used'.[14] The clear implication is that systems that exclude evidence at an early stage, providing that the aim of this is to protect the defence,[15] are just as valid as those which provide for the filtering of evidence by a judge at a later stage, and both methods have the potential to secure compatibility with the demands of 'a fair trial'.

The Court's approach to evidential matters can only be described as cautious. It frequently stresses that the assessment of evidence is primarily a matter for the domestic courts rather than the Strasbourg authorities. The Commission has noted that Art 6 'does not as such prescribe rules of evidence and in particular rules on the admissibility and probative value of evidence, which are essentially matters for the national law'.[16] Thus, it has no capacity 'to decide whether or not domestic courts have correctly assessed evidence' but only 'whether evidence for

---

[10]   RS Frase, 'Introduction' in GL Kock and RS Frase (eds), *The French Code of Criminal Procedure* (Littleton, Colo, FB Rothman,1988) at 16. For further comparisons in relation to the 'exclusion of evidence' see M King, 'Security, Scale, Form and Function: The Search for Truth and the Exclusion of Evidence in Adversarial and Inquisitorial Justice Systems' (2001/02) 12 *International Legal Perspective* 185.

[11]   Including eg unreliability, tendency to mislead or public policy grounds. See F Raitt, *Evidence*, 3rd edn (Edinburgh, W Green/Sweet & Maxwell, 2001).

[12]   See JF Nijboer, 'Common Law Tradition in Evidence Scholarship Observed from a Continental Perspective' (1993) 41 *American Journal of Comparative Law* 299 at 302.

[13]   See eg K Reid, *A Practitioner's Guide to the European Convention on Human Rights* (London, Sweet & Maxwell, 2004) at 85; D Harris, M O'Boyle and C Warbrick, *Law of the European Convention on Human Rights* (London, Butterworths, 1995) at 210; B Emmerson and A Ashworth, *Human Rights and Criminal Justice* (London, Sweet & Maxwell, 2001) at 417. Note however that the obsession with admissibility is predominantly and unsurprisingly confined to the UK commentators. Dutch writers do not mention admissibility: P Van Dijk and GJH van Hoof, *Theory and Practice of the European Convention on Human Rights* (The Hague, Kluwer Law, 1998).

[14]   S Summers, 'The Right to Confrontation after Crawford v Washington: A "Continental European" Perspective' (2004) 2 *International Commentary on Evidence* 1 at 2–4.

[15]   Obviously prosecutorial exclusion is not looked on favourably by the Court. In *Edwards v United Kingdom*, Series A no 247-B, (1993) 15 EHRR 417, the Court held that the prosecution is obliged 'to disclose to the defence all material for or against the accused'.

[16]   See *X v Belgium*, App no 8876/80, decision of 16 Oct 1980, (1980) 23 DR 233 and *X v Belgium*, App no 7450/76, decision of 28 Feb 1977, (1977) 9 DR 108.

and against the accused has been presented in such a manner and the proceedings in general have been conducted in such a way' as to comply with the demands of a fair trial.[17] In the frequently cited judgment in *Schenk v Switzerland* the Court ruled that while 'Article 6 of the Convention guarantees the right to a fair trial, it does not lay down any rules on the admissibility of evidence as such', which is instead 'primarily a matter for regulation under national law'.[18] The Strasbourg authorities have thus made it clear that the role of deciding what evidence should be admitted falls outwith the scope of the Convention and is retained by the national authorities. The Court seeks in this regard to rely on the trial judges of the member states to uphold the fairness requirement.

Although the Court's reticence in this regard might be seen as understandable in view of the complicated nature of the task of deciding what evidence should have been admitted or how this evidence should have been weighed, there is no doubt that the development of a coherent strategy in this regard is essential to the protection of the procedural opportunities of the defence.

The Court is not entirely silent on the subject of evidential issues, however it approaches these in a very specific manner. It is primarily interested in its vision of fairness, which requires that the defence have an adequate opportunity to challenge all the evidence against it. The distinction between adversarial and inquisitorial criminal procedural traditions is frequently commented on by academics, but the reality is that European countries, and even sometimes jurisdictions within countries, differ substantially in the way that they regulate evidence, even though the principles underlying the rules may be similar. Consequently, the notion of ensuring fair treatment of evidence and proof takes on a disproportionate importance for those interested in how the Court reconciles procedural systems within its jurisdiction. Regulation by one set of rules is particularly difficult because the way and the point in time at which the evidence is collected, examined and adjudicated differs in almost every legal jurisdiction. These differences relate essentially to the treatment of all evidence, but witness evidence has proven to be particularly controversial.

Witness testimony, when it exists, has traditionally been considered to be one of the most important sources of evidence for the determination of the guilt or innocence of someone charged with a criminal offence. The corroborating evidence of two witnesses was, in several European jurisdictions, deemed to be sufficient to establish a finding of guilt.[19] In spite of the general movement in the

---

[17] *X v Belgium*, App no 8876/80, citing *X v United Kingdom*, App no 6172/73, decision of 7 July 1975, (1975) 3 DR 77 at 78. See also the report of the Commission in the *Nielsen v Denmark*, App no 343/57, (1961) 4 YB 494, at para 52.

[18] Judgment of 12 July 1988, Series A no 140, (1991) 13 EHRR 242, para 45 ff..

[19] See *Morton v HM Advocate* 1938 JC 50, 55 where Lord Justice-Clerk Aitchison noted that 'no person can be convicted of a crime or a statutory offence except where the legislature otherwise directs, unless there is evidence of at least two witnesses, implicating the person with the commission of the crime or offence with which he is charged'. See also JH Langbein, *Prosecuting Crime in the Renaissance: England, Germany, France: Europe and England and the Ancien Régime* (Cambridge, Mass,

nineteenth century towards oral and immediate proceedings, every European legal system contains provisions that allow for departures from these principles, albeit to varying extents. Even in those legal systems such as Scotland or England, which provide as a general rule for the examination of evidence to take place at trial, there are exceptions to the requirement that the witness appear in court. Written statements will sometimes be allowed if, for instance, the witness has died, providing that the trial judge believes the admission of the evidence to be in the interests of justice.[20] There are moreover a limited number of exceptions to the requirement that witnesses give evidence in person at trial and moves towards weakening the principle, in any form, are often accompanied by substantial debate. Reformers in the United Kingdom have recently succeeded in securing concessions for some types of witnesses, notably children[21] and victims of sexual offences,[22] after a series of studies showed the rigours of the trial process to be particularly distressing for them. Such laws, which also exist in many European legal systems, either enable witnesses to give evidence by other means, such as a video link, or prevent some types of questioning at trial. They were not enacted in response to any perceived improvement in the taking or hearing of evidence, but primarily in order to protect various categories of vulnerable witnesses. Nevertheless they must be construed as representing a move away from the traditional reliance on oral testimony at trial.

Other criminal procedural systems, however, do not place such emphasis on oral testimony. Dutch criminal proceedings have a different basis, described by Beijer, Cobley and Klip as being 'to a large extent shaped as an official inquiry rather than a contest between two parties who are responsible for bringing out the evidence'.[23] As a general rule it is rare for witnesses to appear in

---

Harvard University Press, 1974) at 157; JH Langbein, *Torture and the Law of Proof* (Chicago, Ill, University of Chicago Press, 1977) at 5–8. In modern times the doctrine of corroboration requires two independent pieces of evidence, neither of which has to be in the form of witness testimony: see F Raitt, *Evidence*, 3rd edn (Edinburgh, W Green/Sweet & Maxwell, 2001) at 143: '[t]he reference to testimony must not be taken literally, since what is required is two independent items of evidence which may not necessarily be in the form of testimony'. By the end of the 19th century, the rules on corroboration in 'continental Europe' had been abolished: see, eg, J Glaser, *Beiträge zur Lehre vom Beweis im Strafprozeß* (Leipzig, Duncker & Humblot, 1883) at 23–33.

[20] Ss 23–26 of the Criminal Justice Act 1988 (England); For Scotland see s 259 of the Criminal Procedure (Scotland) Act 1995 which, together with the common law, regulates the rules concerning hearsay (for the statements of dead witnesses see *HM Advocate v Irving* 1978 JC 28).

[21] See s 271 of the Criminal Procedure (Scotland) Act 1995 as substituted by the Crime and Punishment (Scotland) Act 1997, s 29.

[22] In Scotland s 1 of the Sexual Offences (Procedures and Evidence) (Scotland) Act 2002, as amended by s 15 of the Criminal Justice (Scotland) Act 2003, prevents people accused of rape from directly questioning the victim in court. Similar provisions exist in England—see eg s 34 of the Youth and Criminal Evidence Act 1999.

[23] A Beijer, C Cobley and A Klip, 'Witnesses and the Principle of Open Justice' in C Harding, P Fennell, N Jörg and B Swart, *Criminal Justice in Europe* (Oxford, Oxford University Press, 1995) at 287. The Dutch Supreme Court ruled in 1926 in favour of permitting hearsay evidence: Hoge Raad, 20 Dec 1926, [1927] NJ 85.

court;[24] instead they take part (in serious cases, at least[25]) in pre-trial 'confrontations', generally in the presence of the investigating judge and the defence, and their evidence is recorded and delivered to the court in the form of a written file. In some Swiss Cantons,[26] including Zurich, a type of District Attorney (*Bezirksanwalt*) is responsible for organising the pre-trial confrontations between the accused and the witnesses. These are then recorded in a file and submitted to the court. Although the defence can request that the judge or judges hear a witness at trial, this is rare in practice. Germany, meanwhile, has a quite different system which generally places the responsibility for deciding which witnesses should be heard on the judge. Witnesses are examined both at pre-trial confrontation hearings and again at trial. Both parties have however the right to demand, either by way of a *Beweisantrag*[27] or by having the witness directly subpoenaed by the bailiff,[28] that additional witnesses be heard. Although the main responsibility for questioning witnesses lies with the judge, both the defence and prosecution are entitled to ask additional questions.[29]

In view of the fact that these examples are just some of the systems employed by the various European jurisdictions in relation to witness evidence, it is clear that any system seeking to regulate this area must find a method of reconciling these differences, and in particular of deciding when and by whom witnesses should be questioned. The Court's approach to regulating the use of witness evidence and the attempt to reconcile this with its notion of 'fairness' have important implications not only for the definition of fairness, but also for the characterisation of 'the trial'. An examination of the case law in the field of witness evidence will demonstrate that in order to find a way to regulate all procedural systems, the Court has had to re-define the meaning of the 'trial', and has consequently struggled to maintain the sense and structure of the guarantee in Article 6.

---

[24]   Although the Dutch Criminal Code permits the defence to request that a witness be examined in Court (Art. 263 CCP), the court has discretion to refuse this request (Art. 280(4) CCP), **see** Beijer *et al*, above n23.

[25]   Estimated to comprise just 3% of cases that go to court. See authority cited in S Field, P Alldridge and N Jörg, 'The Control of the Police Investigation' in Harding *et al*, above n23, at 240.

[26]   Each Swiss canton has its own criminal procedure law, although a draft federal procedural code has been written by Professor Schmid, Emeritus Professor of Law at the University of Zurich, and is currently being redrafted by the Justice Ministry: see N Schmid, *Vorentwurf zu einer Schweizerischen Strafprozessordung* (Bern, Bundesamt für Justiz, 2001).

[27]   Para 244, ss 3-5 of the Code of Criminal Procedure; this can be rejected by the judge only if it is clearly irrelevant.

[28]   *Ibid*, para 220.

[29]   *Ibid*, para 240. On German criminal procedure generally see T Weigend, 'Germany' in CM Bradley, *Criminal Procedure: A Worldwide Study* (Durham NC, North Carolina Press, 1999) at 187; H Jung, 'The Criminal Process in the Federal Republic of Germany—An Overview' in M Delmas-Marty (ed), *The Criminal Process and Human Rights: Towards a European Consciousness* (Dordrecht, Martinus Nijhoff, 1995).

D   Regulating Witness Evidence: Article 6(3)(d)

Witness evidence is principally governed by Article 6(3)(d) which states that everyone 'charged with a criminal offence' has the right to:

> examine or have examined witnesses against him and to obtain the attendance and examination of witnesses on his behalf under the same conditions as witnesses against him.

The guarantee thus contains two principal aspects: the right to challenge the testimony of prosecution witnesses and the right of the defence to call its own witnesses. The first part of the guarantee, which clearly resembles the principle of cross-examination, naturally lends itself to interpretation in the light of the adversarial procedure requirement. The opportunity to challenge witness evidence is obviously a fundamental part of the right to challenge the prosecution's submissions. This provision looks to be a relatively straightforward guarantee but, in view of the different European mechanisms for recording witness testimony, it has become one of the most controversial provisions of the Convention.

(i)   What is an Adequate and Proper Opportunity to Challenge Witnesses?

In the *Kostovski* case, the Court noted that the possibility of challenging the witness evidence at the pre-trial stage would be compatible with Article 6(3)(d) only if the defence had had an 'adequate and proper opportunity' to exercise this right. Ascertaining what constitutes such an opportunity and what this qualification actually envisages is not entirely simple. Although the Court frequently uses the words 'adequate and proper' to describe the chance that the defence should have to examine witnesses, this is never clearly defined, and is supposed to be applied in the light of the circumstances of each case.

(a)   The Identity of the Witness

One of the most important components of an adequate chance to challenge witness evidence is that the defence know the identity of the witness. This may seem an obvious point, but in fact the problem of anonymous witnesses has arisen in a surprisingly large number of cases. Although Article 6 does not explicitly require the interests of witnesses to be taken into consideration, their:

> life, liberty or security of person may be at stake, as may interests coming generally within the ambit of Article 8 of the Convention. Such interests of witnesses and victims are in principle protected by other, substantive provisions of the Convention, which imply that Contracting States should organise their criminal proceedings in such a way that those interests are not unjustifiably imperilled. Against this background, principles

of fair trial also require that in appropriate cases the interests of the defence are balanced against those of witnesses or victims called upon to testify.[30]

Despite this, the Court has stressed that it is essential to 'have regard to the place that the right to a fair administration of justice holds in a democratic society, any measures restricting the rights of the defence should be strictly necessary. If a less restrictive measure can suffice then that measure should be applied.'[31] A number of competing considerations must be taken into account, but while states may, and indeed in some cases must, take measures to protect victims and witnesses, these measures must not unduly compromise the ability of the defence to challenge the evidence against it. One of the areas in which these conflicting interests have been most clearly evident is in relation to witnesses who, for their safety, wish to remain anonymous. A number of cases have concerned the defence's inability to challenge the testimony of an anonymous witness. The Court has stated that it is fully aware of 'undeniable difficulties' of the fight against, in particular, organised crimes like drug-trafficking—in particular with regard to obtaining and producing evidence—and of the ravages caused to society by the drug problem, but such considerations cannot justify restricting to this extent the rights of the defence of 'everyone charged with a criminal offence'.[32]

In spite of the Court's insistence, however, that it recognises both the difficulties associated with fighting organised crime and the importance of protecting witnesses from the threat of intimidation,[33] it has taken a consistently strict approach to the use of unchallenged testimonies of anonymous witnesses. In *Kostovski*, the applicant's complaint was based on the use as evidence of reports of statements by two anonymous people. The latter had been heard by the police, and in one case by the examining magistrate, but were not themselves heard at either of the trials. Furthermore, their statements were taken in the absence of both the applicant and his counsel, and thus the defence had no opportunity to question them. The Court noted

> [I]f the defence is unaware of the identity of the person it seeks to question, it may be deprived of the very particulars enabling it to demonstrate that he or she is prejudiced, hostile or unreliable. Testimony or other declarations inculpating an accused may well be designedly untruthful or simply erroneous and the defence will scarcely be able to bring this to light if it lacks the information permitting it to test the author's reliability or cast doubt on his credibility. The dangers inherent in such a situation are obvious.[34]

---

[30] *Doorson v Netherlands,* judgment of 26 Mar 1996, Reports 1996-II, 446, (1996) 22 EHRR 330, para 70; *Visser v Netherlands,* no 26668/95, judgment of 14 Feb 2002, para 43.

[31] *Doorson v Netherlands,* judgment of 26 Mar 1996, Reports 1996-II, 446, (1996) 22 EHRR 330, para 70.

[32] *Saïdi v France,* judgment of 20 Sept 1993, Series A no 261-C, (1994) 17 EHRR 251.

[33] See eg *Kostovski v Netherlands,* judgment of 20 Nov 1989, Series A no 166, (1990) 12 EHRR 140, para 44.

[34] *Ibid,* at paras 42–43.

Moreover, as the person who made the statement did not appear in court, the trial court was unable to examine his demeanour under questioning or form its own impression. The Court held that notwithstanding the fact that the Government had sought to protect the witnesses from intimidation, it had failed to lay sufficient weight on the interest that everyone in a civilised society has in ensuring a controllable and fair judicial procedure. The use of the anonymous statements to found the conviction and the limitations on the defence was irreconcilable with the guarantees of Article 6. A violation of Article 6 was also found in the similar case of *Windisch v Austria* where neither the applicant nor his counsel had the chance to examine witnesses whose evidence had been taken by the police and subsequently reported by third persons during the hearings.[35] There is now a fixed line of case law which confirms that in order to ensure adversarial procedure 'a conviction should not be based either solely or to a decisive extent on anonymous statements'.[36]

(b)   The Importance of the Witness

It is unfortunate that from the start of the case law the Strasbourg authorities have framed the test for determining whether or not the witnesses should be examined in terms of the weight of their evidence in securing a conviction. The implication is that the defence need not have the opportunity to challenge every witness, only those whose evidence is particularly important for the prosecution case. In *Unterpertinger* it was decisive that the Austrian Court of Appeal based the applicant's conviction mainly on statements made by the witnesses to the police.[37] In *Kamasinski*, a similar test was used, albeit in the negative sense, when the Court decided that insofar as the applicant's conviction was not attributable to the two witnesses which the defence had requested to examine, their absence from the trial raised no issue under Article 6.[38] In fact, the case law is littered with

---

[35]   *Windisch v Austria*, judgment of 27 Sept 1990, Series A no 186, (1991) 13 EHRR 281, paras 27–32. See similar findings in *Delta v France*, judgment of 19 Dec 1990, Series A no 191-A, (1993) 16 EHRR 574; *Saïdi v France*, judgment of 20 Sept 1993, Series A no 261-C, (1994) 17 EHRR 251.

[36]   *Doorson v Netherlands*, judgment of 26 Mar 1996, Series A no 76, (1996) 22 EHRR 330; *Van Mechelen and others v Netherlands*, judgment of 23 Apr 1997, Reports 1997-III, 691, (1998) 25 EHRR 647; *Delta v France*, judgment of 19 Dec 1990, Series A no 191-A, (1993) 16 EHRR 574, para 37; *Lüdi v Switzerland*, judgment of 15 June 1992, Series A no 238, (1993) 15 EHRR 173.

[37]   *Unterpertinger v Austria*, judgment of 24 Nov 1986, Series A no 110, (1991) 13 EHRR 175, para 33.

[38]   *Kamasinski v Austria*, judgment of 19 Dec 1989, Series A no 168, (1991) 13 EHRR 36, para 91.

such statements: the evidence was (or was not) decisive,[39] the sole basis[40] or the only evidence.[41] These phrases are merged into one standard phase in the *Van Mechelen* case[42] where the Court held:

> In particular, the rights of the defence are restricted to an extent that is incompatible with the requirements of Article 6 if the conviction is based solely or in a decisive manner, on the depositions of a witness whom the accused has had no opportunity to examine or have examined either during the investigation or at trial.

The 'sole or decisive' test has been used in every case subsequently considered by the Court.[43] Thus, in determining whether the defence's rights have been violated, the Court will examine primarily the extent of the evidence against the accused and the weight of the evidence which the defence has been unable to challenge. This can only be described as a wholly unsatisfactory doctrine. It means that where witness evidence led by the prosecution is deemed not to constitute the sole or decisive basis for the conviction, the failure to allow the defence to challenge this witness will not violate Article 6(3)(d). This was the case in *Artner v Austria*,[44] where circumstances meant that it was impossible to organise a confrontation during the pre-trial phase between the witness and the applicant. Despite the fact that the witness did not appear at trial, her testimony was put before the court. On the basis that the witness's statements were not the only evidence before the court, it was held that there was no violation of Article 6(3)(d). The Court noted that as the statements did not constitute the only item of evidence on which the first instance decision was based, the failure to question the witness did not deprive the accused of a fair trial.[45] That the other evidence consisted of documents concerning a loan agreement together with 'the applicant's criminal record and his conviction—against which he did not appeal—in the other case of usury on similar facts' is sufficient to demonstrate the dangers associated with this approach. The Commission also thought there had been no violation, but by only a narrow majority. The dissenting members—Mr Trechsel, joined by Mr Busuttil, Mr Gözübüyük, Mr Weitzel, Sir Basil Hall and Mr

[39] *Delta v France*, above n36, para 37.
[40] *Isgrò v Italy* judgment of 19 February 1991 Series A no 194-A, para 35; *Saïdi v France* judgment of 20 September 1993 Series A no 261-C, para 44 (1994) 17 EHRR 251.
[41] *Asch v Austria* judgment of 26 April 1991 Series A no 203, para 30 (1993) 15 EHRR 597; *Artner v Austria* judgment of 28 August 1992 Series A no 242-A, para 24.
[42] *Solakov v FYROM* no 47023/99 ECHR 2001-X, 29, para 58, citing *Van Mechelen and others v Netherlands* judgment of 23 April 1997 Reports 1997-III, 691 (1998) 25 EHRR 647.
[43] Eg *AM v Italy* no 37019/97 ECHR 1999-IX, paras 25-26; *Lucà v Italy* no 33345/96 ECHR 2001-II, 167, para 43 (2003) EHRR 46; *Sadak and others v Turkey* nos 29900/96, 29901/96, 29902/96, 29903/96 ECHR 2001-VIII, 267, para 66 (2003) 36 EHRR 26; *Solakov v FYROM* no 47023/99 ECHR 2001-X, 29, para 58; *PS v Germany* no 33900/96 judgment of 20 December 2001, para 30 (2003) 36 EHRR 61; *Birutis and others v Lithuania*, nos 47698/99 and 48115/99 judgment of 18 March 2002, para 31; *Hulki Güneş v Turkey* no 28490/95 ECHR 2003-VII, 187, para 96 (2006) 43 EHRR 15.
[44] *Artner v Austria* judgment of 28 August 1992 Series A no 242.
[45] *Ibid*; see also *Asch v Austria*, judgment of 26 Apr 1991, Series A no 203, (1993) 15 EHRR 597.

140

Rozakis—felt that there had been reliance on the witness statements and thus argued that the guarantees of Article 6(3)(d) were essential to ensure that the applicant had a fair trial.

The Court's approach can be criticised on two grounds.[46] First, the Court seems to contradict its earlier statements that it cannot be responsible for determining the importance of each piece of evidence. This argument was taken up by the minority of the Court in *Artner*. Judge Vilhjálmsson stated:

> The case-law of our Court shows that it is not always possible to apply strictly the important rule set out in Article 6(3)(d) of our Convention, despite the fact that it is stated in this very same paragraph that the rights set out therein are minimum rights. Unfortunately, the interpretation of this rule takes our Court into forbidden territory so to say i.e. the assessment of evidence, which should be the domain of the national courts.[47]

The Court's role is neither to determine what evidence a national court should take into consideration, nor to examine the importance of specific pieces of evidence. It must examine only the way in which the evidence has been treated. In this field there is only one approach for the Court which fully respects the guarantee, and that is to ensure that the defence is able to challenge all witness evidence which is put before the court. By leading the evidence, the prosecution or investigating authorities have already made clear their belief in the importance of the evidence; consequently this evidence falls to be treated in the light of both Article 6(3)(d) and the principle of adversarial procedure. The decision by the prosecuting or investigating authorities to put the evidence before the court, or the reliance of the court on this evidence in the reasons supporting the guilty verdict, should be, as it is in relation to documentary evidence, sufficient to convince all involved that the evidence is important for the determination of guilt or innocence. Moreover, the sole or decisive evidence approach falls to be criticised on the basis that, contrary to the aims of the preamble, it inevitably creates different levels of protection, not just between documentary evidence and witness evidence, but also between systems which insist on, or permit, the examination of witnesses at trial and systems which use the pre-trial phase in order to facilitate witness confrontations. In view of the fact that, according to Article 6, the public trial, supervised by an independent and impartial judge, is the forum required to comply with notions of fairness, it is difficult to see how it is acceptable for the evidence to be examined in the non-public, partisan environment of the investigation. Logically, if the principles set out in Article 6(1) are taken as the basis on which to determine the 'fairness' of the proceedings, the examination of evidence solely during the investigation must be seen to be less

---

[46] For criticism see S Trechsel, *Human Rights in Criminal Proceedings* (Oxford, Oxford University Press, 2005) at 297 ff; S Stavros, *The Guarantees for Accused Persons Under Article 6 of the European Convention on Human Rights* (Dordrecht, Kluwer Law, 1993) at 235 who writes in relation to *Asch* that the Court appeared to have 'intentionally undervalued the weight of the untested evidence'.
[47] *Artner v Austria*, judgment of 28 Aug 1992, Series A no 242.

fair than if the examination of the evidence were to be undertaken at trial. In fact, in view of the express requirements of Article 6(1) the use of the investigation as a forum for the examination of the evidence may even be seen to be unfair.

The Court's approach to considering whether the defendant's right to examine prosecution witnesses has been violated appears therefore to be a somewhat unfortunate mix of examining admissibility and policy issues. In particular, and somewhat surprisingly with regard to the examination of whether the defence has had an adequate chance to challenge the submissions and evidence of the other side, the Court has not insisted that those basic, fundamental aspects of Article 6 which are normally associated with challenging evidence, such as the principle of adversarial procedure, be applied. In trying to assess the important of the evidence against the defence, the Court has lost sight of its primary role— that of ensuring that evidence for and against the accused has been presented in a manner compatible with the specific notion of fairness. Moreover by focusing on the issues in each case, be it on the anonymity of witnesses or the extent and scope of the evidence withheld from the defence, the Court has lost sight of the scope of the provision and its own responsibilities. In the context of the Convention the responsibility for assessing the evidence falls to the trial judge, not the Court; that is precisely the reason the evidence must be adjudicated on by an independent and impartial authority in public. Instead of trying to formulate a test to determine how important the evidence must be for the defence to challenge it, the Court ought to insist that the trial judge be able to assess the evidence, and that means insisting on the application of the provision in the context of the general notion of fairness.

(ii) When Should Witnesses be Examined?

If it is clear from Article 6(3)(d) that the defence must be able to challenge the testimony of witnesses, it is considerably less clear when this must occur. A glance at the provision suggests that the intention of the drafters was to enable the defence to challenge witnesses[48] 'live' at trial in the presence of defence counsel and with all the other guarantees set out in Article 6. It is worth noting, too, that the neighbouring provisions, Article 6(3)(c) and (3)(e), have been held to apply predominantly at trial and there have been attempts by applicants to have them applied in the earlier phases of the proceedings which have proven controversial.[49]

---

[48] The term 'witness' is given an autonomous meaning in the Convention, and includes all the people whose evidence has gone before the court: see eg *Delta v France,* judgment of 19 Dec 1990, Series A no 191-A, (1993) 16 EHRR 574, para 34.

[49] The right to a lawyer in the pre-trial/interrogative phases has caused controversy across the continent. See eg S Arquint, 'Anwalt der Ersten Stunde? Ein Positionspapier!' in B Schindler and R Schlauri, *Auf dem Weg zu einem Einheitlichen Verfahren* (Zurich, Schulthess, 2001)—Switzerland; A Eser, 'Aussagefreiheit und Beistand des Verteidigers im Ermittlungsverfahren: Rechtsvergleichende

The initial cases concerning witness evidence highlight indecision on the part of the Strasbourg authorities as to how exactly to approach this provision. The extent of this hesitance was all too apparent in the Commission's report in *Unterpertinger v Austria* where strong doubts were cast on whether the provision required that the witnesses be examined at all, let alone at trial. In this case the applicant complained that he had been convicted solely on the basis of the statements of witnesses to the crime who, as relatives of the accused, had legitimately refused to give evidence during the trial. The applicant had not had, during the trial or earlier in the proceedings, the opportunity to examine the witnesses or to have them examined. The Commission, considering the issue under Article 6(1) rather than Article 6(3)(d) held that there was no violation of the Convention. It held that there was enough evidence before the court to enable it to find the accused guilty without requiring that the witnesses be examined. This was not a unanimous decision, and the dissenters countered that the guarantee of Article 6(3)(d) could be interpreted only as requiring that 'the defendant has an absolute right to question witnesses against him, to put their credibility to the test, to provoke complements to the information already given in an attempt to establish a full picture of the facts and to bring forward elements which are in his favour'. They noted:

> It cannot be accepted that privileges are granted to certain groups of witnesses at the expense of the accused and his right to be heard. In the present case, there ought to have been but one alternative: either the witnesses testify at trial and accept being questioned also by the defence, or their testimony cannot be relied upon at all. Under the Convention it is of no importance whether they made statements before the police or before the investigating judge. What is decisive is, however, whether the accused had the possibility, *at least at one stage of the proceedings*, to examine or have examined witnesses whose testimony is to be relied upon for his conviction.[50]

The Court subsequently agreed with the dissenting opinion and held that there had been a violation of Article 6(3)(d), noting that the applicant had not had 'an opportunity at any stage in the earlier proceedings to question the persons whose statements are read out in the hearing'; however it held that 'in itself, the reading out of statements in this way cannot be regarded as being inconsistent with Article 6(1) and 6(3)(d)'.[51]

Beobachtungen zur Rechtsstellung des Beschuldigten' (1967) 79 *Zeitschrift für die gesamte Strafrechtswissenschaft* 565—Germany; C Grabenwarter, *Verfahrensgarantien in der Verwaltungsgerichtbarkeit: eine Studie zu Artikel 6 EMRK auf der Grundlage einer rechtsvergleichenden Untersuchung der Verwaltungsgerichtsbarkeit Frankreichs, Deutschlands und Österreichs* (Vienna, Springer, 1997), R Soyer, 'Anwesenheits- und Mitwirkungsrechte' in W Schuppich and R Soyer, *Vorverfahren und Verteidigungsrechte* (Vienna, Verlag der österreichischen Staatsdruckerei, 1992)—Austria; E Amodio, 'Das Modell des Anklageprozesse im neuen italienischen Strafverfahrensgesetzbuch' (1990) 102 *Zeitschrift für die gesamte Strafrechtswissenschaft* 171—Italy.

[50] See the dissenting opinions to the Commission's report in *Unterpertinger v Austria*, App no 9120/80, report of 11 Oct 1984, Series B no 93 (emphasis added).

[51] *Unterpertinger v Austria*, judgment of 24 Nov 1986, Series A no 110, (1991) 13 EHRR 175, at para 31.

Although the Court was undoubtedly correct in rejecting the Commission's majority opinion, the way in which it decided to do this was unfortunate. The consequence of the ruling in *Unterpertinger* was to give credence to the argument that the rights set out in Article 6(3)(d) need not be applied in the context of the public, impartially adjudicated trial. The dissenting opinion of the Commission and subsequent comments of the Court constitute the first time in the case law that there is any suggestion that witnesses could be examined outwith the trial setting. The question whether it would be legitimate to challenge witnesses testimony during the pre-trial phase was, however, in this case only *obiter dictum*, as the applicant had not had the chance at any point in the process to challenge the witnesses.

The Court did not seem to adhere immediately to the legitimacy of pre-trial hearings as the sole forum for the questioning of witnesses, noting in *Barberà, Messengue and Jabardo* that, in view of the wording of Article 6 and the Court's ruling that a person subject to a criminal charge is entitled to take part in the hearing and to have the case heard in his presence by a tribunal,[52] Article 6(3)(d) ought to be interpreted as requiring that 'all evidence' must 'in principle' be produced 'in the presence of the accused at a public hearing with a view to adversarial argument'.[53] This seemed to rule out the examination of witnesses at any stage in the proceedings other than at the trial itself, and seemed to uphold the strong emphasis on fairness, requiring that the trial itself be the forum for challenging the evidence. Nevertheless three years later in *Kostovski v Netherlands*, the Court considered again the *Unterpertinger* ruling and cited it as authority in support of its contention that it would be compatible with Article 6(3)(d) to permit the examination of witnesses to take place at an earlier stage in the proceedings, instead of during the trial itself. It again cited the general principle of examination at a public hearing and then qualified this, noting:

> This does not mean, however, that in order to be used as evidence, statements of witnesses should always be made at a public hearing in court: To use as evidence such statements obtained at the pre-trial stage is not in itself inconsistent with paragraphs 3(d) and 1 of Article 6 provided the rights of the defence have been respected.[54]

The Court further clarified this by stating that as a rule this meant that an accused:

---

[52] Referring to *Colozza v Italy*, judgment of 12 Feb 1985, Series A no 89, (1985) 7 EHRR 516, paras 27 and 32.

[53] *Barberà, Messengué and Jabardo v Spain*, judgment of 6 Dec 1988, Series A no 146, (1989) 11 EHRR 360, para 78.

[54] *Kostovski v Netherlands*, judgment of 20 Nov 1989, Series A no 166, (1990) 12 EHRR 140, para 41.

should be given an adequate and proper opportunity to challenge and question a witness against him, either at the time that the witness was making his statement or at some later stage in the proceedings.[55]

In fact, in this case, as in the earlier cases, the question when the accused should be able to examine witnesses testifying against him was never a point at issue, as the applicant had not had, at any stage in the proceedings, a chance to question the witness. There is thus no basis or explanation in the Court's judgment for its decision.

The cases where there has been insistence on the immediate presentation of evidence at trial are the exception rather than the rule. In its admissibility decision in *Cardot*, for instance, the Commission held that 'the requirements of a fair trial and equality of arms generally make it necessary for all prosecutions witnesses to be heard before the trial courts and during adversarial proceedings'. Moreover, it noted that it was 'of the utmost importance that those courts should be able to observe the witnesses' demeanour under questioning and to form their own impression of their reliability'. Although the applicant was 'confronted at the supplementary investigation stage with the persons who had incriminated him', these people were not 'called to give evidence before the trial courts and at a public hearing'. The Commission noted that 'the text of the judgment contains numerous references to the statements of the applicant's former co-accused, which the Court used to establish the facts, without calling those persons to repeat their statements at a public hearing of the parties in the presence of the accused'. It concluded:

> The Commission accordingly finds that the applicant was tried and convicted largely on the basis of evidence from other proceedings to which he had not been a party, and was given no opportunity of discussing in adversarial proceedings at a public hearing the statements made against him by his former co-accused.

It thus held unanimously that there had been a violation of Article 6. Here the Commission seems to take an even stricter approach than that of the Court in *Barberà* and to find pre-trial examinations incompatible with the principle of adversarial procedure. The Court did not rule on the merits in this cases however, as it upheld the Government's preliminary objection that the applicant had failed to exhaust domestic remedies.[56]

Despite such occasional musings in support of the principle that the evidence ought to be challenged and determined at an oral, public and impartially adjudicated hearing, these must undoubtedly be seen as exceptional. The *Unterpertinger/Kostovski* approach has become the dominant force in the application of Article 6(3)(d) and the Court's 'adequate and proper opportunity' test

---

[55]   *Ibid*; see also *Unterpertinger v Austria*, judgment of 24 Nov 1986, Series A no 110, (1991) 13 EHRR 175, para 31.
[56]   *Cardot v France*, judgment of 19 Mar 1991, Series A no 200, (1991) 13 EHRR 853.

prevails.[57] This is an important line of case law as it reflects the fact that the Court does not view the displacement of the defence's right to challenge the submissions of prosecution witnesses from the trial to the pre-trial as compromising or affecting its notion of fairness.

E   The Importance of the Trial as a Forum for Confronting Witness Evidence

Many writers have focused on the importance of the accused's opportunity to examine or confront witnesses as to their testimony, and a wide variety of reasons have been advanced to explain why an accused should be able to question in person those who make incriminating statements again him or her. Confrontation has been said to promote openness and thus guard against coercion;[58] to reinforce the notion of adversarial procedure by ensuring that the accused can challenge any adverse witness evidence;[59] to enable the decision maker to assess the demeanour of the witness and thus aid him or her in determining the truthfulness of the witness statements;[60] and to ensure that only the statements of witnesses who are prepared to testify can be used against the accused and thus guarantee that the evidence is more reliable.[61] Some have even suggested that it has a symbolic purpose and that 'there is something deep in human nature that regards face-to-face confrontation between accused and accuser as 'essential to a fair trial in a criminal prosecution'.[62]

---

[57] *Birutis and Others v Lithuania,* judgment of 28 Mar 2002, para 28; *Visser v Netherlands,* judgment of 14 Feb 2002, para 51; *Doorson v Netherlands,* judgment of 26 Mar 1996, Reports 1996-II, 471; *Saïdi v France,* judgment of 20 Sept 1993, Series A no 261-C, (1994) 17 EHRR 251, para 43.

[58] Eg M Berger, 'The Deconstitutionalization of the Confrontation Clause: A Proposal for a Prosecutorial Restraint Model' (1991) 76 *Minnesota Law Review* 557 at 560.

[59] Eg RS Friedman, 'The Confrontation Clause Re-rooted and Transformed' [2003–04] *Cato Supreme Court Review* 442 at 442.

[60] *Ibid.*

[61] Eg A Choo, *Hearsay, Confrontation and Criminal Trials* (Oxford, Oxford University Press, 1996) at 17.

[62] *Coy v Iowa* 487 US 1012 (1988) at 1017. See also E Scallen, 'Constitutional Dimensions of Hearsay Reform: Towards a Three Dimensional Confrontation Clause' (1992) 76 *Minnesota Law Review* 623; MR Kadish and M Davies, 'Defending the Hearsay Rule' (1989) 8 *Law and Philosophy* 333; CR Nesson, 'The Evidence or the Event: On Judicial Proof and the Acceptability of Verdicts' (1985) 98 *Harvard Law Review* 1357 at 1372; S Clark, 'Who do You Think You Are: The Criminal Trial and Community Character' in A Duff, L Farmer, S Marshall and V Tadros, *The Trial on Trial I: Truth and Due Process* (Oxford, Hart Publishing, 2006). According to the Massachusetts Sup Ct: '[m]ost believe in some undefined but real way recollection, veracity and communication are influenced by face-to-face challenge': *Commonwealth v Bergstrom* 524 N E 2d 366, 371–2 (Mass 1988) citing *United States v Benfield* 593 F 2d 815, 821 (8th Cir 1979). Clark takes a slightly different approach in that his emphasis is firmly on the responsibilities of the witness rather than the rights of the accused. He argues that the confrontation clause provides more than simply ensuring that the witness statement at issue is reliable and accurate. Instead he suggests that the exclusion of out-of-court statements is

Whereas claims based on preventing coercion emphasise the importance of interpreting the principle in the light of a whole host of due process rules sharing the ultimate goal of 'restraining the capricious use of governmental power',[63] those that emphasise its role in ensuring the veracity and accuracy of the statements argue that it offers the greatest chance of obtaining the best evidence. Such claims are based on the belief that it plays a vital role in completing and correcting 'the witness's story',[64] and thereby advances 'the accuracy of the truth-determining process'.[65] These two issues have often been portrayed as irreconcilable opposites, and those in favour of the first interpretation have criticised the courts' tendency to adopt the latter approach as evidence of 'the constitutional provision's subordination to evidence law...'[66] and proof that the court had 'transformed a constitutional guarantee into an evidentiary doctrine....'[67]

In fact neither of these arguments is sufficient, taken alone, to explain the importance of notions such as confrontation or immediacy. While reliance on arguments as to accuracy undoubtedly has the potential to lead to a neglect of the importance of controlling the activities of investigators and prosecutors, the shift towards a more 'procedural' interpretation of the principle means that the principle could become too focused on evidence collected by state authorities at the expense of the defence's right to challenge non-'testimonial' evidence. Neither of these arguments accounts for the institutional importance of immediacy in

---

necessary 'not because testimony without confrontation is necessarily unreliable, but because it is ignoble'. He continues: '[t]he idea is that it is somehow wrong base and cowardly and inconsistent with the respect we owe our fellows to accuse someone without being willing to look them in the eye and stand behind that accusation'.

[63] M Berger, 'The Deconstitutionalization of the Confrontation Clause: A Proposal for a Prosecutorial Restraint Model' (1991) 76 *Minnesota Law Review* 557 at 560; E Scallen, 'Constitutional Dimensions of Hearsay Reform: Towards a Three Dimensional Confrontation Clause' (1992) 76 *Minnesota Law Review* 623; see also RW Kirst, 'The Procedural Dimension of Confrontation Doctrine' (1987) 66 *Nebraska Law Review* 485. This stance was advocated by the US Sup Ct in *Crawford v Washington* 541 US 36 (2004). For an interesting comment on this case see D Nance, 'Rethinking Confrontation After Crawford' (2004) 2/1 *International Commentary on Evidence* 1.

[64] C Allen, *Practical Guide to Evidence* (London, Cavendish, 1998) at 64.

[65] *Dutton v Evans* 400 US 74, 89 (1970); see also *Idaho v Wright* 497 US 805 (1990) 100 S Ct at 3151–2: 'a per se rule of exclusion would... frustrate the truth-seeking purpose of the Confrontation Clause'; *Tennessee v Street* 471 US 409, 415 (1985): 'the Confrontations Clause's very mission [is] to advance "the accuracy of the truth-determining process in criminal trials"' (citing *Dutton*); *White v Illinois* 112 S Ct 736, 743 (1992): 'the Confrontation Clause has as a basic purpose the promotion of the "integrity of the fact-finding process"', citing *Kentucky v Stincer* 482 US 730, 736 (1986). Proponents of this justification point to Viscount Sankey's description of cross-examination as a 'powerful and valuable weapon for the purpose of testing the veracity of a witness and an accuracy and completeness of his story': *Mechanical and General Interventions Co and Lehwess v Austin and Austin Motor Co* [1935] AC 346 at 359 (HL) and to Wigmore's famous statement that it is 'beyond any doubt the greatest legal engine ever invented for the discovery of the truth': JH Wigmore, *Evidence in Trials at Common Law,* 4th edn (Boston, Mass, Little Brown, JH Chadbourne rev, 1974),v, at 32.

[66] RH Jonakait, 'Restoring the Confrontation Clause to the Sixth Amendment' (1988) 35 *University of California Los Angeles Law Review* 557 at 622.

[67] M Berger, 'The Deconstitutionalization of the Confrontation Clause: A Proposal for a Prosecutorial Restraint Model' (1991) 76 *Minnesota Law Review* 557 at 557.

criminal procedural systems that employ a strict division between the investigation and trial stages. Instead, the importance of the examination of evidence at the trial stage must be seen as a logical and necessary consequence of an understanding of criminal proceedings as involving the adversarial determination of the evidence in the context of the accusatorial trinity.

F Reconciling Examination of Witnesses in the Investigation Phase with the 'Accusatorial Trinity'

The decision to legitimise the carrying out of witness examinations during the investigation phase suggests that the Strasbourg authorities believe this opportunity to be equal to the opportunity afforded to the accused who has the chance to examine witnesses at trial. But this gives rise to some serious problems. According to the text of Article 6(1) and to the Court's elucidation of the adversarial proceedings and equality of arms doctrines, the determination of the charge—in the sense of the examination and challenging of the evidence—has to occur at trial precisely because this is the only forum which respects the accusatorial trinity. In this sense it reinforces the sharp distinction between the trial and investigation phases.

Although the Court has had few qualms about moving the guarantee protected by Article 6(3)(d) from the confines of the trial into the pre-trial phase, a considerable number of questions accompany this decision. One fundamental issue is the scope of Article 6(1). The Court has on many occasions noted that Article 6(3) falls to be interpreted in accordance with both the general requirement of the right to a fair trial and Article 6(1). But it is not always clear whether Article 6(1) finds application in relation to the investigative actions of the authorities. If the examination of the evidence takes place in the investigation phase, then it is at least arguable that Article 6(1) is not applicable as there is no 'determination' of the charge *per se*; this occurs later.[68]

On the one hand this could be seen as a failing in the structure of the text of the Convention, in that there is a notable lack of provision in Article 6 for the regulation of the investigation phase. This means that there is little guidance for

---

[68] See eg *IJL, GMR and AKP v United Kingdom*, nos 29522/95, 30056/96 and 30574/96, ECHR 2000-IX, (2001) 33 EHRR 11, para 100: '[t]he Court does not accept that submission and refers in this connection to the nature and purpose of investigations conducted by DTI inspectors. It observes that, in its judgment in the case of *Fayed v United Kingdom* judgment of 21 September 1994 Series A no 294-B, the Court held that the functions performed by the inspectors appointed under section 432(2) of the Companies Act 1985 were essentially investigative in nature and that they did not adjudicate either in form or in substance. Their purpose was to ascertain and record facts which might subsequently be used as the basis for action by other competent authorities—prosecuting, regulatory, disciplinary or even legislative.'

those who believe that it is either unacceptable or undesirable for the examination and challenging of evidence to occur at trial to suggest other acceptable means of regulating the examination of the evidence. On the other hand, however, it could be argued that there is little room for exceptions to the principle that the evidence be examined at trial, precisely because this is what the institutional conception of fairness requires. As can be seen in the works of the nineteenth century writers, the rights of the defence to participate in the proceedings were contingent on the conception of the institutional form of the criminal proceedings.

If it is accepted that the twin requirements of the impartial judge and the principle of 'adversarial procedure' as applied by the Court require that the defence be permitted to challenge evidence in the context of opposing parties and in the presence of an impartial judge, it is difficult to see how this adjudicatory role could be taken on by a partial, at least in the sense of Article 6(1), investigating authority, as is the case in many European jurisdictions.[69] Moreover, the provision undoubtedly requires to be interpreted alongside Article 6(3)(c), which guarantees the right to legal assistance. One of the most important, if not the most important, tasks of the defence counsel is to assist his or her client not only in putting forward a defence but also in challenging the evidence in support of the prosecution's case. It is difficult to see how the right to legal assistance could be 'effectively'[70] applied without enabling the lawyer to take control of this function.

The tacit approval by the Strasbourg authorities of the taking place of witness confrontation hearings in the pre-trial phase has not been accompanied by any requirement that such hearings be impartially supervised or that they take place in the presence of counsel. While these guarantees would be unable to solve other problems such as the lack of publicity or immediacy in the examination of the evidence, they would nevertheless suggest that the Court had recognised the important connection between institutional forms and procedural opportunities. An examination of the case law of the Court reveals that there has been little thought given to ensuring such structural coherence in the interpretation and application of this provision and in identifying the importance of the trial structure in the definition of fairness.

---

[69] See notably the Canton of Zurich in Switzerland where the prosecutor supervises the witness confrontation hearings. See also *De Cubber v Belgium,* judgment of 26 Oct 1984, Series A no 86, (1985) 7 EHRR 236.

[70] See eg *Artico v Italy,* judgment of 13 May 1990, Series A no 37, (1981) 3 EHRR 1, para 33, where the Court noted that the Convention 'is intended to guarantee not rights that are theoretical or illusory but rights that are practical and effective'. For discussion of the principle of the effective assistance of counsel see S Trechsel, *Human Rights in Criminal Proceedings* (Oxford, Oxford University Press, 2005) at 286–90.

(i)   The Presence of Counsel During Pre-trial Examination of Witnesses

In the context of the trial itself it is taken for granted that a lawyer will be present, providing that the accused does not waive his or her right to counsel,[71] and that he or she will be responsible, *inter alia*, for examining the witnesses. Where, however, the examination of the witnesses occurs during the pre-trial phase, the Court's case law makes it clear that these established trial rights are not always mandatory. In *Isgrò v Italy*, the applicant was able, during a 'confrontation' organised by the investigation judge, to put questions directly to the witness. The applicant's lawyer was not present during the confrontation. The authorities were unable to secure the presence of the witness at trial, but his evidence was nevertheless put before the court. Holding that the applicant had 'enjoyed the guarantees secured under Article 6 (3)(d) to a sufficient extent', the Court found no violation. In reaching this conclusion it noted that although the Italian criminal code prevented the applicant's lawyer from attending the confrontation, the public prosecutor was likewise absent, and thus the presence of the applicant's lawyer was not 'indispensable'.[72] This argument seems to be a reply to a claim that the equality of arms has been violated. It does not appear, however, to address incompatibility with the adversarial procedure requirement. Moreover, it seems to apply a lesser test of procedural fairness in relation to the examination of witnesses in the pre-trial procedure than during the trial itself.

In view of the fact that the guarantees of judicial impartiality and publicity are conspicuously absent in the earlier stages of the criminal process, it would seem that the need for counsel is even greater at this stage in the proceedings. Indeed, the Commission had earlier found a violation of the provision, stressing the importance of legal counsel particularly as the witness was not subsequently questioned during the trial hearing. The interpretation of Article 6(3)(d) which does not permit the assistance of counsel at the pre-trial examination is problematic in that it seems to allow for the arbitrary application of Convention rights. Interestingly the dissenters in the Commission—the Italian and British judges— stated:

> we do not attach great significance to the absence of the applicant's lawyer during his confrontation. It cannot be expected, that, in such circumstances, the applicant would receive specific instructions from his lawyer on the events referred to in the confrontation. With regard to any questions that the applicant's lawyer could have asked Mr D. (the witness), the applicant could ask these questions himself, at least through the investigating judge.

---

[71]   See eg *Foucher v France*, judgment of 18 Mar 1997, Reports 1997-II, 452, (1998) 25 EHRR 234, para 35.

[72]   *Isgrò v Italy*, judgment of 19 Feb 1991, Series A no 194-A, (1991) 12 *Human Rights Law Journal* 1000.

This argument, however, seems completely to ignore the reason for the existence of lawyers in the criminal process and casts doubt on the need for a lawyer at trial, if it is sufficient that the judge or the prosecutor can ask the questions for the accused or that he or she can ask them him- or herself. This is a spurious argument at odds with the Court's own definition of fairness and its arguments justifying the right to counsel.

The reluctance of the Court to insist on the presence of counsel during the examination of witnesses in the pre-trial phase can perhaps be explained, in part, by the general controversy associated with even suggesting a right to counsel during the pre-trial phase. Aware that access to counsel in the pre-trial phase is a controversial topic, the Court has been extremely careful not to rock the boat by suggesting that there is an absolute right to counsel during the investigation or interrogation stages.[73] As there is no explicit mention in the Convention of a pre-trial right to counsel and as this is in any case a delicate subject throughout Europe, the Court has approached this question in a relatively conservative manner. In the absence of a specific provision the Court has sought, in a somewhat convoluted manner, to apply a limited right to counsel to the pre-trial phase. But prevented, presumably on political grounds, from applying a clear and consistent right, it has, in a somewhat convoluted manner, attempted to enforce what can only be described as a test of hindsight: counsel will be required in the pre-trial if his or her non-attendance would adversely affect the fairness of the subsequent hearing.[74] This test is essentially retrospective and is unable to offer clear rules as to when counsel is to be permitted to be present. It is thus insufficient adequately to regulate this pivotal aspect of the rights of the defence.

(ii) The Presence of an Impartial Supervisory Authority During the Examination of Witnesses

The Court's understanding of criminal proceedings as based on the accusatorial trinity would also suggest that the examination of witnesses should take place in the presence of an impartial judge.[75] Somewhat surprisingly, this issue appears

---

[73] It should be noted that in this regard the Commission was more progressive. See *Can v Austria*, App no 9300/81, report of 12 July 1984, Series b no 79, paras 50 and 55, where it noted that counsel in the earlier phases was important because 'the investigation phases are of great importance for the preparation of the trial' and that the presence of counsel was important to ensure: 'the control of the lawfulness of any measures taken in the course of the investigation proceedings, the identification and presentation of any means of evidence at an early stage where it is still possible to trace new relevant facts and where the witnesses have a fresh memory'.

[74] 'To deny access to a lawyer for the first 48 hours of police questioning, in a situation where the rights of the defence may well be irretrievably prejudiced, is—whatever the justification for such denial—incompatible with the rights of the accused under Article 6': *John Murray v United Kingdom*, judgment of 8 Feb 1996, Reports 1996-I, 30, (1996) 22 EHRR 29, para 66. See also *Öcalan v Turkey*, no 46221/99, judgment of 12 Mar 2003, (2003) 37 EHRR 10, para 140.

[75] *Ringeisen v Austria*, judgment of 16 July 1971, Series A no 13, (1979–80) 1 EHRR 455, para 95.

not to have been considered at all in the context of Article 6(3)(d). It is however useful to consider the Court's approach to the 'impartiality' of investigating authorities in the context of other aspects of the Convention. As we have seen, the Court in *De Cubber* rejected suggestions that the investigation judge, who was closely related to the prosecution, could be held to be impartial in the sense of Article 6(1):

> One can accordingly understand that an accused might feel some unease should he see on the bench of the court called upon to determine the charge against him the judge who had ordered him to be placed in detention on remand and who had interrogated him on numerous occasions during the preparatory investigation, albeit with questions dictated by a concern to ascertain the truth. Furthermore, through the various means of inquiry which he will have utilised at the investigation stage, the judge in question, unlike his colleagues, will already have acquired well before the hearing a particularly detailed knowledge of the—sometimes voluminous—file or files which he has assembled. Consequently, it is quite conceivable that he might, in the eyes of the accused, appear, firstly, to be in a position enabling him to play a crucial role in the trial court and, secondly, even to have a pre-formed opinion which is liable to weigh heavily in the balance at the moment of the decision.[76]

The Court has also had to consider a number of cases involving the impartiality of investigating authorities in the context of Article 5. Two judgments, both concerning the criminal procedure laws of the Canton of Zurich in Switzerland, are of particular interest in this regard. In the first, *Schiesser v Switzerland*, the Court had to consider, *inter alia*, whether the district attorney (*Bezirksanwalt*) could legitimately be characterised as an 'other officer authorised by law to exercise judicial power' as required by Article 5(3). The Court noted that 'officer' did not have an identical meaning to the term 'judge',[77] but it nevertheless required that the officer have 'some of the latter's attributes, that is to say that he must satisfy certain conditions each of which constitutes a guarantee for the person arrested',[78] including impartiality. It recalled that an officer could be subordinate to another officer or judge providing that he or she was also independent. The applicant and a minority of the Commission argued on the other hand that the District Attorney could not be impartial, not only because he acted in certain cases as a prosecuting authority but also because he was subordinate to the Public Prosecutor (*Staatsanwalt*). These arguments were however rejected by the Court which dismissed the first argument on the basis that:

> In the present case the District Attorney intervened exclusively in his capacity as an investigating authority, that is in considering whether Mr Schiesser (the applicant) should be charged and detained on remand and, subsequently, in conducting enquiries

---

[76] *De Cubber v Belgium*, judgment of 26 Oct 1984, Series A no 86, (1985) 7 EHRR 236, para 29.
[77] Art 5(3) reads: '[e]veryone arrested or detained... shall be brought promptly before a judge or other officer authorized by law to exercise judicial power...'.
[78] *Schiesser v Switzerland*, judgment of 4 Dec 1979, Series A no 34, (1979–80) 2 EHRR 71, para 31.

with an obligation to be equally thorough in gathering evidence in his favour and evidence against him.[79] He did not assume the mantle of prosecutor: he neither drew up the indictment nor represented the prosecuting functions, with the result that the Court is not called upon to determine whether the converse situation would have been in conformity with Article 5(3).[80]

The argument that the District Attorney's subordinate status meant that he could not be considered as an impartial authority was also rejected. The Court accepted the Government's argument that the decision of the District Attorney was taken entirely independently and on the basis that following 'the practice now followed in the Canton of Zurich for more than thirty years, according to which the department of Justice and the Public Prosecutor never give to the District Attorney orders or instructions concerning the placing of a given suspect in detention'. In accepting this view, the Court referred to *Delcourt*[81] and noted that this view corresponded to the 'realities of the situation'.[82] The dissenting judges both emphasised the need for the separation of the functions of prosecuting and judging and argued that this meant that a prosecutor could not be regarded as an officer authorised to exercise judicial power within the meaning of Article 5(3).[83]

The Court had to consider this issue again 10 years later in *Huber v Switzerland*.[84] Here the District Attorney of the Canton of Zurich had ordered the applicant's detention on remand, indicted her and had finally assumed the role of prosecuting authority. The delegate of the Commission urged the Court to depart from its judgment in the *Schiesser* case on the basis that 'the Court's case-law has moved towards the principle that prosecution and judicial functions must be completely separated'; such separation was, he considered, 'necessary at this stage in the development of the protection of human rights in Europe'.[85] Referring to a number of judgments involving military tribunals[86] where the person ruling on the detention of the applicant had the opportunity to assume, in the same case, the role of prosecuting authority had been considered to be partial, the Court found that the officer in the current case could not be said to be independent. It noted:

> Clearly the Convention does not rule out the possibility of the judicial officer who orders the detention carrying out other duties, but his impartiality is capable of

---

[79] As set out in Art 31 of the Criminal Procedure Code (*StPO*) of Zurich.

[80] *Schiesser v Switzerland,* above n78, para 34.

[81] *Delcourt v Belgium,* judgment of 17 Jan 1970, Series A no 11, (1979–80) 1 EHRR 355, para 32; See further Ch 2, above.

[82] *Schiesser v Switzerland,* judgment of 4 Dec 1979, Series A no 34, (1979–80) 2 EHRR 71, para 35.

[83] The decision was reached by a majority of 5:2, with judges Ryssdal and Evrigenis dissenting.

[84] Judgment of 23 Oct 1990, Series A no 188.

[85] *Ibid,* at para 38.

[86] *De Jong, Baljet and van den Brink v Netherlands,* judgment of 22 May 1984, Series A no 77, (1986) 8 EHRR 20, para 49; *Van der Sluijs, Zuiderveld and Klappe v Netherlands,* judgment of 22 May 1984, Series A no 78, (1991) 13 EHRR 461; *Duinhof and Duijf v Netherlands,* judgment of 22 May 1984, Series A no 79, (1991) 13 EHRR 478.

appearing open to doubt if he is entitled to intervene in the subsequent criminal proceedings as a representative of the prosecuting authority.[87]

Only Judge Matscher disagreed with the judgment. In his dissenting opinion, he expresses the view that a combination of the functions of prosecuting, investigating and judging may not necessarily be incompatible with the Convention and that 'the Convention in no way requires separation of the functions in question', although he concedes that this is desirable in the interests of the proper administration of justice, because 'it provides a maximum of guarantees to the individual concerned'. The Government tried to argue that the district attorneys were, despite the name, investigating judges and, although they had to write the indictment, they were also under a statutory obligation to 'take into account exonerating evidence as well as incriminating evidence, without setting out the grounds of suspicion or any legal considerations'.[88]

Although these cases relate to Article 5 and not to Article 6 there are nevertheless distinct parallels. As is clearly demonstrated in the Article 6(1) case law on impartiality and on the adversarial procedural requirement, there is no room within the Convention's conception of criminal proceedings for judicial authorities which undertake a succession of functions. Any authority that has the opportunity negatively to affect the defence's case must be viewed as an opposing party.[89] In the context of the examination of witness evidence it is obvious that similar problems emerge. In many European jurisdictions, investigating authorities are not only responsible for conducting the examination hearings, but are also charged with conducting the prosecution. Indeed in some cases the investigating authority has responsibility not only for determining whether or not to call witnesses but also for putting the defence's questions to the witnesses. It must be questioned how the entrusting of the examination of witnesses to a partial investigating authority, which has been considered insufficiently impartial even for the purposes of Article 5(3), can be reconciled with the institutional fairness requirements of Article 6(1).

(iii)   Immediacy

It goes without saying that the pre-trial examination of witnesses, unless repeated at trial, is incompatible with the immediacy principle. Although it is currently impossible in view of the *Unterpertinger/Kostovski* case law to claim that immediacy is solidly protected by the Convention, some limited references to its importance can be found in the case law. In an inadmissibility decision in 2002 the Court, for the first time, made a direct reference to the principle:

---

[87]   *Huber v Switzerland*, judgment of 23 Oct 1990, Series A no 188, para 43. In the cases cited the Court found that the combination of functions, whether it had actually occurred or whether it was merely theoretically possible, would affect the independence of the 'investigative officer'.
[88]   *Ibid*, at para 39.
[89]   See further Ch 2, above.

The Court considers that an important element of fair criminal proceedings is also the possibility of the accused to be confronted with the witness *in the presence of the judge who ultimately decides the case.* Such a principle of immediacy is an important guarantee in criminal proceedings in which observations made by the court about the demeanour and credibility of a witness may have important consequences for the accused.[90]

This statement was endorsed in *Mellors v United Kingdom* where it was noted:

the Court has had regard to the principle of immediacy, namely, that the decision in a criminal case should be reached by judges who have been present during the proceedings and taking of evidence.[91]

It is telling that neither case was held to be admissible. In spite of the Court's reticence in this regard, there can be little doubt that the dual principles of the oral and immediate examination of the evidence are inherent in the structure of Article 6. In view of this, the failure to insist either on adversarial investigation hearings or on the application of the immediacy principle casts serious doubts on the ability of Article 6 to uphold fairness through guaranteeing the participatory rights of the defence in an adversarial setting.

G The Privilege Against Self-incrimination

The regulation of the position of the accused during the investigation phase is perhaps best illustrated through an examination of the Court's case law on the privilege against self-incrimination.[92] Indeed the emphasis on the privilege against self-incrimination in the Court's case law may be seen as symptomatic of the confusion in its understanding of the institutional form of criminal proceedings. Just as the nineteenth century legislators responded to the importance of the investigation phase by emphasising the voluntary nature of the participation of the accused in the investigation, the Court too has chosen to rely on the privilege against self-incrimination rather than afford the defence a true adversarial role in the investigation phase. While the Court seems to recognise the need for 'pre-trial

---

[90] *PK v Finland*, App no 37442/97, decision of 9 July 2002 (emphasis added).

[91] *Mellors v United Kingdom*, App no 57836/00, decision of 30 Jan 2003.

[92] For an interesting evaluation of the principle see R Schlauri, *Das Verbot des Selbstbelastungszwangs im Strafverfahren: Konkretisierung eines Grundrechts durch Rechtsvergleichung* (Zurich, Schulthess, 2003); See also M O'Boyle, 'Freedom from Self-Incrimination and the Right to Silence: A Pandora's Box?' in P Mahoney, F Matscher, H Petzold and L Wildhaber, *Protection des droits de l'homme: la perspective européenne, Mélanges à la mémoire de Rolv Ryssdal* (Cologne, Karl Heymanns, 2000); IH Dennis, 'Instrumental Protection, Human Right or Functional Necessity? Reassessing the Privilege against Self-Incrimination' (1995) 54 *Cambridge Law Journal* 342; N Oberholzer, *Grundzüge des Strafprozessrechts*, 2nd edn (Bern, Stämpfli, 2005); A Eser, 'Aussagefreiheit und Beistand des Verteidigers im Ermittlungsverfahren: Rechtsvergleichende Beobachtungen zur Rechtsstellung des Beschuldigten' (1967) 79 *Zeitschrift für die gesamte Strafrechtswissenschaft* 565.

safeguards', it appears to rely on the importance of non-compulsion: the accused must not be compelled to co-operate with the investigation authorities. In *John Murray* the Court defined the purpose of the privilege against self-incrimination and the right to silence in the following terms: '[b]y providing the accused with protection against improper compulsion by the authorities these immunities contribute to avoiding miscarriages of justice and securing the aims of Article 6'.[93] The focus of the case law has thus been on attempting to distinguish cases of true compulsion from cases where the accused should have been able to withstand the attempts to get him or her to co-operate.

(i)   Improper Compulsion

The Court has defined 'improper compulsion' in such as way as to encompass laws or regulations which compel those accused of criminal offences to incriminate themselves by threatening them with criminal sanctions in the event that they fail to co-operate. In *Funke v France*, the applicant was convicted and sentenced for refusing to disclose allegedly incriminating documents requested by customs officials. Finding that the obligation to disclose these documents violated Article 6, the Court stated:

> The special features of customs law cannot justify such an infringement of the rights of anyone 'charged with a criminal offence', within the autonomous meaning of the expression in Article 6 to remain silent and not to contribute to incriminating himself.[94]

Similarly, the Court held that there had been a violation of the privilege against self-incrimination in *Heaney and McGuinness v Ireland*, where the applicants were convicted and imprisoned for failing to answer police questions.[95] The Court held that the right not incriminate oneself presupposed that 'the prosecution in a criminal case seek to prove their case against the accused without resort to evidence obtained through methods of coercion or oppression in defiance of the will of the accused'.[96] In this sense the Court noted the obvious correlation with the obligation on the state to prove the guilt of the accused and not leave an accused with the burden of proving his or her innocence. The Court held that the 'degree of compulsion' imposed on the applicants with a view to compelling them to provide information relating to the charges against them 'destroyed the very essence' of their privilege against self-incrimination and the right to remain

---

[93]   *John Murray v United Kingdom*, judgment of 8 Feb 1996, Reports 1996-I, 30, (1996) 22 EHRR 29, para 45.

[94]   *Funke v France*, judgment of 25 Feb 1993, Series A no 256-A, (1993) 16 EHRR 297, para 44.

[95]   *Heaney and McGuinness v Ireland*, no 34720/97, ECHR 2000-XII, (2001) 33 EHRR 12, para 55; see also *Quinn v Ireland*, no 36887/97, judgment of 21 Dec 2000, para 56.

[96]   *Heaney and McGuinness v Ireland*, no 34720/97, ECHR 2000-XII, (2001) 33 EHRR 12, para 40.

silent.[97] Moreover, specifically referring to the terrorist nature of the alleged offences, the Court concluded that the public interest could not be invoked to justify the use of answers compulsorily obtained in a non-judicial investigation to incriminate the accused during the trial proceedings.[98] The Court reached the same conclusion in *JB v Switzerland,* where the applicant was convicted of refusing to submit documents to the tax authorities.[99]

The Court has found no distinction between the imposition of criminal sanctions themselves and the threat to impose them. The threat of criminal prosecution was at issue in *Saunders v United Kingdom,* where the accused was forced to disclose material in connection with a fraud investigation.[100] Failure to do so would have resulted in the possible imposition of penal sanctions. The Commission stated that the 'privilege against self incrimination formed an important element in safeguarding individuals from oppression and coercion, was linked to the presumption of innocence and should apply equally to all types of accused'.[101] The Court held that the right not to incriminate oneself was primarily concerned 'with respecting the will of an accused person to remain silent'.[102] The test for ascertaining whether there had been a violation of the right involved determining 'whether the applicant has been subject to compulsion to give evidence and whether the use made of the resulting testimony at his trial offended the basic principles of a fair procedure inherent in Article 6(1) of which the right not to incriminate oneself is a constituent element'.[103] In this case the obligation to answer potentially incriminating questions and the subsequent use of the statements in court breached the privilege, and thus Article 6. These cases demonstrate the clearest type of compulsion, where failure of the accused to speak results in, or could result in, criminal sanctions. This type of compulsion has been consistently held by the Court to constitute an unacceptable interference with the guarantees protected by Article 6.

(ii)   Indirect 'Acceptable' Compulsion

Inevitably the identification of improper compulsion means that some degree of compulsion or, as the Court has put it, 'a certain level of indirect compulsion' is

---

[97]   *Ibid,* at para 55.
[98]   *Ibid,* at para 57.
[99]   *JB v Switzerland,* no 31827/96, ECHR 2001-III, 435.
[100]   *Saunders v United Kingdom,* judgment of 17 Dec 1996, Reports 1996-IV, 2044, (1997) 23 EHRR 313. See the similar cases of *IJL, GMR and AKP v United Kingdom,* nos 29522/95, 30056/96 and 30574/96, ECHR 2000-IX, (2001) 33 EHRR 11; *DC, HS and AD v United Kingdom,* App no 39031/97, decision of 14 Sept 1999, and *WGS and MLS v United Kingdom,* App no 38172/97, decision of 23 Nov 1999.
[101]   *Saunders v United Kingdom,* judgment of 17 Dec 1996, Reports 1996-VI, 2044, (1997) 23 EHRR 313, para 65.
[102]   *Ibid,* at para 69.
[103]   *Ibid.*

permissible.[104] In several cases the Court held that warning an accused that adverse inferences could be drawn at trial from his or her decision to remain silent during police questioning did not amount to improper compulsion. In *John Murray* the Court stated explicitly that it did not consider it prudent to 'give an abstract analysis of the scope of the immunities and, in particular, of what constitutes in this context "improper compulsion"'. Instead it noted that 'what is at stake in the present case is whether these immunities are absolute in the sense that the exercise by an accused of the right to silence cannot under any circumstances be used against him at trial, or alternatively, whether informing him in advance that, under certain conditions, his silence may be so used, is always to be regarded as "improper compulsion"'.[105]

The Court framed the issue in the following terms:

> On the one hand, it is self-evident that it is incompatible with the immunities under consideration to base a conviction solely or mainly on the accused's silence or a refusal to answer questions or to give evidence himself. On the other hand, the Court deems it equally obvious that these immunities cannot and should not prevent that the accused's silence, in situations which clearly call for an explanation from him, be taken into account in assessing the persuasiveness of the evidence adduced by the prosecution. Wherever the line between these two extremes is to be drawn, it follows from this understanding of the 'right to silence' that the question whether the right is absolute must be answered in the negative. It cannot be said therefore that an accused's decision to remain silent throughout criminal proceedings should necessarily have no implications when the trial court seeks to evaluate the evidence against him. In particular, as the Government have pointed out, established international standards in this area, while providing for the right to silence and the privilege against self incrimination, are silent on this point.'[106]

The Court went on to note that determining whether there had been a violation of Article 6 would depend on the circumstances of each case. In this case the accused had elected to remain silent during police questioning and had opted not to give evidence in the trial proceedings. Although the accused had been warned that inferences might be drawn from his silence, he was not in the Court's opinion subject to direct compulsion of the threat of criminal sanctions. The Court noted that:

> Admittedly a system which warns the accused—who is possibly without legal assistance (as in the applicant's case)—that adverse inferences may be drawn from a refusal to provide an explanation to the police for his presence at the scene of a crime or to testify during his trial, when taken in conjunction with the weight of the case against him,

---

[104] *John Murray v United Kingdom,* judgment of 8 Feb 1996, Reports 1996-I, 30, (1996) 22 EHRR 29, para 46.
[105] *Ibid,* at para 44.
[106] *Ibid,* at para 47.

involves a certain level of indirect compulsion. However, since the applicant could not be compelled to speak or to testify, as indicated above, this factor on its own cannot be decisive.[107]

The Court went on to find that, as there was no direct compulsion and as the domestic court had not relied wholly or mainly on the accused's silence to establish proof of guilt, there had been no interference with Article 6.

The Court continued with this approach in *Averill v United Kingdom*.[108] Here the applicant was refused access to a solicitor for the first 24 hours of police questions. He chose to remain silent, although he did offer some explanations to the Court during his trial. The judge drew 'very strong' adverse inferences from the silence of the accused during police questioning, and rejected his submissions that his silence was motivated by policy considerations. In this case the Court, noting that the trial judge had been able to exercise his discretion, went so far as to state that 'the decision to drawn adverse inferences must be seen only as one of the elements upon which the trial judge found that the charges against the applicant had been proved beyond reasonable doubt'.[109] It concluded that the applicant was fully apprised of the implications of remaining silent and was therefore aware of the risks which a policy-based defence could entail for him at his trial.

In *Condron and others v United Kingdom* the applicants complained that the decision of the trial judge to leave the jury with the option of drawing an adverse inference from their silence during police interview resulted in the denial of their right to a fair trial.[110] Unlike in *Averill* and *John Murray* the accused elected to give evidence at trial. They had been cautioned and had access to legal advice throughout the police interrogations. The applicants stated that their decision not to speak was based on the advice of their lawyer that they were unfit to answer questions. They argued that the terms of the judge's direction were defective since he failed to advise the jury that that it should draw an adverse inference only if it concluded that their silence was attributed to their having no answer to the charges, or none that would stand up to cross-examination. The end result of the direction was to leave the jury free to draw an adverse inference even if it was satisfied that the reason the applicants held their silence was that they were withdrawing from heroin and were acting on the firm advice of their solicitor, reasons which, moreover, could not in any way be construed as probative of their guilt. The Court noted that:

> [T]he formula employed by the trial judge cannot be said to reflect the balance which the Court in its *John Murray* judgment sought to strike between the right to silence and the circumstances in which an adverse inference may be drawn from silence, including by a jury… In the Court's opinion, as a matter of fairness, the jury should have been

---

[107] *Ibid*, at para 50.
[108] *Averill v United Kingdom*, no 36408/97, ECHR 2000-VI, 203, (2001) 31 EHRR 36.
[109] *Ibid*, at paras 50–51.
[110] *Condron v United Kingdom*, no 35718/97, ECHR 2000-V, 1, (2001) 31 EHRR 1.

directed that it could only draw an adverse inference if satisfied that the applicants' silence at the police interview could only sensibly be attributed to their having no answer or none that would stand up to cross-examination.[111]

The Court held that the failure of the judge to issue such a direction fundamentally compromised the fairness of the trial.

(iii) The Relationship Between 'Compulsion' and the Assistance of Counsel

Despite the relatively strict line drawn by the Court between proper and improper compulsion, the Court has accepted that other factors may also be important in the determination of whether the privilege against self-incrimination or the right to remain silent was violated. In *Magee v United Kingdom* the Court considered the effect of restricted access to a solicitor on the applicant's ability to decide whether to co-operate with the police or not, thus considering issues pertinent to Article 6(3)(c) and 6(1) together.[112] It had already considered the same issues, but separately, in *John Murray*, eventually concluding that while there had been a breach of Article 6(3)(c) there had been no breach of Article 6(1). *Magee* concerned the same provisions which had been at issue in *John Murray* and which enabled the court to draw adverse inferences from the accused's decision not to respond to police questioning during detention. Unlike Murray however, Magee broke his silence, and confessed after a prolonged period of detention without access to a lawyer. Consequently there was no opportunity for the trial court to draw adverse inferences.

Referring to *John Murray* the Court accepted that the nature of the caution which warned an accused that adverse inferences might be drawn from his or her silence might place the accused in a dilemma at the beginning of interrogation:

> On the one hand, if he chooses to remain silent, adverse inferences may be drawn against him in accordance with the provisions of the Order. On the other hand, if the accused opts to break his silence during the course of interrogation, he runs the risk of prejudicing his defence without necessarily removing the possibility of inferences being drawn against him.

The Court concluded that 'under such conditions the concept of fairness requires that the accused have the benefit of the assistance of a lawyer already at the initial stages of the police interrogation'.[113]

The Court stated that although Article 6 will normally require that the accused be allowed to benefit from the assistance of a lawyer already at the initial stages of

---

[111] *Ibid*, at para 61.
[112] *Magee v United Kingdom*, no 28135/95, ECHR 2000-VI, 159, (2001) 31 EHRR 35.
[113] *John Murray v United Kingdom*, judgment of 8 Feb 1996, Reports 1996-I, 30, (1996) 22 EHRR 29, para 66.

police interrogation, this right, which was not explicitly set out in the Convention, could be restricted for good cause. The question in each case was whether the restriction, in the light of the entirety of the proceedings, had deprived the accused of a fair hearing.[114] The Court held that 'to deny access to a lawyer for such a long period and in a situation where the rights of the defence were irretrievably prejudiced is—whatever the justification for such denial—incompatible with the rights of the accused under Article 6'.[115] The Court held that, while the confession had been voluntary and there was no evidence that the applicant had been ill treated, the statements had been made after he had spent 48 hours in custody without legal assistance and they had become the 'central platform' of the prosecution's case and subsequently the basis for the applicant's conviction. In such circumstances, this constituted a breach of Article 6.[116] Although encouraging, this is nevertheless far from an unambiguous requirement that defence counsel be present.

(iv) The Privilege Against Self-incrimination as a Substitute for the Refusal to Insist on Adversarial Principles in the Investigation Phase

An important and worrying aspect of the Court's case law is its tendency in determining the extent of the privilege to balance the rights of the accused against the interests of the investigation. So while in *John Murray* it held that 'particular caution was required before a domestic court could invoke an accused's silence against him', it also held that it was 'obvious that the right cannot and should not prevent that the accused's silence, in situations which clearly call for an explanation from him, be taken into account in assessing the persuasiveness of the evidence adduced by the prosecution'.[117] Further, there is evidence in the case law of a reluctance to impose too high guarantees for the accused in the investigative phase for fear that it may compromise the investigation of crime. In a series of cases involving investigations conducted by UK Department of Trade and Industry inspectors liaising with prosecuting officials, the Court held that their functions were 'essentially investigative in nature' as 'they did not adjudicate either in form or in substance Court' stating that; 'a requirement that such a preparatory investigation should be subject to the guarantees of a judicial procedure as set forth in Article 6 § 1 would in practice unduly hamper the effective regulation in the public interest of complex financial

---

[114] *Ibid*, at para 63; *Magee v United Kingdom,* no 28135/95, ECHR 2000-VI, 159, (2001) 31 EHRR 35, para 47.
[115] *Ibid*, para 48.
[116] *Ibid*, at para 49.
[117] *John Murray v United Kingdom,* judgment of 8 Feb 1996, Reports 1996-I, 30, (1996) 22 EHRR 29, para 47.

and commercial activities.'[118] This highlights not only the Court's acknowledgment of criminal proceeding as involving two distinct phases, but also its reluctance to insist on adversarial conditions in the investigation phase.

A view frequently expressed in the Court's case law is that the right to silence and the privilege against self-incrimination lie 'at the heart of the notion of fair procedure in Article 6'.[119] But it must be questioned whether this can really be said to be the case. Although this may be compatible with an understanding of criminal proceedings governed by neutral, impartial investigation authorities it seems somewhat at odds with the adversarial system developed in the course of the nineteenth century and adopted by the Court in its interpretation of Article 6(1). In view of this, its benefit to the accused must be viewed with some scepticism. It is difficult to avoid the impression that the Court's emphasis on the privilege against self-incrimination is intended in some sense to compensate for its refusal to insist on the right of the accused to legal assistance before and during police questioning. Insofar as the Court's notion of fairness is based on institutional adversariality, the privilege against self-incrimination far from lying at the heart of the notion of fairness could even be seen as undermining it.

The appeal to individual autonomy seems to be invoked almost as an alternative to serious consideration of tension between the fairness guarantees of the trial and the under-regulation of the investigation. This situation bears an unmistakable resemblance to the nineteenth century discussions, where considerable emphasis was placed on 'non-compulsion' as a means to avoid the development of a regulatory structure for the investigation phase that would be compatible with the accusatorial concept of the trial. In *Allan v United Kingdom*, for instance, the Court held:

> While the right to silence and the privilege against self-incrimination are primarily designed to protect against improper compulsion by the authorities and the obtaining of evidence through methods of coercion or oppression in defiance of the will of the accused, the scope of the right is not confined to cases where duress has been brought to bear on the accused or where the will of the accused has been directly overborne in some way. The right, which the Court has previously observed is at the heart of the notion of fair procedure, serves in principles to protect the freedom of a suspected person to choose whether to speak or to remain silent when questioned by the police.[120]

This statement must be viewed as somewhat confusing. In particular the reference to 'the will of the accused' seems somewhat out of place in a system in which the accused's position is fundamentally and institutionally connected to his or

---

[118] *Fayed v United Kingdom*, judgment of 21 Sept 1994, Series A no 294-B, (1994) 19 EHRR 393, para 62; see also *Saunders v United Kingdom*, judgment of 17 Dec 1996, Reports 1996-VI, 2044, (1997) 23 EHRR 313, para 67; *IJL, GMR and AKP v United Kingdom*, nos 29522/95, 30056/96, 30574/96, ECHR 2000-IX, (2001) 33 EHRR 11, para 100.

[119] Eg *Condron v United Kingdom*, no 35718/97, ECHR 2000-V, (2001) 31 EHRR 1, para 56; *John Murray v United Kingdom*, judgment of 8 Feb 1996, Reports 1996-I, 30, (1996) 22 EHRR 29, para 47.

[120] *Allan v United Kingdom*, no 48539/99, ECHR 2002-IX, (2003) 36 EHRR 12, para 50.

her role as part of the defence. The focus on the accused as an individual, far from taking seriously his or her 'will', serves in fact to undermine the institutional position of the defence. The right to 'choose' whether to speak or remain silent when questioned by the police would undoubtedly be better guaranteed by allowing the accused to consult with counsel. The argument here is not that the privilege against self-incrimination and the assistance of counsel during the investigation hearings should be seen as alternatives, but merely that the former should not be seen as sufficient compensation for the absence of the latter. But it is more than that, because the case law on the privilege against self-incrimination expressly focuses on the autonomy of the accused and thereby neglects the importance of the defence role in the institutional understanding of fairness. There is a danger, therefore, that the importance of the privilege against self-incrimination is exaggerated precisely in order to obscure the deficiencies of the institutional position of the defence during the investigative phases of the proceedings.

Pre-trial safeguards are absolutely essential, but if the Court is serious about employing an adversarial conception of fairness, it must focus more on the regulation of the investigation phase. As the nineteenth century jurists noted, it is insufficient and inconsistent continually to emphasise the importance of the adversarial trial and yet to neglect the ways in which this can be undermined.[121] The introduction of, and reliance on, evidence at trial which the accused was able to challenge only in the non-adversarial investigation phase is fundamentally at odds with the understanding of fairness which the Court has itself set out as essential to a fair trial. Recourse to the privilege against self-incrimination to uphold the legitimacy of the investigation is incoherent and problematic, not least because it emphasises the role of the accused as an individual rather than as part of the defence, thereby undermining the essence of the Court's approach to fairness.

H   The Root of the Problem: Defining the 'Trial'

(i)   The Investigation Phase Lacuna

The essence of the confusion lies in the fact that the definition of the trial, and in particular the distinction between the trial and the investigation, has been ignored. Resembling a system of common law, but lacking a strong doctrine of precedent to lend the judgments consistency, the case law of the Court is susceptible to criticism that it lacks coherence. In most cases the relatively rigid

---

[121] Eg J Vargha, *Die Verteidigung in Strafsachen* (Vienna, Manz'sche k. k. Hof-Verlag und Univ. Buchhandlung, 1879) at 395.

structure of the Convention itself provides sufficient support to thwart such criticism, but in those areas where the text of the Convention provides little guidance the deficiencies of this system are exposed. This is undoubtedly the case in relation to the lack of regulation of the investigative phases of criminal proceedings. Although the Convention sets out guidelines in Article 6 for the regulation of the trial and although it is well established that in relation to arrest and detention Article 6 should give way to Article 5,[122] there is no mention of the procedure to be followed in relation to proceedings before trial. As the investigation phase follows the detention but precedes the trial, it seems to slip between these two provisions. This lacuna has had a substantial effect on the interpretation of Article 6.

As is illustrated above in relation to witness evidence, the Court has chosen to interpret Article 6 as permitting the hearing and challenging of evidence to take place during the investigation phase. In doing so it has suggested that it is legitimate for the defence's right to be heard (to hear and to challenge the evidence against it) to be exercised during the pre-trial phase; this however has called into question the distinction, central to the European procedural tradition, between the determinative trial and the investigative phase. It also raises doubts about the coherence of Article 6(1). If the Court's own concepts of fairness in Article 6(1), ie the principle of adversarial proceedings and the equality of arms, are to be taken seriously it would seem that the they will have to be exercised in conditions compatible with the other aspects of Article 6(1), namely at a public trial adjudicated by an impartial judge.

The lack of regulation specific to the investigation phase has also created a number of problems in relation to other aspects of Article 6. The extent to which a lawyer should be present in the interrogative stages is, for instance, left under-regulated and the Court has to struggle to incorporate into the investigation phase guarantees that were designed to be applied at trial.

(ii) Explaining the Investigation Phase Lacuna: *Les Travaux Préparatoires?*[123]

The reason for the investigation phase lacuna lies partly in the drafting of the text of Article 6. There can be no doubt that the provision is clearly orientated towards the trial at the expense of the investigation phase, which is almost entirely ignored. If this seems to represent a rather trial-based, perhaps even Anglo-Saxon, approach to criminal procedure, this can perhaps, at least in part,

---

[122] *Imbrioscia v Switzerland*, judgment of 24 Nov 1993, Series A no 275, (1994) 17 EHRR 441.
[123] See also the discussion of the fair trial provisions during the drafting of the United Nations Declaration of Human Rights in D Weissbrodt, *The Right to a Fair Trial: Articles 8, 10 and 11 of the Universal Declaration of Human Rights* (The Hague: Kluwer Law, 2001) and S Trechsel, *Human Rights in Criminal Proceedings* (Oxford, Oxford University Press, 2005).

be explained by the drafting process. The *travaux préparatoires* show that originally the provisions concerning both legality of detention and the right to a fair trial were combined, in rather vague terms, in one provision:

3a) No one shall be subject to arbitrary arrest, detention or exile.

b) Everyone is entitled in full equality to a fair and public hearing by an independent and impartial tribunal, in the determination of his rights and obligations and of any criminal charge against him.[124]

There was considerable discussion in both the Committee of Experts responsible for drafting the Convention and, later, in the Council of Ministers about whether this draft or a rival draft based on proposals by the British delegation should be accepted. The United Kingdom representative was unhappy with the possibility of concluding a Convention, which did not contain 'as precise a definition of these rights as possible'.[125] On this basis they decided to submit 'precise proposals' drawn up by the Government and to be submitted to the Committee of Experts. These read as follows:

Art. 8. 1) In the determination of any criminal charge against him or of his rights and obligations in a suit at law everyone is entitled to a fair and public hearing by an independent and impartial tribunal established by law.

Judgment shall be pronounced publicly but the press and public may be excluded from all or part of the trial in the interests of morals, public order or national security, or where the interests of juveniles or incapacitated persons so requires.

2) Everyone charged with a penal offence has the right to be presumed innocent until proved guilty according to law. In the determination of any criminal charge against him, everyone is entitled:

to be informed promptly of the nature and cause of the accusation against him;

to defend himself in person or through legal assistance of his own choosing and if he has not sufficient means to pay for such assistance, to be given it free when the interests of justice so require;

to examine or have examined the witnesses against him and to obtain compulsory attendance of witnesses on his behalf;

to have the free assistance of an interpreter if he cannot understand or speak the language used in court.[126]

This proposal, which clearly resembles the current Convention, includes the first reference not only to the right to examine and call witnesses[127] but also to all of

---

[124] Council of Europe, *Collected Edition of the 'Travaux Préparatoires' of the European Convention on Human Rights* (The Hague, Martinus Nijhoff, 1975–85), iii, at 320.
[125] Sir Oscar Dowson (UK representative) in *ibid*, iii, at 258.
[126] See Council of Europe, *Collected Edition of the 'Travaux Préparatoires' of the European Convention on Human Rights* (The Hague, Martinus Nijhoff, 1975–85), iii, at 284.
[127] *Ibid.*

the specific provisions of Article 6(3) except Article 6(3)(e). Following the British proposal there was no consensus in the Committee of Experts as to which to adopt. The Committee decided that it was 'impossible to amalgamate the text of the Articles defining Human Rights in the United Kingdom Proposals and the text of the Articles listing these rights in the Assembly's draft since the systems on which these two drafts were based were essentially different'. But on the other hand the Committee felt that the 'choice between the two systems should be decided in the light of political rather than legal considerations'.[128] In the end it was decided to put these alternatives to the Committee of Ministers. The Committee of Ministers, comprising senior officials mainly from the interior ministries of the member states, then met to consider the drafts. The British representative (Mr Hoare) based his case for the British proposal on two principal grounds. First, the treaty would create obligations which states would be bound to perform, and they had to know 'the precise extent of their undertakings' and, secondly, if the rights were defined in more general terms it would be 'easier to avoid observing them'. The following discussion is more or less confined to these arguments. There is almost no discussion of the substance of the texts. Indeed the Greek representative noted that 'not being a lawyer he could not help with the redrafting of the various alternatives, which was essentially legal work'.[129] The Irish supported a general discussion, while the Italians favoured a 'comparative study' on an article-by-article basis. In the end the Chairman decided on a general discussion based on political principles. The final texts of Articles 5 and 6 are clearly those proposed by the British representative with minor amendments. Thus it seems that the decision to include the right to examine witnesses at trial was made by British legal experts and accepted by politicians who had no special expertise in the field of criminal procedure law and who made the decision on which proposal to accept on the basis of whether a more explicit or a more general text would be preferable and without any discussion of the effects of the substantive provisions themselves.

(iii)   Resolving the Fairness Deficit: Acknowledging the European Procedural Tradition

If the nature of the drafting process can help to explain the lack of provision for regulation of the investigation, an Anglo-Saxon bias cannot be held to be the reason for the creation of the equality of arms and adversarial procedure doctrines. Rather these are based on an understanding of criminal proceedings as developed across Europe in the nineteenth century as based on the accusatorial trinity of impartial judges, partisan prosecutors and defence teams, comprising

---

[128]   *Ibid*, iv, at 16.
[129]   Council of Europe, *Collected Edition of the 'Travaux Préparatoires' of the European Convention on Human Rights* (The Hague, Martinus Nijhoff, 1975–85), iv, at 106.

both the accused and counsel, equipped with certain procedural opportunities. The importance of this procedural form was based on acceptance of the accusatorial trinity, and thus the evidence was to be examined at a public, oral trial, supervised by an impartial judge, while the investigation phase was to be primarily orientated towards allowing the parties to prepare for the trial. Most importantly, the participatory opportunities to be afforded to the accused were developed in the context of this institutional structure. This means that fairness is dependent not just on the exercise of certain procedural opportunities, but on the exercise of these procedural opportunities in a specific institutional environment: the oral, public, impartial trial.

Insofar as the Court's approach to witness evidence fails to acknowledge this relationship it not only defies the European procedural tradition, but also compromises its claim to apply one notion of procedural fairness by disregarding the fact that its own concept of fairness is heavily dependent on its vision of the structure of the trial. In view of this, it can be characterised only as wholly unsatisfactory. In essence, the Court has sought to minimise perceived differences in the procedural laws of the member states by altering the notion of what constitutes a 'trial', extending it into the investigation phase while simultaneously reducing the extent of the guarantee and creating a two-tier standard of fairness. The procedural opportunities of an accused who can examine witnesses at trial differ from those of an accused who has the chance to question witnesses in a partisan pre-trial environment. Moreover the main aspect of the Court's case law on the privilege against self-incrimination must be seen to be quite at odds, in the absence of further regulation, with the otherwise resolutely adversarial nature of the Court's understanding of criminal proceedings.

It is essential to see that the controversies involving the regulation of witness evidence are not merely symptomatic of differences between European criminal procedural systems but are rather indicative of a wide-ranging European-wide failure to address the consequences of the strict separation of the trial and investigation phases. The introduction of evidence at trial which could be challenged only in non-accusatorial circumstances is incompatible with a system based on the accusatorial trinity and an adversarial conception of the trial, and thus fundamentally undermines the trial's claim to legitimacy through fairness.

These problems can be solved only by recognising the deficiencies of the comparative criminal law scholarship's characterisation of European criminal proceedings as divided into accusatorial and inquisitorial procedural systems, and acknowledging instead the legacy of the nineteenth century developments in which the European procedural tradition originated. This would mean accepting the importance of the separation of prosecuting and judging or examining the evidence and recognising that this requires a strict distinction between the investigative pre-trial stage and the determinative trial. The Court's case law on the 'equality of arms' and 'adversarial procedure' requirements suggests recognition of the first element; as regards the second element there is still some way to go.

It is difficult to avoid the conclusion that in regulating the 'fair trial' the Court has focused primarily on the right to hear and challenge the evidence. This guarantee, related as it is to notions of communication and participation, is undoubtedly an important element of the notion of a fair trial, but it represents only part of the picture. Regulation of the institutional setting in which these rights can be exercised is equally important. The failure to acknowledge the dependency of the procedural rights of the defence on the institutional form of the proceedings has led to inconsistency in the creation of a European standard of fairness in criminal proceedings.

6

Reassessing Fairness in European Criminal Law: Procedural Fairness, Individual Rights and Institutional Forms

A Procedural Fairness as Individual Rights

THERE CAN BE little doubt that fairness in criminal proceedings has become synonymous with procedural rights, and more specifically with ensuring that those accused of criminal offences have an adequate opportunity to exercise certain rights. Those charged with a criminal offence have the 'right' to a fair trial, the 'right' to present evidence in their defence and the 'right' to remain silent. Even in legal systems such as those of the United Kingdom, where theorising in terms of rights was traditionally unpopular,[1] scholars have increasingly turned to considering the 'advantages of conceptualizing the criminal process in terms of rights in general and human rights in particular'.[2]

---

[1] G Maher, 'Human Rights and the Criminal Process' in T Campbell, D Goldberg, S McLean and T Mullen (eds), *Human Rights: From Rhetoric to Reality* (Oxford, Basil Blackwell, 1986) at 199 argued that British lawyers do not 'have much place for human rights as part of their conceptual map: human rights play only a minor part in how the criminal process is understood and justified'.

[2] *Ibid*, at 197. Developments in the UK at the end of the 20th century, and in particular the 'incorporation' of the ECHR, seem to have contributed to this, see T Mullen, J Murdoch, A Miller and S Craig, 'Human Rights in the Scottish Courts' (2005) 32 *Journal of Law and Society* 148; L Farmer and S Veitch, *The State of Scots Law* (Edinburgh, Butterworths, 2001) at 1–10; R Reed and J Murdoch, *A Guide to Human Rights Law in Scotland* (Edinburgh, Butterworths, 2001), especially ch 1; J Jackson, 'The Impact of Human Rights on Judicial Decision Making in Criminal Cases' in J Jackson and S Doran (eds), *The Judicial Role in Criminal Proceedings* (Oxford, Hart Publishing, 2000) at 109–25; ATH Smith, 'The Human Rights Act and the Criminal Lawyer: The Constitutional Context' [1999] *Criminal Law Review* 251. It is worth noting that in a later article Maher expresses doubt whether 'the concept of human rights has sufficient substance in its own right' to support a theory of the criminal process: G Maher, 'Dialogue and the Criminal Process' in E Attwool and D Goldberg (eds), *Criminal Justice: papers from the Twentieth Annual Conference of the UK Association for Legal and Social Philosophy* (Stuttgart, Franz Steiner Verlag, 1995) at 43.

169

Procedural rights are said to operate as 'procedural restraints on state power to ensure that the individual is treated with dignity and respect', thereby limiting (as well as legitimising) the application of the substantive law.[3] A theory, so the argument goes, 'which uses the notion of human rights has the effect of blocking arguments which allow or require the interests of individuals in the criminal process to be overridden' by, for example, 'the social value in increased fact-finding'.[4] It is precisely this 'constitutional type' character of rights that lends them their strategic importance, particularly when they are viewed in Dworkinian terms as 'trumps' able to defeat collective social goals.[5] Principles expressed as rights have more protection from interference from politicians and the electorate than norms expressed as mere laws. Indeed this would seem to be precisely the reason for the creation of the European Convention on Human Rights. In the aftermath of the Second World War, there was a desire to find legal means to try and prevent the types of atrocities which took place in Europe in the first half of the twentieth century. The Convention can therefore be seen in the context of an international attempt to set standards which could not be overridden by the competing aims of the various legislatures.[6] This was to be achieved first by way of collective inter-state agreement on those principles which were to be deemed 'inviolable'—thus providing for the potential for collective disapproval in the event that a member state did in fact violate the provisions—and secondly though the setting out of these principles in the language of 'human rights'. The expression of the Convention guarantees as 'rights' afforded them not just greater symbolic importance than would have been attributed to them had they been expressed simply as legal norms, it also conferred significant concrete benefits for those seeking to have them applied in practice.[7]

In spite of the very real advantages of expressing fairness in terms of rights, it is impossible to avoid the conclusion that this focus on rights has been at the expense of consideration of the institutional context of criminal proceedings. This is highlighted by the tendency to shoehorn principles into the language of rights—even if this classification is not entirely accurate. Questioning the accuracy of the designation of the standards set out in Article 6 as 'rights' may seem overly pedantic. In fact ambiguity as to the character of some principles set out in Article 6 provides a valuable insight into the problem of construing fairness in terms of rights. This issue is perhaps best exemplified by one 'institutional-type' value, which the Court has been forced by virtue of its inclusion in the text of

---

[3] P Arenella, 'Rethinking the Functions of Criminal Procedure: The Warren Courts and Burger Courts' Competing Ideologies' (1983) 72 *Georgetown Law Journal* 185 at 200.

[4] G Maher, 'Human Rights and the Criminal Process' in T Campbell, D Goldberg, S McLean and T Mullen (eds), *Human Rights: From Rhetoric to Reality* (Oxford, Basil Blackwell, 1986) at 218.

[5] R Dworkin, *Taking Rights Seriously* (Cambridge, Mass, Harvard University Press, 1977) at p xi

[6] See T Buergenthal, 'International Human Rights Law and Institutions: Accomplishments and Prospects' (1988) 63 *Washington Law Review* 1.

[7] L Sohn, 'The New International Law: Protection of the Rights of Individuals Rather than States' (1982) 32 *American University Law Review* 1.

Article 6 to regulate, namely the public hearing requirement. Several commentators have cast doubt on the characterisation of the publicity of the trial as an individual right.[8] The fact that 'many an accused, including those who ultimately secure an acquittal, would opt—if given the choice—for avoiding the stress and ignominy of publicity'[9] makes it difficult to characterise it as something, which has been 'chosen' by the accused. Moreover, the fact that an accused does not have an '*ex ante* power' to waive the possibility to be tried in public leads Jaconelli to suggest that it cannot accurately be described from the perspective of 'will theory'[10] as a 'right'.[11] He also highlights problems with its characterisation as a 'right' from the perspective of 'interest theory', not least because it is by no means clear (especially when the public trial requirement is examined from an historical perspective) that the accused can be identified as the 'intended beneficiary'.[12] The fact that neither of the main rights theories can support the categorisation of the public trial as a right leads him to conclude that 'no such right exists: however valuable the open conduct of trials may be, it can be explained in terms other than those of rights'.[13]

If it is accepted that the public hearing requirement cannot (or at least cannot always[14]) be construed as a 'right', this has serious ramifications for a system, such as that of the ECHR, which is dependent on individual applicants claiming 'their rights'. If a public hearing is viewed by applicants rather as a burden than as something beneficial, then it would appear that there is no way of insisting that member States uphold this aspect of the fair trial. Trechsel recognises this when he notes that other interested parties could exercise their right to information under Article 10 ECHR to gain access to the hearing.[15] But this solution necessarily raises issues of the legitimacy of the inclusion of the principle in a provision directed towards protecting the rights of those charged with a criminal offence. Moreover other institutional values may not be capable of being enforced by anyone.

Arguments based solely or principally on 'rights' seem to ignore the possibility that procedural fairness may require something else. The failure to recognise the relationship between individual rights and the institutional form of the proceedings is also a failure to understand that rights alone offer insufficient restraints on the procedural law to guarantee procedural fairness. Other values, even if they are

---

[8] Eg S Trechsel, *Human Rights in Criminal Proceedings* (Oxford, Oxford University Press, 2005) at 121: '[i]t is even doubtful whether it is correct to characterize the rule that trials have to be held in public as an individual right'.

[9] J Jaconelli, 'Rights Theories and Public Trial' (1997) 14 *Journal of Applied Philosophy* 169.

[10] See H Steiner, *An Essay on Rights* (Oxford, Blackwell, 1994) at 57 ff.

[11] J Jaconelli, 'Rights Theories and Public Trial' (1997) 14 *Journal of Applied Philosophy* 169 at 170.

[12] *Ibid*, at 174. On interest perspective in this context see N McCormick, 'Rights in Legislation' in PS Hacker and J Raz, *Law, Morality and Society* (Oxford, Oxford University Press, 1977) at 202.

[13] J Jaconelli, 'Rights Theories and Public Trial' (1997) 14 *Journal of Applied Philosophy* 169 at 174.

[14] In some cases, of course, an accused may actually desire a public trial.

[15] S Trechsel, *Human Rights in Criminal Proceedings* (Oxford, Oxford University Press, 2005) at 122–3.

not principally orientated towards the individual interests of the accused person, may also be essential to a comprehensive conception of procedural fairness.

B Procedural Rights and Institutional Forms

As was argued in Chapter 2, acknowledgment of the development of the institutional role of the defence within the criminal procedural system makes it clear that the extent of the rights of the accused will depend on the institutional form of the proceedings. The regulation of the institutional setting must therefore be seen to be a prerequisite to enabling the consistent application of procedural rights and to the creation of a uniform standard of procedural fairness across different jurisdictions. The disregarding of the importance of regulating the institutional form of criminal proceedings has led to the propagation of the erroneous view that fairness can be achieved through requiring the implementation of defence rights regardless of the institutional form of the procedural system. Procedural rights, however, cannot be seen to be capable of application irrespective of the institutional context in which they are expected to operate. This raises serious questions about the possibility of achieving 'procedural fairness' through the prescription of various defence rights in the absence of a clear understanding of the setting in which these are to be applied.

The historical analysis of the development of European criminal procedure in the course of the nineteenth century demonstrates that those principles, which are now commonly thought of as instrumental 'defence rights', developed as part of the institutional and structural form of the criminal procedural system. The development of the 'defence role' was precipitated principally by other institutional developments—notably the separation of judging and prosecuting—rather than as a means to enhance the autonomy of the accused or as a constraint on the criminal justice authorities. Indeed this is evidenced by the fact that developments towards an increased role for the defence were accompanied by considerable scepticism by commentators as to whether they could truly be seen to be in the interests of individual accused persons.[16] This suggests not only that any attempt to regulate 'fairness' solely on the basis of individual rights and without regard for the institutional context in which these are to be applied will be necessarily incomplete, it also calls into question the understanding of criminal proceedings as principally focused on the accused.

---

[16] JF Stephen, *A History of the Criminal Law of England* (London, Macmillan, 1883), i–iii; see also Ch 3, above.

While the nineteenth century has been characterised by some as a period in which 'individualism was valued in social and political form',[17] the writings of the nineteenth century jurists seem to call into question suggestions that the autonomy of the accused represented the primary concern in the development of criminal proceedings. Rather, after the institutional development of the criminal justice system, the defence was given certain procedural rights within this setting. This is clearly emphasised by the treatment of the importance of the accused's participation. Those accused of criminal offences were not (and are not) given the opportunity to decide whether to participate or not; whether to accept the jurisdiction of the court or not; whether to acknowledge the criminal law as their law or not (it is quite legitimate for states to punish foreign nationals who commit crimes; similarly people can be punished for acts committed in a different jurisdiction). Instead they are compelled to submit to the state's monopoly to prosecute and punish. These comments should not be misunderstood as suggesting that the participation requirement is unfavourable or of dubious validity, but rather they serve to suggest that it may have value beyond that of guaranteeing the rights of an accused. It promotes recognition of the states' power to prosecute, it serves to legitimise the criminal process and, most importantly from a practical perspective, it enables enforcement of the verdict. As was argued in Chapter 3, the historical development of criminal proceedings must be viewed as having been primarily concerned, not with the institutional role of the individual accused in the proceedings, but rather with the role of the defence.[18] This is an important distinction as it reflects an understanding of criminal proceedings as based fundamentally on the relationship between the defence and the prosecution. It is this relationship which should be pivotal to an adequate understanding of the modern conception of fairness in criminal proceedings.

Individual rights and autonomy must be viewed from an historical perspective as having been constrained by the desire to create a standardised criminal justice system capable of regulating the prosecution of a diverse group of criminal offences and an assorted group of criminals. In this regard the principal concern was not for the individual right to a fair trial but for some sort of equality before the law, which was able to guarantee that everyone caught violating the criminal law would be subject to prosecution on the same basis. Inherent in this is an understanding of the importance of the standardisation of criminal procedure enabling the criminal law to be applied in an equal manner, free from claims of

---

[17] CJW Allen, *The Law of Evidence in Victorian England* (Cambridge, Cambridge University Press, 1997) at 173.

[18] Cf A Duff, L Farmer, S Marshall and V Tadros, *The Trial on Trial II: Judgment and Calling to Account* (Oxford, Hart Publishing, 2006) at 3, who argue that trials should 'give the defendant a central, and at least ideally an active, role in the trial—as the person to whom the criminal charge is addressed; who is summoned to answer that charge, and to answer for his conduct if it is proved to be criminal; and who is expected to accept responsibility for what he has done, and to accept the condemnation that a conviction expresses if his guilt is proved'.

arbitrariness, to a vast number of people.[19] It was this, and not individual procedural rights, which was seen to be key to acceptance of criminal proceedings.[20] Any notion of fairness couched only in terms of individual rights will fail to account for the fact that the 'morality of fairness is also the morality of comparison'.[21]

The reluctance to acknowledge the importance of the relationship between defence rights and the criminal justice system not only compromises the chance to apply one consistent standard of fairness, it also threatens to undermine the benefits afforded by the rights. Improving defence rights without making provision for institutional developments to accommodate these changes could result in the development of mechanisms to undermine the position of criminal proceedings[22] or even neutralise the benefits brought about by the creation of these rights:

> the criminal justice system is characterized by extraordinary discretion—over the definition of crimes (legislatures can criminalize as much as they wish), over enforcement (police and prosecutors can arrest and charge whom they wish, and over funding (legislatures can allocate resources as they wish). In a system so dominated by discretionary decisions, discrimination is easy, and constitutional law has surprisingly little to say about it.[23]

Merely insisting on the creation of procedural rights without considering the context of their application could, moreover, reduce the guarantees afforded to some accused persons; in the absence of system-wide regulation, the creation of rights may cause unfairness instead of guaranteeing fairness. Stuntz, for instance, has drawn attention to the ways in which procedural rights and laws which are

---

[19] P Ramsay, 'The Responsible Subject As Citizen: Criminal Law, Democracy and The Welfare State' (2006) 69 *MLR* 29.

[20] H Arendt, *The Origins of Totalitarianism* (San Diego, Cal, Harvest, 1968) at 91, writing about the Dreyfus Affair, seems to hint at this when she notes that while it 'in its broader political aspects belongs to the twentieth century... the various trials of the Jewish Captain Alfred Dreyfus, are quite typical of the nineteenth century, when men followed legal proceedings so keenly because each instance afforded a test of the century's greatest achievement, the complete impartiality of the law... The doctrine of equality before the law was still so firmly implanted in the conscience of the civilised world that a single miscarriage of justice could provoke public indignation from Moscow to New York.' See also P Ramsay, 'The Responsible Subject As Citizen: Criminal Law, Democracy and The Welfare State' (2006) 69 *MLR* 29.

[21] E Colvin, 'Conceptions of Fairness in the Criminal Process' (2000) Occasional Paper delivered at the International Society for the Reform of Criminal Law Conference, 9 July 2004, available at www.isrcl.org/papers/colvin.pdf (last visited 13 Apr 2006).

[22] There is some suggestion that this occurred in the United States where the due process reforms instituted by the Warren Court coincided with an exponential rise in plea-bargaining: P Arenella, 'Rethinking the Functions of Criminal Procedure: The Warren Courts and Burger Courts' Competing Ideologies' (1983) 72 *Georgetown Law Journal* 185 at 200. SR Moody and J Toombs, *Prosecution in the Public Interest* (Edinburgh, Scottish Academic Press, 1982) have suggested, moreover, that if the outcome of the trial is uncertain then either the defence or the prosecution or both may be more willing to seek a guilty plea than risk the uncertainty of the trial.

[23] W Stuntz, 'The Uneasy Relationship Between Criminal Procedure and Criminal Justice' (1997) 107 *Yale Law Journal* 1 at 5.

supposed to restrict both the law and those responsible for its application and to uphold equality can actually contribute to a bias in the law.[24] He notes that despite a significant rise in crime in the USA since the 1960s there was no corresponding increase in the number of prosecuting officials. The considerable and ever-increasing volume of alleged crimes forced prosecutors into limiting the number of cases that they could prosecute, enabling them in effect to 'choose among winners'. While in a 'low crime-to-law-enforcement-budget society' the constitutional procedural reforms instituted by the Warren Court might have proven hugely controversial, in a high-crime society (with a restricted prosecutorial budget) they had relatively little effect, precisely because the police and prosecutors were able to select those cases that they could successfully prosecute. Successful prosecution rate thus remained constant in spite of the increasing number of procedural rights.

Although the Warren Court increased the volume of procedural rights, it did not, for instance, insist on regulating the fees of state-appointed defence counsel. As a result, although the procedural reforms vastly increased the cost of prosecuting those able to exercise their procedural rights, this was kept in check by the low level of funding for defence counsel which limited the potential for poor defendants to 'litigate aggressively'. The consequence was therefore a considerable increase in 'the gap between the cost of prosecuting the rich and the cost of prosecuting the poor'.[25] In essence, he suggests that the granting of these procedural rights, far from ameliorating a class bias in the criminal law, actually contributed to it. The essential characteristic of the potential for unfairness identified by Stuntz is that it is not an individual conception of unfairness in a particular case (although this may certainly also be a consequence), but rather unfairness between those who are suspected of having committed a crime. As such it seems to have a closer affinity to concepts such as equality before the law than to notions of individual rights or autonomy.

In this regard it is also important to give some consideration to the importance of the substantive criminal law.[26] Those that rely on the procedural law to ensure fairness generally do so on the basis of an understanding that the necessary morality of the law lies in the way in which it is enacted or applied. Although procedural rights play a crucial role in regulating, and thereby legitimising, the whole enterprise of criminal prosecutions, these are only part of the picture. Other essential restraints include the principles of generality, legality, clarity and the requirement that laws are not retrospective.[27] But can there be said to be a role for procedure law in constraining the substance or content of the criminal law?

---

[24] *Ibid.*

[25] *Ibid*, at 31.

[26] IH Dennis, 'Reconstructing the Law of Criminal Evidence' [1989] *Current Legal Problems* 21 at 35: 'theorising about the law of criminal evidence needs to begin with the substantive law. Evidence like procedure, is adjectival law; we cannot properly understand its purposes without reference to its context.'

[27] The most famous account of the role of such restraints on the enactment and application of laws in upholding the morality of the law is undoubtedly that of L Fuller, *The Morality of Law* (New

It would seem relatively clear that there is little role in this regard for procedural rights, seeing as these are restricted to regulating how the law is applied (eg criminal law should be applied equally, consistently, not retrospectively etc by impartial judges or in oral proceedings). Similarly principles such as the burden of proof or the *mens rea* requirement are limited to regulating when the law can be applied and are unable to provide guidance on the substance of the criminal law itself. The most pressing issue in this regard is still that which was identified in 1959 by Henry Hart in his famous article on the aims of the criminal law:

> What sense does it make to insist on procedural safeguards in criminal prosecutions if anything can be made criminal in the first place? What sense does it make to prohibit ex post facto laws (to take the one explicit guarantee of the Federal Constitution on the substantive side) if a man can, in any event, be convicted of an infamous crime for inadvertent violation of a law of the existence of which he had no reason to know and which he had no reason to believe he was violating, even if he had known of its existence?[28]

This question engages with the limitations on the ability of procedural law to play a role in restraining the substantive criminal law in relation to the critical question of what conduct can be criminalised.[29] That there is considerable potential for injustice in society to be reflected in unjust criminal law is a point which has often been expressed and is openly conceded in criminal legal theory. But there is less willingness to consider either the effect of this realisation on ensuring fairness in criminal procedure law or the role of criminal procedure in contributing to such injustice. This issue is usually considered from the opposite perspective: the symbiotic relationship between the procedural and the substantive criminal law means that substantive fairness will depend on the fair application of the law. It is not enough that criminal laws apply to everyone; it is essential that they be applied to everyone. Discriminatory application of the law has been accepted on the social, legal and political levels as a problem with the potential to undermine confidence in the criminal justice system.[30]

But just as the failure to apply the substantive law in an equal manner endangers acceptance of the substantive law, so too can unfairness in the

---

Haven, Conn, Yale University Press, 1964), especially at 33–94. He outlines 8 requirements: generality, promulgation, non-retroactivity, clarity, freedom from contradictions, the possibility that the law can be upheld, constancy and congruence.

[28] HM Hart, 'The Aims of the Criminal Law' (1959) 23 *Law and Contemporary Problems* 401.

[29] The extent of the reliance on procedural law to uphold the 'morality of the law' is criticised by Fletcher who writes that 'the paradox of criminal law reform in the United States is that we are so engaged by the glittering constitutional issues of criminal procedure that we hardly notice the injustices rampant in the substantive criminal law': GP Fletcher, 'The Theory of Criminal Negligence: A Comparative Analysis' (1971) 119 *University of Pennsylvania Law Review* 401 at 401.

[30] A good example of this is provided by the comments of Amiri Howe in an interview with D Aitkenhead, 'Interview: Darcus and Amiri Howe', *Guardian*, 15 Oct 2005: '[i]t was just, like, 'cause I'm in England and I'm not accustomed to this kind of stuff or whatever. Police officers would stop and search you all the time and let white kids walk, so it's just a matter of time before you think ahhh, well, just fuck it man, you know? You just think, just forget a' dis.'

substantive law compromise the fairness of criminal proceedings. This is the challenge set out by Veitch who suggests that 'the right to a fair hearing is perfectly consistent and compatible with the reality of injustice in a democratic society'. He notes that this 'in one crucial sense' means that 'the meaning of a fair trial in an unfair society is similar in effect to that of an unfair trial in an unfair society'.[31] Any attempt to legitimise criminal justice through an appeal to the fairness of the trial must therefore be able to account for the gap between the substantive law and its application. It must recognise both that fair procedure may not be able to remedy inherent unfairness in the substantive law and that such unfairness must in turn inevitably compromise the trial's claim to fairness.[32]

The power attributed to procedural rights to restrain criminal procedure fails adequately to recognise the relationship between criminal law, criminal procedure law and procedural rights and to account for the ways in which each part of the criminal process has the potential to compensate for, or indeed interfere with, the other parts, and thus to assist or hinder the due process ideals. This is compounded by the division of responsibility for defining the nature of the rights and the nature of the justice system. As long as the judicial 'constitutional-type' regulation extends only to regulating procedural rights, there will be potential for the legislature to interfere with the manner and the context in which these rights can be applied.[33] This creates an imbalance that negatively impacts on procedural rights and on the potential for fair proceedings. This failure to appreciate the central importance of links between the institutional form of the proceedings and the extent of the applicable rights of the accused also highlights

---

[31] S Veitch, 'Judgement and Calling to Account: Truth, Trials, and Reconciliation' in RA Duff, L Farmer, S Marshall and V Tadros (eds), *The Trial on Trial II: Judgment and Calling to Account* (Oxford, Hart Publishing, 2006).

[32] It is also worth noting the implications of this: if the rights and restraints said to guarantee fairness in criminal proceedings are unable to ensure that the proceedings are in fact fair, then there is a danger that the criminal proceedings legitimate an oppressive criminal justice system: see eg D Rudovsky, 'The Criminal Justice System and the Role of the Police: A Progressive Critique' in D Kairys (ed), *The Politics of Law* (New York, Pantheon, 1982) at 242–3.

[33] Some commentators have argued for constitutional restraints on the criminal law. Dubber, for instance, outlines a role for constitutional regulation of the substantive criminal law based on notions of a return to autonomy, while Finkelstein argues for greater emphasis to be placed on the actus reus and on Millian notions of 'harm': MD Dubber, 'Towards a Constitutional Law of Crime and Punishment' (2004) 33 *Hastings Law Journal* 509; C Finkelstein, 'Positivism and the Notion of an Offense' (1999) 88 *California Law Review* 335. Dubber goes so far as to suggest that 'it has become commonplace [in the US literature] that there are no meaningful constitutional restraints on substantive criminal law'. See in particular: W Stuntz, 'The Substantive Origins of the Criminal Procedure' (1995) 105 *Yale Law Journal* 393; W Stuntz, 'Substance Process and the Civil–Criminal Line' (1996) 7 *Journal of Contemporary Legal Issues* 1; W Stuntz 'The Uneasy Relationship Between Criminal Procedure and Criminal Justice' (1997) 107 *Yale Law Journal* 1; LD Bilionis, 'Process, the Constitution, and Substantive Criminal Law' (1998) 96 *Michigan Law Review* 1269. See also W Hassemer, *Theorie und Soziologie des Verbrechens: Ansätze zu einer praxisorientierten Rechtsgutlehre* (Frankfurt, Europäische Verlagsanstalt, 1980) and RA Duff, 'Strict Liability, Legal Presumptions, and the Presumption of Innocence' in AP Simester, *Appraising Strict Liability* (Oxford, Oxford University Press, 2005) at 134, who argues for a broad understanding of the presumption of innocence so as to require 'that defendants be convicted only on proof beyond reasonable doubt of what the law legitimately defines as culpable wrongdoing'.

deficiencies in the understanding of the nature of procedural rights and their relationship to the procedural criminal law. This in turn has serious implications for a comprehensive understanding of procedural fairness.

C   Article 6 ECHR and the European Criminal Procedural Tradition

The overriding impression conveyed by the academic literature on comparative criminal procedure law is of a discipline preoccupied with an understanding of criminal proceedings as fundamentally divided into two predominant legal traditions.[34] This has remained the case despite the emergence of Article 6 ECHR as the most important benchmark, at least within Europe, for assessing the fairness of criminal proceedings. The apparent ease with which the principles set out in Article 6 have been applied across the various procedural systems represents, on one level, a direct challenge to the prevailing orthodoxy. How can procedural systems, which have been shown to be so different, be successfully regulated by one notion of fairness?

One response has been to argue that the broad, European-wide application of Article 6 implies that the procedural differences are not actually as significant as they are often made out to be: '*[e]benso könnte dies aber bedeuten, dass die strukurellen Unterschiede in Wahrheit gar nicht so groß sind, wie dies immer behauptet wird*'.[35] This argument is however seldom taken seriously. Instead it is linked to the claims about the importance of the Court maintaining a neutral stance in its application of Article 6.[36] The success of Article 6 is explained on the one hand by playing down the differences in the procedural systems of the member states, while maintaining on the other a 'neutrality' requirement in the application of Article 6 for the event that significant differences do in fact emerge. It is not clear however why, if the procedural differences are in fact minimal, it is necessary for the Court to maintain a 'neutral' stance. Such hypotheses moreover tell us little about the Court's notion of fairness, and even less about the nature of the procedural systems in which it is to be applied.

---

[34]   See the literature cited in Ch 1, above.

[35]   R Esser, *Auf dem Weg zu einem europäischen Strafverfahrensrecht* (Berlin, De Gruyter, 2002) at 856: 'At the same time however this might mean that the structural differences in reality are not as big as is always claimed'.

[36]   *Ibid*, at 855–6: '[d]eshalb ist es wichtig, dass sich der EGMR nicht auf die Seite eines adversatorisch ausgestalteten Strafverfahren schlägt, das der Rechtstradition des common law entspricht, sondern von einer prinzipiellen Gleichwertigkeit aller in Europa vorhandenen Strafrechtssysteme ausgeht'.

Others have suggested that the success of Article 6 can be attributed to the fact that the member states are being required 'to realign their processes in accordance with what is better described as a new model of proof altogether'.[37] Jackson has identified in the case law the emergence of a 'participatory model of proof':

> as the European Court refines and develops its vision of participatory proof in the light of modern day conditions and takes criminal procedure beyond the traditional boundaries of adversarial/ inquisitorial discourse, the European states are given considerable freedom of manoeuvre in realigning their procedures in a manner that respects the rights of the defence.[38]

According to Jackson, the member states are being encouraged by the case law of the Court to realign their procedural systems in order to be able to accommodate the rights of the accused. Implicit in this argument is an understanding of the ECHR as a new influence, able to mould old procedural traditions. To some extent this is undoubtedly correct. It seems inevitable that the rights case law of the Court will impact upon the procedural systems of the member states. The question is the extent of this influence—to what extent can these trial rights shape the proceedings or constrain the power of the state authorities?

There is a tendency evident in both the case law of the Court and in the work of many commentators to view the principles set out in Article 6 as autonomous concepts, existing outside the socio-historical context which typically serves to constrain national procedural systems. But the analysis of the writings of the nineteenth century European jurists suggests that the rights of the defence, far from being 'discovered' in the middle of the twentieth century, developed much earlier. That many of the principles set out in Article 6 are as easily applicable in Switzerland as they are in Scotland can be explained not because they are contemporary standards impacting on traditional principles of criminal procedure, but because, on the contrary, these principles form part of the foundations on which modern European criminal procedure law is based. The identification of a European criminal procedural tradition not only emphasises the fundamental importance of the institutional role of the defence within the criminal procedural system, it also casts doubt on the relevance of much of the current writing on European comparative criminal procedure law.

If the principles identified in the works of the nineteenth century jurists are clearly visible in the structure of Article 6 and indeed in the case law, they have not been acknowledged either by the Court or by modern commentators. Institutional procedural norms have been seriously neglected as the focus has been firmly on protecting individual rights.

The reluctance of the Strasbourg authorities to elucidate and insist on institutional norms has been exacerbated by the comparative law scholarship's persistent emphasising of the divide between adversarial and inquisitorial forms of

---

[37] JD Jackson, 'The Effect of Human Rights on Criminal Evidentiary Processes: Towards Convergence, Divergence or Realignment' (2005) 68 *MLR* 737 at 747.

[38] *Ibid,* at 763.

procedure and its firm rejection of the notion that there could be one institutional form common to all European jurisdictions. There has been almost universal silence on aspects of the Court's case law, such as its acceptance of the pre-trial/investigation phase as an acceptable forum for the defence to challenge witness evidence, despite the manifest failure of the pre-trial phase to fulfil the criteria of judicial impartiality and publicity. This is no doubt attributable to the prevailing opinion that any insistence on the trial as the only forum for hearing the evidence would be unacceptable in 'inquisitorial' systems. Nevertheless, there can be little disagreement with the assertion that the defence right to challenge witness evidence before an impartial judge in a public forum differs from the defence right to challenge witness evidence in the context of a non-public forum supervised by a prosecuting or investigating authority which does not meet the impartiality criteria set out in Article 6(1). Moreover using the Court's own criteria for determining fairness it can be legitimately claimed that the treatment of the accused in the latter context is less fair than his or her treatment in the context of the former.

Although inconsistencies in the Court's notion of fairness are particularly evident in relation to the case law on the right to question witnesses, they are also reflected in the failure to address serious institutional flaws in various European criminal procedural systems. There can be little doubt that the coherence and consistency of procedural fairness could be improved through an acknowledgment of the reliance of its adversarial proceedings and equality of arms doctrines on the accusatorial trinity. A more sound approach to the regulation of fairness in European criminal trials requires recognition both of the European procedural tradition and of the common institutional values which it implies.

This need not necessarily prove hugely problematic. Indeed some of these values, notably the public trial requirement, are already accepted as applicable across Europe and are set out in Article 6. We have seen that the failure to uphold the requirement that the tasks of examining the evidence and prosecuting the charge be attributed to different institutions within the criminal justice system is a matter of particular concern. It seems impossible to reconcile the concept of the prosecutor conducting or supervising the examination of the evidence with the concept of institutional fairness inherent in the European procedural tradition. This practice is common in many European jurisdictions.[39]

---

[39] Eg in the Canton of Zurich where it is quite common for the investigating judge responsible for the investigation hearings (at which the defence was given the opportunity to examine the evidence, confront witness etc) to be resurrected at trial as the prosecutor: see A Donatsch and N Schmid, *Kommentar zur Strafprozessordnung des Kantons Zürich* (Zurich, Schulthess, 1996–) at para 25 II and Vorbemerkung zu paras 128.5; R Hauser, E Schweri and K Hartmann, *Schweizerisches Strafprozessrecht*, 6th edn (Basel, Helbing & Lichtenhahn, 2005) at paras 26.8–26.10 and 62.31–62.33a. See also paras 161a and 168b of the German Criminal Procedural Code which allow for the prosecutor to conduct the investigation confrontations with witnesses. The protocols of these hearings are then submitted to the court by way of the file. See L Meyer-Goßner, *Strafprozessordnung*, 48th edn (Munich, Beck, 2005).

The Court's interpretation of the right to confrontation is symptomatic of a broader failure to come to terms with the relationship between the trial and the pre-trial phase. The investigation is recognised across Europe as an important aspect of criminal proceedings, albeit one which differs substantially in character from the trial. The European procedural tradition suggests that criminal proceedings must be seen as made up of two distinct phases, each governed by its own regulatory structure. Accepting the characterisation of criminal proceedings as comprising oral trials and secret investigations necessitates consideration not just of trial norms but also of those principles which are to regulate the investigation.

The current regulation of the investigation by the Court is patchy and incoherent. The inadequacy of the status quo is demonstrated by the reasoning in the case law on the role of counsel in the investigation phase, which is dominated by recourse to a necessarily retrospective determination of whether it could be said that the measures undertaken, or not as the case may be, significantly affected the subsequent fairness of the trial. A good example of this methodology is clearly evident in the judgment in *John Murray v United Kingdom*, where the applicant complained that the failure to allow him access to counsel in the investigative stages of the proceedings had violated his right to a fair trial. According to the Court:

> National laws may attach consequences to the attitude of an accused at the initial stages of police interrogation which are decisive for the prospects of the defence in any subsequent criminal proceedings. In such circumstances Article 6 will normally require that the accused be allowed to benefit from the assistance of a lawyer already at the initial stages of police interrogation. However, this right, which is not explicitly set out in the Convention, may be subject to restrictions for good cause. The question, in each case, is whether the restriction, in the light of the entirety of the proceedings, has deprived the accused of a fair hearing.[40]

The problem with this is that 'the behaviour of the suspect immediately after arrest will always have consequences';[41] the Court however has not accepted this. Although it upheld the applicant's complaint in *John Murray*, there are nevertheless several other examples where it determined that the fact that the applicant had not had access to counsel following arrest was not such as to compromise the fairness of the trial.[42] As a result, it is virtually impossible to tell from the Court's case law when the right to counsel actually arises.

---

[40] *John Murray v United Kingdom,* judgment of 8 Feb 1996, Reports 1996-I, 30, (1996) EHRR 29, at para 63.
[41] S Trechsel, *Human Rights in Criminal Proceedings* (Oxford, Oxford University Press, 2005) at 283.
[42] Eg *Brennen v United Kingdom,* no 39846/98, ECHR 2001-X, 211, (2002) 12 EHRR 217, where the fact that the applicant had not had access to a lawyer earlier was not 'attributable to any measure imposed by the authorities'—ie the Court determined that the accused would have been entitled to the assistance of counsel had he expressly requested it; or *Sarikaya v Turkey,* no 36115/97, judgment of 22 Apr 2004, where the Court did not find a violation even though the applicant had been in custody for 20 days without access to counsel. This judgment is strongly criticised by S Trechsel, *Human Rights in Criminal Proceedings* (Oxford, Oxford University Press, 2005) at 285; see also J-M Verniory, *Les droits de la défense dans les phases préliminaires du procès pénal* (Bern, Staempfli, 2005) at 148.

Moreover the judgment in *John Murray* demonstrates how the Court's approach to regulating the pre-trial phase principally involves reference to the fairness of the trial. This is also evident in *Imbrioscia* where it was held that 'Article 6 may be relevant before a case is sent for trial if and in so far as the fairness of the trial is likely to be seriously prejudiced by an initial failure to comply with its provisions'.[43] This test is inadequate for several reasons. First, it is vague and retrospective: determining whether the pre-trial circumstances are acceptable will be possible only through either an hypothetical assessment of the effect on future fairness or through a retrospective examination of the influence of the pre-trial factors on the fairness of the trial. This makes it of little use for criminal justice authorities seeking guidance on how they should conduct the investigation proceedings. Secondly, it fails to take account of the systematic importance of the fairness of the investigation phase to the fairness of the trial.

Ambiguity in relation to the regulation of the pre-trial phase is by no means confined to the issue of access to counsel; rather this subject is representative of the failure to establish an effective and adequate strategy for the regulation of the pre-trial investigative phases of the proceedings. This is partly due to deficiencies in the text of Article 6, which is silent as to the pre-trial phase, but this must be seen in itself as an insufficient excuse, particularly in the light of the judicial activism in other areas such as in relation to the privilege against self-incrimination.[44] The more plausible explanation lies, not least because of the differences frequently emphasised by the comparative criminal law scholarship and the underplaying of the institutional context, in the lack of coherent theorising about the connection between the form of the trial and the investigation, and the consequent differences in the nature of the rights that are required in the respective phases. An effective regulatory strategy for the investigation phase is dependent on an understanding of the division of labour within criminal proceedings as set out by the European jurists in the nineteenth century. Only by accepting this will the Court be able to progress towards its ultimate aim of guaranteeing the consistent application of one European-wide standard of fairness.

More troubling, particularly in view of the fact that tensions between the trial and investigation phases have existed since the origins of the modern system of European criminal procedure law, is the possibility that the under-regulation of the investigation phase is not merely an oversight, but is representative of a systematic prioritising of the effectiveness of prosecuting crime over the importance of the adversarial conception of fairness and the legitimacy of the criminal procedural system. This suggests that the emphasis on the 'fair trial' becomes a

---

[43] *Imbrioscia v Switzerland,* judgment of 24 Nov 1993, Series A no 275, (1994) 17 EHRR 441, at para 36.
[44] S Trechsel, *Human Rights in Criminal Proceedings* (Oxford, Oxford University Press, 2005) at 340–59; R Schlauri, *Das Verbot des Selbstbelastungszwangs im Strafverfahren: Konkretisierung eines Grundrechts durch Rechtsvergleichung* (Zurich, Schulthess, 2003) at 82–4 and 357–97.

crucial means of diverting attention away from the unfairness of the most important part of the proceedings, namely the investigation. This gives rise to the rather unpalatable conclusion that acceptance of the 'fairness' of the modern European criminal trial is heavily dependent on the 'unfairness' of the investigation.

One response to these criticisms might be to question whether, even if the institutional conception of fairness implied by the European criminal procedural tradition is accepted, it is reasonable or indeed realistic to expect the Court to apply an institutional conception of fairness. In view of the fact that the Convention is based on individual human rights and personal autonomy, might it not be seen as self-evident that it would resist conceptions of criminal proceedings stated in institutional terms of fairness and efficiency? Even if, however, the Court might be seen to be in some way tied to, or restrained by, its 'rights mandate' there is no escaping the fact that the principles of Article 6 are not, and cannot be, applied in a structural vacuum. The extent of any participatory rights will depend on the surroundings in which they are to be exercised. The aim of ensuring the consistent application of these rights can be achieved only if there is consideration of the institutional context. Further, the Court has, albeit unconsciously, adopted an institutional conception of the trial which is consistent with the European criminal procedural tradition. Thus, although Article 6 may be seen to be based on an understanding of criminal proceedings as rights-based, it is impossible to ignore the influence of the procedural tradition, not just on text of the Article, but also on its interpretation in the case law of the Court.

D   Towards an Institutional Understanding of Fairness in Criminal Proceedings

The examination of the works of the nineteenth century jurists reveals an understanding of the institutional basis of criminal proceedings which is essential not only to the correct functioning of the defence rights but also to an understanding of procedural fairness in modern European criminal proceedings. The identification of a type of European criminal procedural tradition suggests that underlying the various superficial differences in the regulation of criminal proceedings is deep-seated agreement on how these should take place. Acknowledgement of this tradition would represent a first important step in improving both consistency in the application of Article 6 and the European conception of fair trials.

An institutional understanding of criminal proceedings however has the potential to afford something more than just the basis on which to construct a standardised European notion of procedural fairness. It also provides a new framework for thinking about criminal proceedings as concerned with maintaining the equilibrium between the defence and the prosecution rather than simply in terms of the rights of the accused. To some extent the Court has accepted this in its case law on the equality of arms and its notion of adversarial proceedings. On the other hand however, its failure adequately to regulate the investigation and pre-trial phases of the proceedings can be seen to be symptomatic of its failure fully to come to terms with the institutional understanding of procedural fairness. As we have seen, such an understanding requires recognition not just of the capacity of rights to unbalance the institution, but also more generally of the interdependent nature of procedural laws, procedural rights and the criminal law.

Index